Happy Christmas
Grandpa.

NATIONAL GEOGRAPHIC
KiDS

INFOPEDIA
2022

NATIONAL GEOGRAPHIC
KiDS
INFOPEDIA
2022

NATIONAL GEOGRAPHIC
WASHINGTON, D.C.

NATIONAL GEOGRAPHIC KiDS

Welcome to National Geographic Kids' fantastic new *Infopedia 2022!*

Are you looking for adventure, fun and games? Then this is the book for you! *Infopedia 2022* is packed with all the incredible facts and stories that you'll find each month in *National Geographic Kids* magazine — from awesome animals and spectacular science to intrepid explorers and mind-bending puzzles!

Learn all about our world in this year's Wonders of Nature, Geography Rocks, History Happens, Amazing Animals and Space and Earth chapters. Then discover how YOU can help tackle our planet's plastic problem in the *Infopedia*'s brilliant new Kids vs. Plastic section. Find out how creatures have coped during COVID-19 in the Your World pages, and then dive into our Culture Connection chapter to read some of the wackiest stories from around the globe. Looking for laughs? Then don't miss the jokes, comics, puzzles and brain-teasing quizzes in our bumper Fun and Games section, and make sure you amaze your mates with hundreds of Bet You Didn't Know facts!

Bursting with fantastic photos, inspiring interviews, exciting things to do and wonderful places to see, National Geographic Kids *Infopedia 2022* is the perfect read for children who want to know about everything and more.
So what are you waiting for?

Get ready to explore!

Tim Herbert
Editor, *National Geographic Kids* magazine

If you enjoy *Infopedia 2022*, look out for *National Geographic Kids* magazine — it's jam-packed with adventure and fun every month!

Subscribe to *Nat Geo Kids* now by visiting natgeokids.com/subscribeuk and enter code NGKIP225 at checkout to receive £5 off the subscription price!

Contents

NATIONAL GEOGRAPHIC KiDS
INFOPEDIA CHALLENGE 2022

THE RESULTS ARE IN!

Which plastic-reducing idea won our 2021 Infopedia Challenge? *See page 27.*

Want to become part of the 2022 Infopedia Challenge? Go to page 27 to find out more.

YOUR WORLD 2022

ANIMALS DURING QUARANTINE

When COVID-19 hit, these headline-making critters got all the clicks.

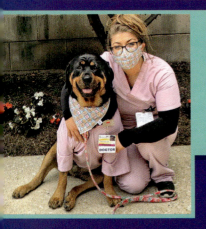

'Dogtor' Cares for Hospital Heroes

Not all heroes wear capes; some wear collars! Second-year University of Maryland medical student Caroline Benzel and her pet Rottweiler 'Dogtor' Loki brought cheer and smiles to the University of Maryland Medical Center in Baltimore, Maryland, U.S.A. They delivered 'hero healing kits' filled with tea, skin lotion, lip balm and more to the dedicated nurses and doctors working tirelessly to care for coronavirus patients. Benzel even arranged for Loki to 'visit' patients virtually.

Sea Turtles Get a Boost

When tourism to Thailand and Florida, U.S.A., drastically slowed during the pandemic, leatherback sea turtles levelled up. After all, with fewer people and pets walking on the beaches and over the turtles' nests, their eggs had a much better chance of surviving. Thailand and Florida both saw an increase in successful nests. Sounds like these turtles are really coming out of their shells.

Penguins Waddle Around

What's a penguin to do during a pandemic? When the Shedd Aquarium in Chicago, Illinois, U.S.A., shut down, its resident penguins had free rein to roam. Aquarium employees allowed rockhoppers Eddie and Annie to wander — and waddle — around and check out their finned friends. Another pair, Magellanic penguins Izzy and Darwin, visited SUE the *T. rex* at the neighbouring Field Museum.

Goats Go to Town

When residents of Llandudno in northern Wales, U.K., were asked to stay inside during the pandemic lockdown, a herd of wild mountain goats took advantage of the empty streets and pavements. They strolled around, grazed on grassy lawns and feasted on flower beds. Sounds like those goats had it good!

COOKIES *IN SPACE*

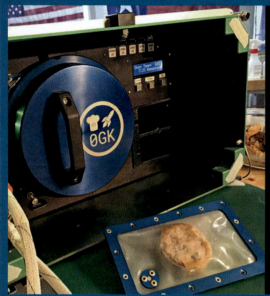

Forget freeze-dried ice cream: Astronauts living at the International Space Station (ISS) may soon be able to satisfy their sweet tooth with freshly baked cookies! Thanks to a special zero-gravity oven, astronauts made a small batch of chocolate chip cookies, the first food ever baked in space from raw ingredients. Although the astronauts didn't get to snack on the cookies (experts had to analyse them first to make sure they were safe to eat), it showed what may be possible in the unique environment of the ISS with limited power supply and no gravity. As for what happened to the cookies? They were returned to Earth and preserved so people can one day check out the made-in-space snacks.

MYSTERY FOSSIL
Discovery

Did a tiny lizard with a skull the width of a thumbnail slither around Earth during the age of the dinosaurs? That's what scientists suspect after discovering a fossil of the extra-small animal encased in amber at an amber mine in Southeast Asia. After initially believing it to be a birdlike dinosaur, experts now think that the species was, in fact, a type of lizard that lived around 100 million years ago. The reptile weighed just a few grams and is thought to have been a fierce predator that feasted on bugs with its numerous jagged teeth. It also had huge eyes, suited for seeking out prey in the trees. As for the difference between dinosaurs and lizards? The two groups of animals actually diverged from one another some 270 million years ago, well before this lightweight lizard lived.

A TINY FOSSILISED SKULL PRESERVED IN AMBER

PINK
MANTA RAY

Think pink! This rare manta ray — thought to be the only one in the world to boast the bubblegum shade — was photographed swimming around Australia's Great Barrier Reef. Nicknamed Inspector Clouseau after the detective in the Pink Panther movies, the ray has only been seen a few times. At first, experts thought the ray's rosy hue came from a skin infection or from its diet, much like how flamingos get their pink shade from eating tiny crustaceans. But after doing a small skin biopsy, they determined that a genetic mutation actually causes its skin pigment (which is usually black, white or black-and-white) to be pink. That makes this 3.5-metre (11-ft) ray a true standout of the sea!

Ancient Lines Revealed

Did ancient people use emojis? Some archaeologists believe that prehistoric land art discovered in Peru may have been a way for the inhabitants of the desert coastal area to express themselves — or at least what was going on around them. The giant images, some taller than the Statue of Liberty in New York, U.S.A., are also known as Nasca Lines and were first discovered in the area in 1927. Recently, experts using high-tech scanning gear uncovered even more images etched into the ground in an area south of Peru's capital of Lima. Some theorise that the images — which depict humans, fish and birds — represent constellations. Others suggest they were part of ancient rituals. But there's no question that these mysterious works of art were a way for the Nasca civilisation to tell a story.

AN ANCIENT HUMANOID IMAGE CAPTURED BY A LOW-FLYING DRONE CAMERA IN SOUTHERN PERU

Let the Games Begin!

BEIJING NATIONAL STADIUM — THE 'BIRD'S NEST'

BEIJING 2022

BIG-AIR SKIER

When the XXIV Olympic Games kick off in February 2022, it will mark the very first time one city has served as host of both the Winter and Summer Games. That city is Beijing, China, which also hosted the 2008 Summer Games. To prepare for the historic double, Beijing will once again use its famous Olympic stadium — also known as the Bird's Nest — to hold the opening and closing ceremonies. The Beijing National Aquatics Center, nicknamed the 'Water Cube' during the 2008 games, will become the 'Ice Cube' and will hold the curling competition. And the Capital Indoor Stadium, which hosted the volleyball events in 2008, will now be the site for figure skating and short-track speed skating. As for the outdoor events like skiing, snowboarding and bobsleigh? Those will take place in the mountains outside of Beijing. Because the region averages less than 20 centimetres (8 in) of snowpack a year, the white stuff will be made by machines.

TOKYO ~~2020~~ 2021

The Olympics was meant to be held in Tokyo, Japan, in 2020, for the first time in 56 years. But when it became clear that it would not be safe to bring thousands of athletes and fans to the capital city due to the spread of COVID-19, the Games were postponed until 2021. If COVID-19 remains a concern, they will consider safety measures such as rapid testing for the virus, limited spectators and 'bubbles' for athletes.

NOTE: This information is current as of press time.

BOOKSTORE KITTENS

We're not *kitten:* Otis & Clementine's, a secondhand bookstore and café in Upper Tantallon, Nova Scotia, Canada, is one of the most adorable around! What makes the shop so, well, *aww*-some? A handful of foster kittens can often be found hanging out among the stacks and shelves! Otis & Clementine's owner took in the cats as foster pets and let them live in the store with the hope that customers would want to adopt them. But no worries for those who don't want a pet: It's *purr*-fectly fine to just enjoy the free kitten cuddles instead.

THE OWNER'S DAUGHTER, INGRID, HOLDS TWO KITTENS AT OTIS & CLEMENTINE'S.

SlothBot

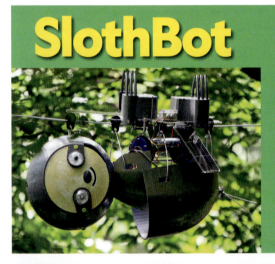

If you're ever at the Atlanta Botanical Garden in Georgia, U.S.A., look up! You may spot the SlothBot slowly creeping along a cable above the ground. The bot, made with a 3D-printed shell, runs on batteries powered by solar energy and even locates the sunlight when its batteries need to be recharged. But the SlothBot isn't just there to look cute: It's equipped to monitor info like weather, temperature and carbon dioxide levels. The SlothBot's developers — engineering experts at the Georgia Institute of Technology — hope that it can one day be used in places like South America, where it could provide key data that might help monitor orchid pollination or the lives of endangered frogs.

Harry Potter Turns 25!

Happy birthday, Harry! While the fan-favourite fictional wizard will be forever young in readers' eyes, 2022 marks 25 years since J.K. Rowling's legendary book series launched. The first title in the Harry Potter series was published in the United Kingdom on 26 June 1997, with just about 500 copies sent to bookstores and libraries. The book took off, and today, the original Harry Potter series, which includes seven books, has sold more than 500 million copies, and the franchise features eight blockbuster movies, theme parks, a West End play and more.

HARRY POTTER and the Philosopher's Stone
J.K. ROWLING

GOODY TESTS HER NEW FLIPPER.

Sea Turtle Gets New Flipper

When Goody lost her flipper after becoming entangled in a fishing net, it could have been a tragic ending for the olive ridley sea turtle. But thanks to some kind — and crafty — humans, Goody got a second lease of life. After being rescued in Thailand and later fitted with a prosthetic flipper by researchers at a nearby university, Goody is now able to float freely. And although her injury means she cannot return to the sea, Goody's new life is going just, er, swimmingly.

HOUND HER⭐ES

South Africa is home to about 80 percent of the world's last remaining rhinos. But more than 8,000 rhinos have been poached, or illegally hunted, in South Africa since 2008. To help protect the species, officials came up with a clever idea that was perfect for sniffing out bad guys: Texas hound dogs. These dogs have excellent scent-tracking skills and use their barking abilities to alert their human helpers to where they are at any time. A pack of hounds travelled from Texas, U.S.A., to South Africa to nab poachers. And the approach is working: Before the Texas hounds arrived, rangers were nabbing only about 5 percent of known poachers. But with the new dogs on the prowl, more than half of the bad guys are now being caught. As the hounds in South Africa have puppies, rangers hope that the young dogs can be trained and then sent to other areas of Africa. That way, more rhinos and many other animals will get a chance to roam free.

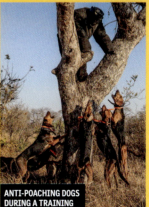

ANTI-POACHING DOGS DURING A TRAINING EXERCISE

15

Cool Events 2022

INTERNATIONAL GUIDE DOG DAY

Pay tribute to all of the dogs who work hard to help visually impaired humans.

27 April

INTERNATIONAL KITE DAY

GO FLY A KITE!

This celebration, which began in Gujarat, India, marks the end of the short, cold days of the winter season.

14 January

WORLD REEF DAY

It's never been more important to protect the ocean's coral reefs. Some 25 percent of sea life depends on them.

1 June

INTERNATIONAL DAY OF HAPPINESS

DON'T WORRY, BE HAPPY!

Make it a goal to keep grinning all day long in this observance of everything that brings you joy.

20 March

INTERNATIONAL JOKE DAY

LOL ALL DAY

by telling your best jokes and riddles — and encourage your friends and family to get funny, too!

1 July

WORLD DOLPHIN DAY

Flip out over our finned friends on this day dedicated to dolphins.

14 April

INTERNATIONAL PUZZLE DAY

Exercise your brain by solving a sudoku or get clever with a crossword today!

13 July

WORLD ART DAY

Promote creativity worldwide by painting, drawing or sculpting something today!

15 April

WORLD LEMUR DAY

Celebrate the lovable lemur while helping to raise awareness for these amazing — and endangered — animals.

28 October

Tortoise Turns 100

Tuki, an Aldabra tortoise living in a zoo in Turkey, recently hit a mega milestone: He turned 100 years old! The centenarian celebrated alongside some llama friends at the zoo with balloons and a giant cake made of lettuce and vegetables. While Tuki's age is impressive, it's not entirely unusual: Aldabras, one of the world's largest land tortoises, can live for more than 150 years!

New Species Name Honours Climate Activist

One tiny mollusc was recently given quite a big name! The two-millimetre (.08-in)-long *Craspedotropis gretathunbergae* was named after teen climate change activist Greta Thunberg. Citizen scientists, together with Taxon Expeditions, discovered the snail in a rainforest in Brunei on the island of Borneo. They say this type of tiny critter is sensitive to drought, extreme temperatures and other hallmarks of climate change. So they chose the name to honour Thunberg's efforts in speaking up about climate change as well as to encourage future generations to continue to fight to protect the planet—and all of the species living on it.

RED PANDAS might be TWO SPECIES

Red pandas are super rare—it's estimated that there are as few as 2,500 in the wild—and now scientists say those left are actually two species. The difference? It's observed that Chinese red pandas have redder fur and striped tail rings, while the Himalayan red pandas have whiter faces. Scientists hope this discovery will help them better protect the animals' habitats and save *all* red pandas from extinction.

Constructed of plastic waste, this art installation in Kochi, India, was created to remind people of the threat plastics pose to marine life.

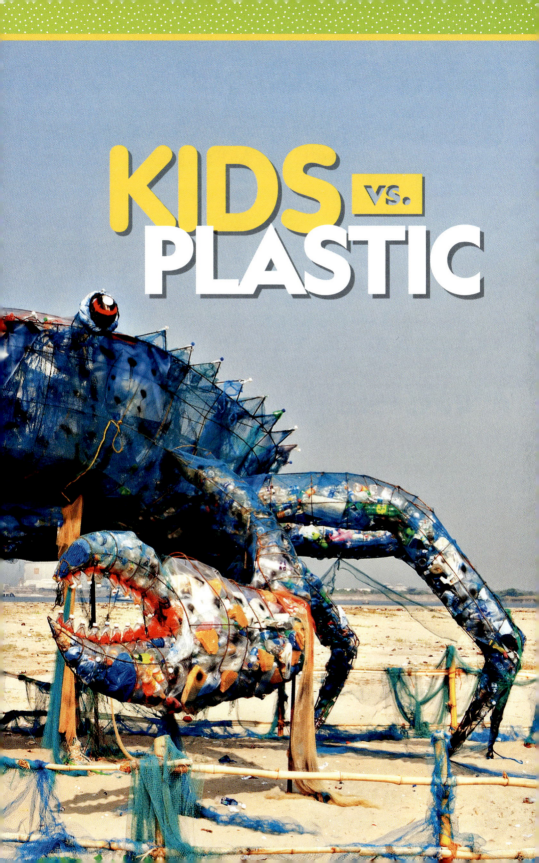

WHAT IS PLASTIC?

» **P**lastic can be moulded, coloured and textured to make, well, just about anything. That begs the question: What precisely is this wonder product?

THE BASICS:
Plastics are polymers, or long, flexible chains of molecules made of repeating links. This molecular structure makes plastic lightweight, hard to break and easy to mould — all of which makes it extremely useful.

WHERE DO POLYMERS COME FROM?
Polymers can be found in nature, in things like the cell walls of plants, tar, tortoiseshell and tree sap. In fact, nearly 3,500 years ago, people in what is today Central America used the sap from gum trees to make rubber balls for games. About 150 years ago, scientists began replicating the polymers in nature to improve on them — these are called synthetic polymers.

WHO INVENTED PLASTIC?
In 1869, an American named John Wesley Hyatt created the first useful synthetic polymer. At the time, the discovery was a big deal: For the first time, manufacturing was no longer limited by the resources supplied by nature like wood, clay and stone. People could create their own materials.

WHAT IS SYNTHETIC PLASTIC MADE FROM?
Today, most plastic is made from oil and natural gas.

WHEN DID IT BECOME POPULAR?
During World War II, from 1939 to 1945, nylon, which is strong and light like silk but made of plastic, was used for parachutes, rope, body armour and helmet liners. And aeroplanes used in battle had lightweight windows made of plastic glass, also known as Plexiglas. After the war, plastic became a popular material. Everything from dishes to radios to toys hit the market. A few decades later, plastic bottles became a lightweight nonbreakable alternative to glass bottles, and food stores switched from paper bags to cheaper thin plastic ones.

THAT BRINGS US TO TODAY.
Look around: Are you more than a few feet away from something plastic? Probably not! Plastic is all around us.

AMERICANS use an average of ONE plastic shopping bag A DAY. People in DENMARK use an average of FOUR plastic shopping bags A YEAR.

WHERE DOES ALL THE PLASTIC GO?

Only a small percentage of all the plastic that has ever been made has been recycled to make other things. Most has been tossed out and left to slowly biodegrade in landfills, a process that can take hundreds of years. The other option for getting rid of plastic is to burn it. But because plastic is made from fossil fuels, burning it releases harmful pollutants into the air. Here is a breakdown of where all the plastic has gone since people started making it, and how long it takes to biodegrade if it does end up as landfill.

9% Recycled

12% Burned, releasing toxins into the air

79% Sent to landfills or wound up in the natural environment (like oceans)

THE LIFE SPAN OF PLASTIC

PLASTIC BAG 20 YEARS

PLASTIC-FOAM CUP 50 YEARS

Plastic that's sent to landfill doesn't just disappear — it stays there for a really long time. Different types of plastic take different lengths of time to biodegrade.

DRINKING STRAW 200 YEARS

BOTTLE 450 YEARS

SODA SIX-PACK RING 450 YEARS

FISHING LINE 600+ YEARS

21

DEADLY DEBRIS

THE INS AND OUTS OF THE (NOT SO) GREAT PACIFIC GARBAGE PATCH

On a map, the space between California and Hawaii, U.S.A., looks like an endless blue sea, but in person, you'll find a giant floating island — made up of plastic. Plastic can be found in all the oceans of the world, but currents and winds move marine debris around in certain patterns that create huge concentrations, or patches, of plastic in some spots. The biggest one is the Great Pacific Garbage Patch. Scientists estimate that there are about 1.8 trillion pieces of plastic in the patch, and 94 percent of them are microplastics. So, don't try walking on it; it's definitely not solid! Some of the patch is made up of bulky items, including fishing gear like nets, rope, eel traps, crates and baskets. The patch is also made up of debris washed into the sea during tsunamis. A tsunami is a series of waves caused by an earthquake or an undersea volcanic eruption. It can pull millions of tonnes of debris — from cars to household appliances to pieces of houses — off coastlines and into the ocean. Scientists and innovators are working on ways to clean up the patch, although with more plastic constantly entering waterways, the effort will inevitably be ongoing.

TANGLED NYLON ROPE WASHED ASHORE OFF THE COAST OF PHUKET, THAILAND.

SMASHED-UP SHIPS EVENTUALLY MAKE THEIR WAY TO A SWIRLING MASS OF DEBRIS IN THE GREAT PACIFIC GARBAGE PATCH.

GARBAGE PATCH ZONES

ARCTIC OCEAN

ASIA

NORTH AMERICA

ATLANTIC OCEAN

AFRICA

Great Pacific Garbage Patch

AFRICA

PACIFIC OCEAN

SOUTH AMERICA

INDIAN OCEAN

AUSTRALIA

Warm Ocean Current

Cold Ocean Current

ATLANTIC OCEAN

ANTARCTICA

CANADA

Garbage patch area with low concentration of plastics

PACIFIC OCEAN

UNITED STATES

California

PACIFIC OCEAN

MEXICO

Hawai'i (United States)

Garbage patch area with high concentration of plastics

There are five large systems of circulating ocean currents around the world called gyres. Plastic and other rubbish travel with the currents and get trapped in the gyres. The gyre that the Great Pacific Garbage Patch swirls in is the largest of them all.

THE GREAT PACIFIC GARBAGE PATCH MEASURES 1.6 MILLION SQUARE KILOMETRES
(618,000 SQ MILES)

That's about:

3 TIMES THE SIZE OF FRANCE

2 TIMES THE SIZE OF TEXAS

There are 250 PIECES OF PLASTIC in the Great Pacific Garbage Patch for EVERY HUMAN on Earth.

SEA TURTLE RESCUE

RESCUERS SWOOP IN TO HELP A SEA TURTLE THAT SWALLOWED A BALLOON.

A young green sea turtle bobbed along the surface of the water off the coast of Florida, U.S.A. Young turtles usually don't hang out at the surface — that's where predators can easily spot them, plus their food is deeper underwater. But something was keeping this 30.5-centimetre (1-ft)-long turtle from diving.

Luckily, rescuers spotted the struggling turtle and took it back to the Clearwater Marine Aquarium, where they named it Chex. Staff placed Chex in a shallow kiddie pool so that the turtle wouldn't waste energy trying to dive. They tested Chex's blood and ran x-rays but couldn't figure out what was wrong. "Then one day Chex started pooping out something weird," biologist Lauren Bell says. The weird object turned out to be a purple balloon and an attached string.

SOS (SAVE OUR SEAGRASS)!

Sea turtles often mistake floating rubbish for food. "Even some *people* can't tell the difference between a plastic grocery bag and a jellyfish in the water," Bell says. But plastic doesn't just hurt sea turtles: It hurts their habitat.

Green sea turtles often hang out close to the shore near seagrass, one of their favourite snacks. Plastic waste left on the beach or coming from rivers that empty into the sea often ends up in this habitat. When it settles on the seagrass, the rubbish can smother the grass, causing it to die. That can mean trouble for green sea turtles like Chex that rely on the seagrass for food or shelter.

During one three-hour cleanup on a beach in Virginia, U.S.A., volunteers collected more than 900 balloons.

TURTLE POWER

BALLOON STRING

PIECE OF BALLOON

1 CHEX THE GREEN SEA TURTLE PROBABLY MISTOOK A 0.6-METRE (2-FT)-LONG STRING FOR FOOD.

2 CHEX RECOVERED AT THE CLEARWATER MARINE AQUARIUM, SPENDING LOTS OF TIME IN A KIDDIE POOL. ONCE THE TURTLE STARTED EATING SOLID FOODS AGAIN, RESCUERS DECIDED CHEX WAS READY TO RETURN TO THE OCEAN.

GREEN SEA TURTLE
Redington Beach, Florida, U.S.A.

ARCTIC OCEAN

NORTH AMERICA

EUROPE

ASIA

PACIFIC OCEAN

ATLANTIC OCEAN

AFRICA

PACIFIC OCEAN

SOUTH AMERICA

INDIAN OCEAN

AUSTRALIA

ANTARCTICA

Seagrass

BYE, BALLOON

After several days at the aquarium, Chex started to improve as the balloon made its way through the turtle's digestive system. Chex eventually passed the entire balloon, plus a 0.6-metre (2-ft)-long string. A few months later, after aquarium staff had successfully introduced solid food back into Chex's diet, rescuers declared the turtle was ready to return to the sea. Bell stood hip deep in the waves as another staff member handed Chex to her. She carefully placed the little turtle in the water and watched it paddle away. "Chex was like, 'Oh, there's the ocean! Okay, bye!'" Bell says. Chex's rescue is worth celebrating ... but maybe without the party balloons.

POLLUTION SOLUTION · PLASTIC PREDATOR

The ocean is full of trillions of pieces of rubbish called microplastics that are smaller than the full stop at the end of this sentence—which makes them really hard to clean up. But the solution might be in tadpole-like creatures called larvaceans (lar-VAY-shuns). These marine animals eat by filtering tiny food particles out of the water and through their bodies. The particles are first trapped in what's called a mucus house—a thin, see-through bubble of, well, mucus that surrounds the larvacean as it travels. Scientists are studying this behaviour to see if a similar process could pull harmful microplastics out of the water.

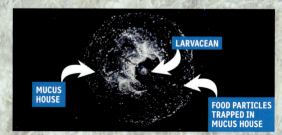

LARVACEAN

MUCUS HOUSE

FOOD PARTICLES TRAPPED IN MUCUS HOUSE

3 BIOLOGIST LAUREN BELL PREPARES TO RELEASE THE LITTLE TURTLE BACK INTO THE SEA.

OUR AWESOME OCEAN
SHOW & TELL!

NATIONAL GEOGRAPHIC KiDS

INFOPEDIA CHALLENGE 2022

Earth is sometimes called the blue planet because more than 70 percent of its surface is covered by ocean. Award-winning underwater photographer and National Geographic Explorer Brian Skerry has travelled the world to capture images of some of the oceans' most elusive creatures. From the fiercest fish to the most wondrous whales, Skerry has just about seen everything in the sea. Here, he shares more about life behind the lens, as well as why it's so key we all work together to protect our oceans.

What inspired you to become an underwater photographer?

I grew up in Massachusetts, and my parents would take me to the beach as a young boy. There was something so magical in the ocean. It was a place that was ripe for discovery, and the idea of exploring the ocean really appealed to me. I also loved photography and the idea of exploring the ocean with a camera and telling stories with pictures.

Are you ever afraid of swimming in the ocean or diving with sharks?

I've never been afraid of the water. It has always seemed so natural and comfortable to me. But I do have a healthy fear of predators like sharks. I know there are risks, and I try to do things as carefully and safely as possible.

What is one of your best memories of interacting with sharks?

I have thousands of memories! One of my favourites is swimming with oceanic whitetip sharks, one of the most dangerous species in the world. After 16 days, we only had one encounter, a female. She came right towards me! There I was, spinning around in the beautiful blue water of the Bahamas. She was very curious and swam big, lazy circles around us as I took her picture. I was pleasantly surprised about how polite she was. It was magical.

Besides sharks, what other animals have you worked with?

I love whales, and I recently had the opportunity to photograph multiple species. Through my work, I discovered that whales have a culture that's not that much different than humans'. They have different languages and dialects. Humpback whales have singing competitions. Some whale families even have babysitters! It's so fascinating, and I hope it gives people more appreciation for whales.

Why is it so important that we take care of our oceans?

The ocean is everything. Even though we live on land, we live on a water planet. About 72 percent of Earth's surface is ocean, and 98 percent of where life can exist on our planet is water. Everything from the weather to the air we breathe comes from the sea. The oceans are essential to human life: Our own survival depends on us understanding the ocean and protecting it.

THIS YEAR'S CHALLENGE

Now it's your turn! Help celebrate Our Awesome Ocean by showing and/or telling us all about your favourite ocean animal. There are so many cool animals: whale, octopus, sea turtle, dolphin, sea otter, walrus, seahorse, clownfish, jellyfish and so many more. Choose the animal and method (show or tell — or both) that's right for you.

Show: Draw a picture of your favourite ocean animal in its environment. Be as accurate as you can about how it looks, so that we can appreciate it as you do. With your drawing, include the name of the animal, where in the world it lives and one important fact about it.

Tell: Write a short essay, biography or poem about your favourite ocean animal, including its name, where in the world it lives, basic information like how big it grows and what it eats and why it's your favourite. Be informative and creative in writing about the creature, so that we can appreciate it as you do.

The most creative visual and written pieces will be featured in next year's Infopedia!

Find inspiration and details on how to enter at **natgeokids.com/almanac**.

LAST YEAR'S CHALLENGE

Kids proved they can be part of the plastic pollution solution! Last year more than 35,000 kids took the Nat Geo Kids pledge to reduce their plastic waste. And most of them aren't doing it alone. They're involving their families and friends to have an even bigger positive impact on the planet.

The 2021 Infopedia Challenge winner is Mary Rose Farinella, age 9, for her entry, Planet Protector: Making a Difference, One Sip at a Time.

Mary Rose inspired her family to recycle more and cut down on their use of plastic straws and plastic shopping bags. But the most significant thing she did was to replace plastic water bottles with reusable metal ones. Nearly one million plastic drink bottles are sold every minute around the world, so choosing a reusable bottle can make a huge difference. Plus, it's something everyone can do! You can read Mary's entry and more at **natgeokids.com/almanac**.

Certificate of Heroism
This hereby recognises
Mary Rose Farinella
as a PLANET PROTECTOR, pledging to help save the world by decreasing the use of straws, water bottles and other single-use plastic items.

GARY E. KNELL
Chief Executive Officer
National Geographic Partners

NATIONAL GEOGRAPHIC KIDS.

kids PLASTIC

10 EASY WAYS TO CUT BACK ON PLASTIC

Encourage your parents to shop with **REUSABLE TOTES** instead of **PLASTIC** shopping bags.

MUNCH ON FRUIT like apples, bananas or oranges instead of snacks that come in plastic packaging.

SKIP THE PLASTIC BOTTLES AND OPT FOR A **REFILLABLE WATER BOTTLE.**

ENJOY your ice cream in a cone and **AVOID** using plastic cups and spoons.

Encourage your family **to shop for snacks, cereal and pasta in** bulk, and store them in **glass containers.**

USE BARS OF SOAP
rather than liquid soap, which is dispensed from a **PLASTIC BOTTLE.**

Stock up on METAL or PAPER STRAWS — **and STOP USING** PLASTIC STRAWS **altogether.**

Carry cutlery or chopsticks with you to cut back on using plasticware at restaurants.

Use a **BAMBOO** toothbrush

instead of a plastic one.

BIRD FEEDER

Try to REPURPOSE, or UPCYCLE, plastic containers into toys, art and other useful things, instead of tossing them away.

kids VS. PLASTIC

Do your part to help prevent single-use plastic items from reaching the ocean. Check out ideas here, and then grab an adult and go online for more.
natgeokids.com/KidsVsPlastic

CHOOSE THIS

NOT THAT

WHY?

You might use plastic bags for snacks, but for many animals, the plastic bag *is* the snack!

The glint of a plastic goodie bag floating in the water can look like a fish. As the plastic fills the animal's stomach, it blocks food from travelling through its intestines, causing it to starve. In fact, one Cuvier's beaked whale was recently discovered with more than 39 kilograms (86 lb) of plastic—including snack bags, shopping bags and nylon ropes—in its stomach.

So instead, store your treats in reusable containers, and then toss them in your backpack for on-the-go grub.

Grab an adult and go online to pledge to reduce your single-use plastic waste!

TAKE THE PLASTIC PLEDGE!
natgeokids.com/
KidsVsPlastic

Pick Your Perfect SNACK SACK.

Find a reusable food container by choosing the phrase that fits you best.

1 I don't want my sandwich to get squished. — **Stash it in a sturdy container.**

2 I want a light and flexible wrap. — **Use a cloth or beeswax wrap.**

3 I need a container for messy munchies. — **Grab a glass jar.**

4 I want a pouch that's flexible yet sturdy. — **Stuff it in a silicone sack.**

LAST BAG If you have a few plastic snack bags left at home, keep using them! After each use, wash the bags with soap and water, let them air-dry and then keep reusing. Once they wear out, find a place to recycle them: Many supermarkets accept the bags for recycling.

YOUR **PLASTIC-FREE** GUIDE TO
SNACKS

Chew on these three ideas for plastic-free snacking.

1 TRAIL MIX

Just mix all your favourite treats from the bulk section of the supermarket together in a bowl, and then eat! You can even sprinkle your mixture with sea salt, cinnamon or another of your favourite spices for more flavour. Check out these ideas for ingredient inspiration.

- ☐ Pretzels
- ☐ Nuts like almonds, pistachios or peanuts
- ☐ Pumpkin or sunflower seeds
- ☐ Dried fruit like apricots, raisins or banana chips
- ☐ Chocolate chips
- ☐ Whole-grain cereal
- ☐ Desiccated coconut

2 HOB POPCORN

You'll need a paper bag full of popcorn kernels, some cooking oil and a big pan with a lid. Make sure to get a parent's help with this recipe.

- ☐ Pour a splash of oil into the pot, using just enough to cover the bottom.
- ☐ Grab a parent and heat the pot on the hob over medium heat.
- ☐ Pour in enough popcorn kernels to create one layer along the bottom of the pan.
- ☐ Cover the pan with the lid.
- ☐ After a few minutes, listen for popping sounds. When the popping slows, remove the pan from the burner, take off the lid and put the popcorn in a bowl.
- ☐ Top off your treat with salt, melted butter or other spices.

3 BAKED APPLES

Turn this packaging-free fruit into a special snack with brown sugar, butter and cinnamon. Make sure to get a parent's help with this recipe.

- ☐ Grab a parent and preheat the oven to 175°C (350°F). (You can also use the microwave.)
- ☐ Cut the apple in half, then scoop out the core.
- ☐ Put the apples in an ovenproof baking dish, and then spread a tablespoon of brown sugar and a tablespoon of butter on the inside of each apple half. Then sprinkle the apples with cinnamon.
- ☐ Bake the apples in the oven for about half an hour, in the microwave for about three minutes or until the fruit softens.

DIY Ice Pops

Help keep Earth healthy by ditching single-use plastic items. Make your own ice pops so you can skip the plastic-wrapped shop-bought version.

YOU'LL NEED

- 350 grams (12 oz) fresh fruit like strawberries, blueberries, peaches and bananas
- 30 millilitres (2 tbsp) honey
- 60 millilitres (10 fl oz) juice or water
- Blender
- 8 small paper cups
- Baking tin (optional)
- Aluminium foil or 8 foil muffin cases
- 8 wooden craft sticks

Left in outdoor waste bins, plastic wrappers can easily be blown into the environment, where animals might mistake them for food.

STEP ONE

Grab a parent and put the fruit, honey and juice (or water) into the blender.

STEP TWO

Put the lid on the blender, and then blend the mixture until it's smooth.

STEP THREE

Fill the paper cups 3/4 full with the blended mixture. (You can put the cups in a baking tin to keep them stable while you pour.)

STEP FOUR

Cover the top of each paper cup with a piece of aluminium foil or a foil muffin case.

STEP FIVE

Carefully poke a craft stick through the centre of the foil on each cup.

STEP SIX

Slide each craft stick about halfway down into the mixture.

STEP SEVEN

Place the cups on a flat surface in the freezer for about four hours, or until the mixture is fully frozen.

STEP EIGHT

Take the cups out of the freezer, remove the foil, peel away the paper cups and enjoy!

QUIZ WHIZ

What's your eco-friendly IQ? Find out with this quiz!

Write your answers on a piece of paper. Then check them below.

1 **True or false?** Burning plastic is harmful to the environment because it releases toxins into the air.

2 **What is a way to keep plastic out of the ocean?**
a. opt for package-free snacks
b. avoid using plastic bags in your lunch box
c. shop with a reusable tote bag
d. all of the above

3 **About how many pieces of plastic can be found in the Great Pacific Garbage Patch?**
a. 180,000
b. 1.8 million
c. 1.8 billion
d. 1.8 trillion

4 **Sea turtles often mistake _____ for their favourite food, seagrass.**
a. seaweed
b. eels
c. floating rubbish
d. fish

5 **True or false?** Plastic and other rubbish get trapped in circulating ocean currents around the world called gyres.

Not **STUMPED** yet? Check out the *NATIONAL GEOGRAPHIC KIDS QUIZ WHIZ* collection for more crazy **ENVIRONMENT** questions!

ANSWERS: 1. True; 2. d; 3. d; 4. c; 5. True

HOMEWORK HELP

Write a Letter That Gets Results

Knowing how to write a good letter is a useful skill. It will come in handy when you want to persuade someone to understand your point of view. Whether you're emailing your Member of Parliament or writing a letter for a school project or to your grandma, a great letter will help you get your message across. Most important, a well-written letter makes a good impression.

CHECK OUT THE EXAMPLE BELOW FOR THE ELEMENTS OF A GOOD LETTER.

Your address

Date

Salutation
Always use 'Dear' followed by the person's name; use Mr, Mrs, Ms or Dr as appropriate.

Introductory paragraph
Give the reason you're writing the letter.

Body
The longest part of the letter, which provides evidence that supports your position. Be persuasive!

Closing paragraph
Sum up your argument.

Complimentary closing
Sign off with 'Yours sincerely' or 'Thank you'.

Your signature

Maddie Smith
1234 Main Street
London
SW7

22 April 2022

Dear Owner of the Happy Hamburger,

I am writing to ask you to stop using single-use plastic at the Happy Hamburger.

This is my favourite restaurant. My family and I eat there almost every Saturday night. I always order the bacon cheeseburger with mac and cheese on the side. It's my favourite meal, ever!

The other day, my Dad brought home a takeaway order from your restaurant. The order contained a plastic fork, knife and spoon, all wrapped in plastic. It also came in a plastic bag. Now that's a lot of plastic!

I am concerned because plastic is a huge problem for the planet. Did you know that nine million tonnes of plastic waste end up in the ocean every year? Even worse, scientists think that the amount of plastic might triple by 2050.

Some other restaurants in town have cut back on their single-use plastic. The Hotdog Hangout uses paper bags instead of plastic bags for takeout. And servers at the Weeping Onion ask customers if they'd like plastic cutlery, instead of automatically including it in takeaway orders.

These are simple changes that I hope you can make at the Happy Hamburger. That way, not only would you be serving the best burgers around, but you'd also be helping to protect the planet.

Thank you very much for your time.

Yours sincerely,

Maddie Smith
Maddie Smith

COMPLIMENTARY CLOSINGS

Yours sincerely, Thank you, Regards, Kind regards, Best wishes, Respectfully

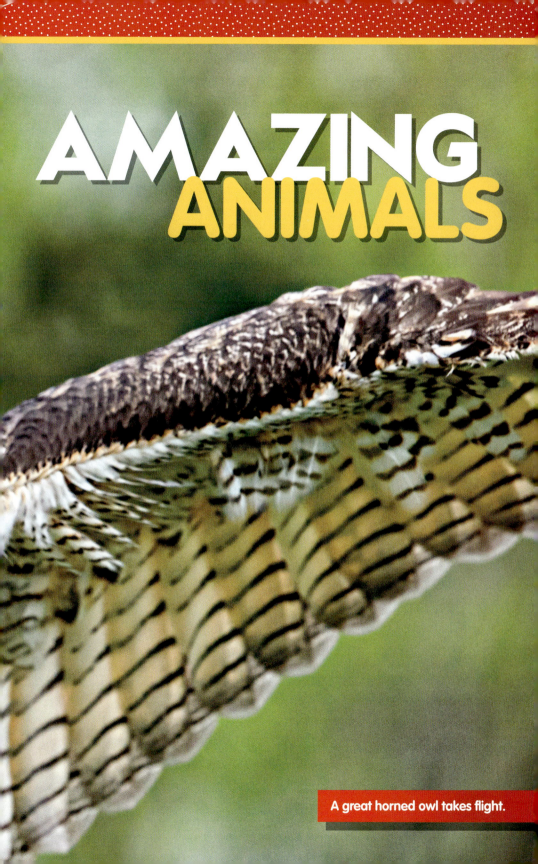

AMAZING
ANIMALS

A great horned owl takes flight.

WHAT IS Taxonomy?

Because there are billions and billions of living things, called organisms, on the planet, people need a way of classifying them. Scientists created a system called taxonomy, which helps to classify all living things into ordered groups. By putting organisms into categories, we are better able to understand how they are the same and how they are different. There are eight levels of taxonomic classification, beginning with the broadest group, called a domain, followed by kingdom, down to the most specific group, called a species.

Biologists divide life based on evolutionary history, and they place organisms into three domains depending on their genetic structure: Archaea, Bacteria and Eukarya. (See page 101 for 'The Three Domains of Life'.)

Where do animals come in?

Animals are a part of the Eukarya domain, which means they are organisms made of cells with nuclei. More than one million species of animals, including humans, have been named. Like all living things, animals can be divided into smaller groups, called phyla. Most scientists believe there are more than 30 phyla into which animals can be grouped based on certain scientific criteria, such as body type or whether or not the animal has a backbone. It can be pretty complicated, so there is another, less complicated system that groups animals into two categories: vertebrates and invertebrates.

HEDGEHOG

SAMPLE CLASSIFICATION
PHILIPPINE TARSIER

Domain:	Eukarya
Kingdom:	Animalia
Phylum:	Chordata
Class:	Mammalia
Order:	Primates
Family:	Tarsiidae
Genus:	*Carlito*
Species:	*syrichta*

TIP: Here's a sentence to help you remember the classification order: **Did King Phillip Come Over For Good Soup?**

BY THE NUMBERS

There are 13,730 vulnerable or endangered animal species in the world. The list includes:

- **1,220 mammals,** such as the snow leopard, the polar bear and the fishing cat
- **1,492 birds,** including the Steller's sea eagle and the black-banded plover
- **2,494 fish,** such as the Mekong giant catfish
- **1,367 reptiles,** including the Round Island day gecko
- **1,597 insects,** such as the Macedonian grayling
- **2,157 amphibians,** such as the emperor newt
- **And more,** including 183 arachnids, 733 crustaceans, 239 sea anemones and corals, 187 bivalves and 2,039 snails and slugs

ROUND ISLAND DAY GECKO

Vertebrates
Animals WITH Backbones

Fish are cold-blooded and live in water. They breathe with gills, lay eggs and usually have scales.

Amphibians are cold-blooded. Their young live in water and breathe with gills. Adults live on land and breathe with lungs.

Reptiles are cold-blooded and breathe with lungs. They live both on land and in water.

Birds are warm-blooded and have feathers and wings. They lay eggs, breathe with lungs and are usually able to fly. Some birds live on land, some in water and some on both.

Mammals are warm-blooded and feed on their mothers' milk. They also have skin that is usually covered with hair. Mammals live both on land and in water.

BIRD: MANDARIN DUCK

AMPHIBIAN: POISON DART FROG

Invertebrates
Animals WITHOUT Backbones

Sponges are a very basic form of animal life. They live in water and do not move on their own.

Echinoderms have external skeletons and live in seawater.

Molluscs have soft bodies and can live either in or out of shells, on land or in water.

Arthropods are the largest group of animals. They have external skeletons, called exoskeletons, and segmented bodies with appendages. Arthropods live in water and on land.

Worms are soft-bodied animals with no true legs. Worms live in soil.

Cnidaria live in water and have mouths surrounded by tentacles.

MOLLUSC: MAGNIFICENT CHROMODORID NUDIBRANCH

SPONGE: SEA SPONGE

ARTHROPOD: PRAYING MANTIS

Cold-Blooded versus Warm-Blooded

Cold-blooded animals, also called ectotherms, get their heat from outside their bodies.

Warm-blooded animals, also called endotherms, keep their body temperatures level regardless of the temperature of their environment.

39

10 ADORABLE FACTS ABOUT ANIMAL BABIES

BABY HEDGEHOGS — also known as **HOGLETS —** are BORN with TINY, SMOOTH SPIKES, which eventually turn into **PRICKLY QUILLS.**

BABY RABBITS are called **KITTENS.**

Cotton-top tamarin monkeys have TWINS MORE OFTEN than they have SINGLE BABIES.

PUPPIES SLEEP as many as **20 hours** a day.

BABY RHINOS aren't born with a **HORN —** it takes a **FEW MONTHS** to start to **GROW IN.**

A **BABY GIRAFFE** can **STAND SOON AFTER** its **BIRTH** and learns to **WALK WITHIN AN HOUR.**

A newborn **DOLPHIN** is born with a **TINY PATCH** of **HAIR** on its chin.

Baby deer — called **fawns** — are born with **white spots** that look like **spots of sunlight** to help them **hide from predators.**

FEMALE RED SQUIRRELS are known to **'ADOPT'** ABANDONED SQUIRREL BABIES — CALLED PUPS — and RAISE THEM as THEIR OWN.

A **PANDA CUB** is about the **SIZE** of a **NEWBORN CAT** AT BIRTH — about 1/900th the size of its mother.

EXTRAORDINARY ANIMALS

Bears Get Backs Scratched

Aah, that's the spot!

THE CUB, ON THE RIGHT AND BELOW, IS LIKELY ABOUT TWO AND A HALF YEARS OLD.

THE METAL POLES HELP MARK THE ROAD WHEN SNOW FALLS.

Yukon Territory, Canada

When a mum grizzly bear and her nearly full-grown cub spotted a metal road sign, the pair could *bearly* contain their excitement. The two stood up on their hind legs and rubbed their backs and faces against the pole like they were scratching bear-sized itches!

But the two probably weren't itchy, says Tom Smith, a bear biologist at Brigham Young University in Utah, U.S.A. "Bears use these scratching behaviours to lay down their scent," he says. "It tells other bears that live there that these two are nearby, which can help bears avoid fights or find mates."

Bears living in forested areas often leave their scent on tree trunks. But in the treeless Canadian tundra, grizzlies spread their odour on boulders, muddy areas and human-made objects like buildings and signposts. Sort of like a smelly text message!

Clean Sea = Happy Birds!

Flamingo Says "Save the Earth!"

BOB THE FLAMINGO SWIMS IN THE CARIBBEAN SEA.

Willemstad, Curaçao

Bob the flamingo likes taking dips in his own salt-water pool and getting foot massages on the beach. This hardworking bird deserves all the pampering: He's teaching kids about conservation.

Veterinarian and wildlife sanctuary founder Odette Doest rescued Bob after he flew into a hotel window. After rehabilitating him, she realised he wouldn't be able to survive in the wild. So Doest decided to keep Bob at her sanctuary and use the friendly bird to help educate people.

She often brings Bob to schools to teach kids about plastic pollution, which can harm wildlife when the animals become entangled in fishing gear or mistake discarded balloons as food. Bob helps people understand how a small change in their habits can have a big impact on his life, Doest says. Best bird ever!

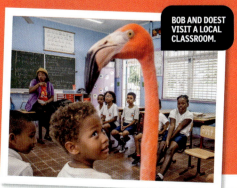

BOB AND DOEST VISIT A LOCAL CLASSROOM.

Dog Flies Away

Rochester Hills, Michigan, U.S.A.

Tinkerbell the Chihuahua was relaxing with her owners at an outdoor market when a blast of wind tore through the area at 113 kilometres an hour (70 mph). Tables and chairs flew into the air—and so did the 2.7-kilogram (6-lb) pup. Her frantic owners chased after her, but the wind carried Tinkerbell away like a furry paper aeroplane.

For two days, owners LaVern and Dorothy Utley searched the area. But the only sign of Tinkerbell was her lead, found about 0.4 kilometre (0.25 mile) away. Desperate, the Utleys wandered along a footpath and called the dog one final time. She came running!

No one is sure how Tinkerbell survived her journey—or her landing. "She was probably only six or eight feet off the ground," meteorologist Dave Rexroth said. "I suspect she was tossed around like a tumbleweed until she got caught in small trees." Her owners, however, didn't care how she managed to survive. "We were just totally tickled to have her back," LaVern Utley said.

I must be part bird!

43

Hen Sails the World!

Sailing is so much easier than flying.

Brittany, France

Why did the chicken cross the sea? To keep the sailor company!

Guirec Soudée and Monique have been sailing buddies for years, visiting places such as Antarctica, the Caribbean islands and South Africa. The hen stands beside Soudée while he hoists the sails, and she catches fish that have flopped onto the deck. "I knew that this little chicken was as adventurous as I am," says Soudée, author of *The Hen Who Sailed Around the World: A True Story.*

Monique lives in her own cabin filled with straw, and she's been known to lay an egg on board. Chicken behaviour expert K-lynn Smith says Monique probably has a better life than most chickens, with more space and sunshine. This chicken definitely isn't cooped up!

SOUDÉE SAYS THAT MONIQUE OFTEN 'SINGS' FOR HIM AS THEY SAIL.

Let me steer the boat.

MONIQUE USUALLY STAYS CLOSE TO HER OWNER, GUIREC SOUDÉE.

ANIMAL MYTHS BUSTED

Some people mistakenly think adult opossums hang by their tails or that porcupines shoot their quills. What other misconceptions are out there? Here are some common animal myths.

MYTH Elephants are afraid of mice.

HOW IT MAY HAVE STARTED People used to think that mice liked to crawl into an elephant's trunk, which could cause damage and terrible sneezing. So it makes sense that elephants would be afraid of the rodents.

WHY IT'S NOT TRUE Although elephants do get anxious when they hear sounds they can't identify, their eyesight is so poor that they could barely even see a mouse. Plus, if an elephant isn't afraid to live among predators such as tigers, rhinos and crocodiles, a mouse would be the least of its worries!

Who are you again?

MYTH Goldfish only have a three-second memory.

HOW IT MAY HAVE STARTED While an adult human's brain weighs about 1.4 kilograms (3 lb), an average goldfish's brain weighs only a tiny fraction of that. So how could there be any room for memory in there?

WHY IT'S NOT TRUE Research has shown that goldfish are quite smart. Phil Gee of the University of Plymouth in the United Kingdom trained goldfish to push a lever that dropped food into their tank. "They remembered the time of day that the lever worked and waited until feeding time to press it," Gee says. One scientist even trained goldfish to tell the difference between classical and blues music!

MYTH Touching a frog or toad will give you warts.

HOW IT MAY HAVE STARTED Many frogs and toads have bumps on their skin that look like warts. Some people think the bumps are contagious.

WHY IT'S NOT TRUE "Warts are caused by a human virus, not frogs or toads," says dermatologist Jerry Litt. But the wart-like bumps behind a toad's ears *can* be dangerous. These parotoid glands contain a nasty poison that irritates the mouths of some predators and often the skin of humans. So toads may not cause warts, but they can cause other nasties. It's best not to handle these critters — warty or not!

45

Cute Animal
SUPERLATIVES

Funky features. Super senses. Sensational speed. No doubt, all animals are cool. But whether they've got goofy grins, funky hair or endless energy, some species are extra adorable. Here are 15 of the cutest creatures on Earth.

FURRIEST

Thick, white fur helps polar bears blend in with the ice and snow of their Arctic habitat. This fur even grows on the bottom of their paws! It gives them a better grip on the ice and protection from frozen surfaces.

BEST SNUGGLER

The smallest raptor in Africa, African pygmy falcons only grow to be about the length of a pencil. To stay warm in winter, these pint-sized predators spend up to 15 hours a day snuggling together in their nests.

BEST CAMO

Is that a leaf — or a sea dragon? Thanks to leaf-shaped appendages that cover their bodies, these fish easily blend into the seaweed and kelp that grow in their underwater habitats.

BEST AT HANGING OUT

Spending more than 90 percent of their waking time in trees, orangutans — who have much longer arms than legs — are well suited for life in the forest canopy.

BEST HOPPER

Leaping lambs! All sheep are playful, but the young ones are especially energetic. They spend their days jumping, running around and head-butting their pals for fun.

BEST HAIR DAY

Polish chickens sometimes go by the nickname of 'top hat' because of the funky feathers at the top of their head, or crest. Their unique appearance made them prized birds among the rich and royalty in the 1700s. Despite their name, the breed known today comes from the Netherlands.

BEST DRESSED

Native to Madagascar, panther chameleons can be identified by their brightly coloured skin, which ranges from blue and green to pink and yellow. It only takes a few minutes for a panther chameleon to change its colouring.

BEST SENSE OF SMELL

Elephants are super smellers. They use the nostrils at the edge of their trunks to sniff out sources of water and food from several miles away.

SMALLEST HOOVES

About the size of a rabbit, the Vietnamese mouse-deer — also known as a chevrotain — is the world's smallest hoofed animal. After not being seen in the wild in nearly 30 years, it was photographed in Vietnam in 2017.

BEST STRETCH

What's the benefit of having an extra-long neck? It's better to catch prey with! Snake-necked turtles use their stretchy necks — which can grow to be more than half the length of their shells — to strike at shrimp, worms or fish.

FASTEST

Cheetahs are the swiftest species on land. When hunting prey, the big cats can accelerate to speeds of more than 97 kilometres an hour (60 mph) in just three seconds.

BEST ACROBAT

Inchworms have a funny way of walking: With legs at both ends of their bodies but none in the middle, they shift from the front end to go forwards, creating an awesome arch with their bodies as they move.

SLEEPIEST

Koalas sure catch a lot of z's! In fact, the marsupials sleep up to 22 hours a day, allowing their body to conserve plenty of energy, which is required to digest their food.

BEST WARNING

If you spot a poison dart frog in the wild, watch out! These teeny amphibians are among the world's most toxic animals. Their brightly coloured skin — which can be yellow, gold, copper, red, green, blue or black — sends a message to predators to stay away.

SLOWEST

Never expect a sloth to make it anywhere on time! The sluggish species travels at a top speed of some 1.8 to 2.4 metres (6 to 8 ft) a minute. Otherwise, it sleeps in treetops for about 20 hours a day.

Bet You Didn't Know!

6 facts that will BUG you!

1 **Dragonflies** appeared on **Earth 140 million years before** the **first birds.**

2 **Mosquitoes** prefer to **bite people** who have **smelly feet.**

3 **Raw termites** taste like **pineapple.**

4 **A housefly** can **turn somersaults** in the **air.**

5 **Tiny bugs** called **mites** live in your **eyebrows.**

6 **Most female fireflies can't fly.**

SPIDER'S WEB STATS

A single spider can eat up to 2,000 insects every year. How do spiders catch all of those tasty treats? Using silk from special glands called spinnerets, spiders weave sticky webs to trap their delicious prey. But this silk can do much more than simply catch dinner. Stick around and learn more about the incredible spider's web.

.001–.004
millimetre
(.00004–.00016 in)
Thickness of silk a spider uses to build webs

-60°C TO 150°C
(-76°F to 302°F)
The extreme range of temperatures that a spider's silk can withstand

ORB WEAVER SPIDER

25
METRES (82 ft)
Diameter of webs woven by Darwin's bark spider —the largest spider's webs in the world!

5
Number of times stronger a spider's silk is compared to steel of the same diameter

2–8
Pairs of spinnerets, the glands a spider uses to make silk

Age of oldest spider's web ever found embedded in amber:

140 MILLION YEARS OLD

51

SUN BEAR RESCUE

How kind carers helped an orphaned cub return to the wild

These bears are named for the golden or white 'rising sun' patch on their chests, which experts think might help the bears seem bigger than they are.

A three-month-old sun bear huddles alone in a metal cage. A few days ago, poachers snatched the cub from the wild and brought her to a town in Malaysia, an island country in Southeast Asia, where she was sold as a pet, which is illegal. Now the orphan is stressed and hungry. If she stays in the cage, she may not survive.

BEAR AID

That's when carers from the Bornean Sun Bear Conservation Centre step in. They give the cub a name — Natalie — and take her in, giving her a special milk with extra protein, plus plenty of comfort and care. Within a few weeks, Natalie grows strong enough to head outside with a carer. She even climbs a tree! Soon, she joins three other bears in an outdoor enclosure. Together, the bears lounge, play and learn to forage for their favourite treats of termites, earthworms and honey.

WILD AGAIN

After five years at the rescue centre, Natalie is ready to be released in the wild. A team of veterinarians gives the 45-kilogram (100-lb) bear one last checkup before fitting her with a tracking collar so that they can watch where she goes for the first few months. They fly her on a helicopter in a crate to a protected wildlife reserve where people don't live. The rescuers use a long rope to open Natalie's crate from afar. She bursts out into the woods — finally a free bear again.

Scientists have spotted mother sun bears cradling cubs in their arms while walking on their hind legs.

WONG SIEW TE FEEDS NATALIE A SPECIAL MILK TO HELP HER GAIN WEIGHT.

WONG WATCHES OVER NATALIE LIKE HER MOTHER WOULD HAVE DONE IN THE WILD.

ASIA
AREA ENLARGED
PACIFIC OCEAN
INDIAN OCEAN
AUSTRALIA

A S I A
BANGLADESH
INDIA
MYANMAR (BURMA)
LAOS
THAILAND
VIETNAM
CAMBODIA
South China Sea
INDIAN OCEAN
BRUNEI
MALAYSIA
INDONESIA

Where sun bears live

PREPARE TO BE
AMAZED BY THIS
ACROBAT
OF THE FOREST ...

THE INCREDIBLE
RED PANDA

A red panda totters along the branch of an evergreen tree, placing one paw in front of the other like a gymnast on a balance beam. But then ... whoops! The panda loses its footing. A fall from this height — about 30 metres (100 ft) — could be deadly. But the panda quickly grips the branch with all four paws and some seriously sharp claws, steadies itself and keeps moving.

Red pandas spend about 90 percent of their time in the trees, says Mariel Lally, a red panda keeper at the Smithsonian's National Zoo in Washington, D.C., U.S.A. In fact, red pandas have adapted so well to life in the trees that they're famous for their incredible acrobatic skills. Check out three ways that red pandas land a perfect score with their amazing aerial act.

ASIA

Bay of Bengal

South China Sea

INDIAN OCEAN

Where red pandas live

BUILT-IN BALANCE

A tightrope walker is all about balance. But red pandas can't exactly extend their arms like an acrobat. Instead, they hold their tails straight behind them. "If they start to swing in one direction, they can move their tails the opposite way," Lally says. "It's sort of like a tightrope walker's pole."

UNDER FUR COVER

What's the best way to avoid a hungry snow leopard? Never let it see you in the first place! The small red panda's fiery coat sticks out at the zoo, but in the fir trees of the Himalayan mountains, the fur hides the panda in the reddish moss and white lichen (a plantlike organism) that often hang on the trees. Red pandas are so hard to spot that even scientists have trouble locating these creatures.

FAKE THUMB

A trapeze artist needs her thumbs to wrap her whole hand around the trapeze as she swings. Otherwise she might fly off! Same idea with red pandas. They have a special thumb-like wrist bone that gives them an extra grip when climbing down trees headfirst.

RED PANDA ON THE RUN

Smithsonian's National Zoo, Washington, D.C., U.S.A.

Ashley Wagner was out with her family when she spotted an animal crossing the street. At first Wagner's mum thought they'd seen a raccoon, but as soon as the creature turned its face towards them, Wagner knew it was a red panda.

Rusty the runaway red panda had arrived at the zoo just a few weeks before. As he scampered under a fence, Wagner snapped photos, shared them on social media and called the zoo. Soon a team came to the rescue, eventually nabbing him from a tree.

Today, Rusty has retired from his life on the run and settled down. The father of three red panda cubs, he lives at the Smithsonian Conservation Biology Institute.

SAVING THE RED PANDA

With their kitten-like faces, fluffy fur and waddling walk, red pandas are adorable. But these endangered animals are also ideal targets for the illegal pet trade.

Luckily, people are trying to help them. There's the Red Panda Network, which hires local people to keep watch over the red pandas in Nepal, replant bamboo and help paying tourists observe them without disturbing the creatures. Other organisations track poachers by using DNA samples from red pandas rescued from the black market to learn where the animals are being taken from.

You can help by asking your parents and older siblings not to 'like' photos and videos of red pandas on social media unless you know that the group or person posting them is trustworthy (like a wildlife photographer or a conservation group).

BIG CATS

A young male jaguar

The National Geographic Big Cats Initiative's goal is to stop the decline of lions and other big cats in the wild through research, conservation, education and global awareness. Visit natgeo.org/bigcats to learn more.

Not all wild cats are big cats, so what are big cats? To wildlife experts, they are tigers, lions, leopards, snow leopards, jaguars, cougars and cheetahs. The first five are members of the genus *Panthera*. They can all unleash a mighty roar, and, as carnivores, they survive solely on the flesh of other animals. Thanks to powerful jaws; long, sharp claws; and daggerlike teeth, big cats are excellent hunters.

WHO'S WHO?

BIG CATS IN THE *PANTHERA* GENUS MAY HAVE a lot of features in common, but if you know what to look for, you'll be able to tell who's who in no time.

FUR

SNOW LEOPARD

A snow leopard's thick, spotted fur helps the cat hide in its mountain habitat, no matter the season. In the winter its fur is off-white to blend in with the snow, and in the summer it's yellowish-grey to blend in with plants and the mountains.

JAGUAR

A jaguar's coat pattern looks similar to that of a leopard, as both have dark spots called rosettes. The difference? The rosettes on a jaguar's torso have irregularly shaped borders and at least one black dot in the centre.

TIGER

Most tigers are orange-coloured with vertical black stripes on their bodies. This colouring helps the cats blend in with tall grasses as they sneak up on prey. These markings are like fingerprints: No two stripe patterns are alike.

LION

Lions have a light brown, or tawny, coat and a tuft of black hair at the end of their tails. When they reach their prime, most male lions have shaggy manes that help them look larger and more intimidating.

LEOPARD

A leopard's yellowy coat has dark spots called rosettes on its back and sides. In leopards, the rosettes' edges are smooth and circular. This colour combo helps leopards blend into their surroundings.

BENGAL TIGER
109 to 227 kilograms
(240 TO 500 LB)
1.5 to 1.8 metres long
(5 TO 6 FT)

JAGUAR
45 to 113 kilograms
(100 TO 250 LB)
1.5 to 1.8 metres long
(5 TO 6 FT)

LEOPARD
30 to 80 kilograms
(66 TO 176 LB)
1.3 to 1.9 metres long
(4.25 TO 6.25 FT)

AFRICAN LION
120 to 191 kilograms
(265 TO 420 LB)
1.4 to 2 metres long
(4.5 TO 6.5 FT)

SNOW LEOPARD
27 to 54 kilograms (60 TO 120 LB)
1.2 to 1.5 metres long (4 TO 5 FT)

Weirdest. Cat. Ever.

THE SERVAL MIGHT LOOK STRANGE, BUT THAT'S A GOOD THING WHEN IT COMES TO HUNTING.

SERVALS CAN CATCH UP TO 30 FROGS IN THREE HOURS WHILE HUNTING IN WATER.

SERVAL KITTENS STAY WITH MUM UP TO TWO YEARS BEFORE LIVING ON THEIR OWN.

Servals can chirp, purr, hiss, snarl and growl.

A serval sits patiently in a grassy field, swiveling its head back and forth like a watchful owl. The predator is scanning the savannah for a meal not with its eyes, but with its oversize ears. An unseen rodent stirs under the thick brush, and the wild cat tenses. It crouches on its legs and feet before launching itself up and over the tall grass. Guided only by sound, the serval lands directly on the once invisible rat.

Thanks to its extra-long legs, stretched-out neck and huge ears, the serval is sometimes called the 'cat of spare parts'. The wild cat might look weird to some people. "But put together, their bizarre-looking body parts make them really successful hunters," says Christine Thiel-Bender, a biologist who studies servals in their African home.

In fact, servals catch their prey in more than half of their attempts, making them one of the best hunters in the wild cat kingdom. That's about 20 percent better than lions hunting together in a pride.

ALL EARS

The serval's big ears are key to the animals' hunting success. Servals rely on sound more than any other sense when they're on the prowl. Thanks to their jumbo ears—the biggest of any wild cat's relative to body size—a serval can hear just about any peep on the savannah. (If a person had ears like a serval's, they'd be as big as dinner plates!) To make the most of their super hearing, servals avoid creating noise while hunting. So instead of stalking prey like some cats do, servals squat in clearings and sit still—sometimes for several hours—as they listen for food.

THE
MYSTERY OF THE
BLACK
PANTHER

Are you superstitious? Do you think it's bad luck if a black cat crosses your path?

Many people once believed that black cats partnered with the devil. They show up regularly in comic books, posters and movies. But in real life these big cats are as rare as parents who allow kids to eat dessert before dinner. What are these mysterious black cats, and where do they live?

"Black panthers are simply leopards with dark coats," says scientist John Seidensticker. "If you look closely, you can see the faint outline of spots in the dark fur," he adds.

Biologists used to think that black panthers were a separate species of leopard. The fierce black cats had a reputation for being more aggressive than spotted leopards, the way dark-maned lions are more aggressive than those with lighter manes. But zookeepers noticed that spotted leopards and black leopards can sometimes be born in the same litter (see below) — just as kids in the same family can have blue eyes or brown eyes.

BLENDING IN

Overall, black leopards are extremely rare in the wild. They are almost never seen in the leopard's range in Africa, and only occasionally in India. But surprisingly, these black cats are the only leopards known in the forests of Malaysia, in Southeast Asia. Black leopards are so much more common there that the people living in the country's forests don't even have a word in their vocabulary for *spotted* leopards.

Scientists don't really know why black leopards are the norm in Malaysia. One theory is that animals living in dark, humid forests like those in Malaysia tend to have darker fur for

camouflage. African leopards spend most of their lives in grasslands and forests, where spots may be the best disguise.

The black cats are not evil creatures of witches and devils. They are cats at their best — evolving to blend with their habitat.

59

TIGERS in the Snow

These wild cats survive the cold of eastern Russia.

Many Amur tigers have beachfront access—they live in Russian forests on the edge of the Sea of Japan.

Silently moving through the trees, a tigress stalks her prey. Deep snow covers the ground, and with each step the big cat sinks to her belly. She knows the snow will muffle any sounds, so she can sneak up on a wild boar that is rooting around for pine nuts. A few yards away, the tiger pauses, crouches and then launches her 127-kilogram (280-lb) body towards her prey. Snow sprays up with each leap as she prepares to pounce on the boar with her plate-sized paws. A powdery cloud fills the air. Then the snow settles, revealing the 0.9-metre (3-ft)-long tail and orange, black and white body. Now stained red, the tigress grasps the boar in her mouth.

She carries her catch behind some larch trees, and her two cubs join her from a nearby hill. Camouflaged in the trees, they were watching their mother hunt. Soon, they'll start hunting for themselves. But for now, they are content with the meal their mother has provided, followed by a nap.

These Siberian, or Amur, tigers live in the eastern reaches of Russia—further north than any other tiger subspecies. Thick coats of fur insulate their bodies from the freezing winter temps. In the summer, their coats blend in with the forest, making them nearly impossible to see.

HUNGER GAMES

The tiger trio is among the some 600 Amur tigers that researchers think are left in the wild. As recently as 50 years ago, there were plenty of deer and wild boar, staples of a tiger's diet. Today, those prey animals are harder to find. People hunt

A TIGER CUB STICKS WITH MUM FOR AT LEAST 18 MONTHS.

them, and logging companies and fires destroy the forest where they live. Some tiger habitat is protected, but the cats wander beyond these safe zones in search of prey. Half of all tiger cubs die young because they are sick, killed by hunters or orphaned. Cubs that survive leave Mum at about 18 months old, relying on the hunting skills they learned growing up. Sometimes a young male must travel far to find unclaimed land that has enough food. But the odds are that his journey will take him through areas where people live.

TROUBLESHOOTING

It is late winter when the male tiger leaves his mother's care. When he scratches against a tree, he catches his paw on something. He's walked into a wire snare, and the more he moves, the tighter it gets. A little while later, he hears voices. People. They stay behind the trees, and one of them raises a gun. The tiger roars at the sharp pain in his backside, then lies down and falls asleep. He's been shot by a researcher's tranquilliser gun, not a hunter. Unable to find enough food in the snowy forest, this tiger started taking livestock and dogs in a nearby town. Dale Miquelle and his team are called in to fix the problem. "Relocating them gives them a second chance," Miquelle says. Otherwise, the farmer would track down the tiger and shoot him.

The researchers quickly weigh and measure the tranquillized tiger. Then they fit a collar with a radio transmitter around his neck. This will let Miquelle's team keep track of the tiger's whereabouts for at least three years.

NEW TERRITORY

Two hours later, the tiger wakes up in the back of a truck about 241 kilometres (150 miles) from the town. The cage gate opens, and the wild cat leaps out. Unfamiliar with the territory, he searches for signs of other tigers. He comes across a birch tree with a strong odour. Another male sprayed the tree and left scrape marks and urine on the ground to tell others, "Occupied. Keep moving."

The young tiger walks on. Miquelle's team monitors his movements using signals from the radio collar. They hope he can find food, avoid other males, find his own territory and eventually mate with a local female. The tiger spots a deer ahead. Melting snow drips from the trees, masking his footsteps as he ambushes his prey. His odds just got a little better.

THIS TIGER'S SCRATCHES ON TREES ARE MESSAGES FOR OTHER TIGERS.

In the 1930s, only about 30 Amur tigers were left in the wild.

ICE-COLD WATER QUENCHES THIS TIGER'S THIRST.

A HIPPOPOTAMUS HELPS BABY ANIMALS CROSS A RAGING RIVER.

It's rush hour in Africa. Every October, thousands of wildebeest and zebras gather along the banks of the Mara River. They wait to cross the deep, rushing waters as part of their seasonal journey from the Masai Mara National Reserve in Kenya to the Serengeti National Park in Tanzania. The river flows so fast that fully grown animals struggle to swim to the other side. "When the river is full, lots of animals drown trying to cross," says Tom Yule, who ran the nearby Lemala Mara safari camp. Watching from the river's edge, Yule sees a wildebeest calf and later a zebra foal jump into the water. But he doesn't expect what happens next.

wild CROSSING GUARD

1

The little wildebeest tries to paddle across the river but is swept away by the strong current. The calf tries to keep its head above water while floating downstream. Suddenly something rises out of the water: a large, dark head followed by the hulking body of a hippopotamus. "The hippo was lying in the water near where the animals jump in, and it immediately goes after the calf," Yule says. Hippos can be very aggressive and even deadly when defending territory, so he wonders whether the hippo will attack the baby wildebeest.

The strong hippo defies the current and uses its body to stop the wildebeest calf's scary ride downstream. Like a tugboat guiding a ship filled with precious cargo, the hippo shepherds the youngster to the other side of the river. Yule and other bystanders watch in disbelief. "I have never witnessed anything like this," he says. The wildebeest reaches the opposite bank and runs back upstream to rejoin its herd.

WILDEBEEST CALF

ZEBRA IN TROUBLE

2

Yule thinks the drama is over when suddenly the river grabs hold of a small zebra foal. He watches as the tiny striped head dips underwater and then resurfaces. Just when it looks like the zebra won't make it, the hippo suddenly appears. Again, the huge hippo helps the baby across to the shallow water on the other side. But the exhausted foal can barely stand. Gently, the hippo nudges the zebra into a safe nook between two large rocks. "The hippo gets out of the water and starts to nuzzle the foal with its great jaws," Yule says. "And then the hippo coaxes the zebra to cross a small channel and climb up the slope of the opposite bank to its mum."

SAFE ON LAND

3

Yule thinks the hippo would be too exhausted for any more superhero moments. But instead, it settles back into the river to keep a watchful eye. "Animals are unpredictable, and each one has its own unique personality," Yule says. "This hippo's instincts are to help those that need assistance. It's just like protective people who say, 'Not on my watch!' as they help others."

UNICORNS
OF THE SEA

SCIENTISTS TRY TO **SOLVE THE MYSTERY** OF THE NARWHAL'S **GIANT TUSK.**

Chilly water laps against an iceberg in the Arctic Ocean. Suddenly a pod of narwhals—a species of whale that sports a unicorn-like horn on its head— emerges from the sea near the iceberg's edge.

Narwhals live in the Arctic Ocean. Like most whales, they're jumbo-sized—up to 1,588 kilograms (3,500 lb)— and surface to breathe. And like some whale species such as orcas, they live in pods. (Narwhals usually have 15 to 20 in their group.) But there's one thing a narwhal has that no other whale does: a giant tusk growing out of its noggin.

For centuries people have been trying to figure out what this tusk—actually an enlarged tooth—is used for. Luckily scientists have come up with some theories that may help solve this gnawing puzzle.

SURFACING ABOVE WATER, A GROUP OF NARWHALS TAKES A BREATH OF AIR.

TUSK, TUSK

A narwhal's swordlike tusk first pokes from their jaw through the animal's upper lip when it's about three months old. This is the only tooth the whale develops. Over time, the tusk can grow to be half the length of the whale's body. New research shows that narwhals may use these long appendages to snag prey like arctic cod, using quick jabs to stun the fish before they eat them.

TOOTH SLEUTHS

Another theory is that male narwhals use the tooth to attract females. Similar to a peacock's flashy feathers, the tusk makes them stand out to potential mates. The animals have been observed scraping their tusks together, as though they are in a fencing match. This may be a way for male members of the pod to identify each other.

Although there's still plenty scientists don't know about narwhals, they will continue to look for answers. In the meantime, it appears that these mysterious whales still have a few secrets up their tusks.

THIS POD OF MALES SWIMS THROUGH ARCTIC WATERS.

A NARWHAL MUM TRAVELS WITH HER BABY.

ROCK 'EM SOCK 'EM SHRIMP

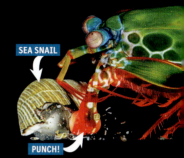

SEA SNAIL

PUNCH!

THESE TINY CRUSTACEANS WILL KNOCK YOU OUT.

Burrowing under the sand near coral reefs lives a pint-sized punk. Sure, this crustacean has a colourful shell and adorable eyes — but don't let that fool you. Although the peacock mantis shrimp is only 2.5 to 17.8 centimetres (1 to 7 in) long, it's a fearsome ocean predator. Dig deeper to discover some stunning facts about this tiny toughie.

PERFECT PUNCH

Many of the peacock mantis shrimps' favourite snacks — like crabs, clams and sea snails — are protected by superhard shells. Good thing the shrimps have **two hinged, hammer-like limbs** that can thwap their targets with a force that's more than 2,500 times stronger than their body weight. (That'd be like you punching through a steel wall!) These animals also use their powerful punchers to defend their territory against other peacock mantis shrimps. In fact, they're so brawny that they've been known to **shatter aquarium tanks' glass.**

SPEED DEMON

Don't blink around peacock mantis shrimps: They strike so quickly that they could knock out 50 punches in the time it takes you to bat your eye. This swift motion forms a bubble of vapour around the prey's shell, which collapses less than a nanosecond later. If the prey hasn't escaped yet, watch out. The water briefly heats up to **4704°C (8500°F)**, and a wave of energy thumps the victim like a tiny implosion.

BRAINIAC ATTACK

One reason peacock mantis shrimps are so tough is their braininess: They have to be smart about how — and when — they wield their weapons. "They can remember another mantis shrimp they've fought before, and whether they **won or lost**," says Roy Caldwell, a biologist and professor at the University of California, Berkeley, U.S.A. And when they're going after a tricky meal, peacock mantis shrimps go in with a game plan. "If they're dealing with a crab, they'll first knock off the deadly claws, then the legs, then use their own limbs to hold the crab in just the right place for **a shell-shattering punch,**" Caldwell says.

A male's shell is more colourful than a female's.

EYES

PUNCHING LIMBS

FEEDING LIMBS

SWIMMING LIMBS

WALKING LIMBS

65

THE SECRET LIVES OF

Orcas don't often dive very deep — their food is usually near the surface, so they are as well.

You'd need more than 650 cans of tuna to keep an orca full!

Orcas

'FRIENDING' OTHER DOLPHINS. 'LIKING' FUN ACTIVITIES. 'CHATTING'. ORCAS MIGHT HAVE THE BEST SOCIAL NETWORK EVER.

A bottlenose dolphin flips its tail as it swims with its dolphin friends. A baby chimpanzee watches closely as its mum shows it how to crack a nut. A male wolf howls to gather the pack for a hunt.

Playing, teaching and working together are known as social skills. Humans, of course, are social animals. So are bottlenose dolphins, chimps and wolves. And according to scientists, it's time to move one animal higher up the list: orcas!

Orcas are dolphins, so scientists already knew about some of their social behaviours. "We knew orcas travel in pods," says biologist Janice Waite of the National Oceanic and Atmospheric Administration (NOAA), in the United States. But new research shows that the school-bus–sized swimmers have more complex social behaviours than previously understood.

Could orcas be among the most social animals of all? Here are five stories to help you decide.

Orcas 'adopt' orphans.

Springer watched curiously as a boat approached her. The young orca had been orphaned as a calf, so no one had taught her that boat propellers could injure her. Wanting to take a closer look, Springer swam closer until ... *whoosh!* An older female orca called Nodales forcefully shoved her away from danger.

"Nodales took Springer under her wing, even though they weren't related," says Paul Spong, co-director of OrcaLab, a research station in Canada. "It didn't take long for the young orca to understand she should keep away from boats." Today, Springer is a mother herself — and she stays out of water traffic.

Orcas 'babysit' other orcas.

One day a female named Sharky moved close to a group of newborn orcas and their mothers. Sharky swam near a calf, and then led it away to play with her — giving the mums a break. Waite observed Sharky behave like that with other calves as well. "She's not the only young female we've seen 'babysit' other orcas," Waite says. "We think they do it as practice for when they have calves of their own."

ORCAS APPROACH A WEDDELL SEAL, HOPING TO MAKE IT THEIR MEAL.

Orcas are team players.

A Weddell seal lies on a sheet of floating ice in Antarctica. Suddenly five orcas begin nudging the ice. Then, a large female orca begins to make whistling and clicking noises. It's like a signal: The other orcas line up, swim towards the ice and create a wave that knocks the seal into the water. Oddly, the orcas let the seal escape.

Some experts believe that the female orca was teaching hunting and teamwork to her calves. And as with any new skill, practice makes perfect!

Orcas put family first.

Researchers rarely spotted Plumper and Kaikash apart. But when older brother Plumper became ill, the researchers worried that he wouldn't be able to keep up with his younger sibling. But the brothers were inseparable. Kaikash would swim a short distance, and then wait for Plumper to catch up. "This went on for hours," Spong says. "Kaikash didn't seem to mind. Like human brothers, these two had each other's backs."

Researchers now know that orca families spend most of their days together. Although adults — especially males — sometimes split from the group to hunt, they stay close enough to hear family members. Says Waite, "They're probably as close with their families as we are with ours."

Orcas play together.

Orcas are known for breaching — or leaping out of the water — to show their playful side. "They get most excited when they meet up in groups," says biologist Candice Emmons of NOAA. She's seen orcas from different pods brush against each other to say hello. She's also watched orcas smacking their tails against the water (called lobbing) to show excitement. But Emmons's favourite thing to observe is 'pec slapping'.

"That's when they touch each other with their pectoral fins, which are like their arms," Emmons says. Sort of like orca high fives!

An orca's diet consists of whales, sea lions, penguins, seals, walruses and a variety of fish and squid. *Chomp!*

SURF Pups

5 WAYS COASTAL WOLVES THRIVE BY THE SEA

Coastal wolves are valued in many indigenous cultures; some groups consider them ancestors.

Wolves often howl in a chorus.

A wolf steps out onto a sandy beach. Catching a scent, it paws at the wet sand in search of a buried clam. *Crunch!* The wolf crushes the clam in its jaws and swallows. Still hungry, it splashes into the ocean waves and swims to a nearby island to find more food.

Wolves on the beach might sound strange, but these special grey wolves have been living by the seaside for thousands of years. Known as coastal wolves, about 2,000 of these individuals make their homes among the islands and coastal rainforest of western British Columbia in Canada. (Another population lives in southeast Alaska, U.S.A.) "Their environment is so different from that of any other wolf," wildlife researcher Chris Darimont says. "So they've had to adapt to this unique place." Check out five ways these howlers are living their best life on the beach.

BEACH HAIR, DON'T CARE

Unlike most grey wolves, coastal wolves' fur is often streaked with reddish orange highlights. The colour matches seaweed found on the shore, likely helping to camouflage these predators as they hunt on the beach.

Coastal wolves also have less underfur than other grey wolves. The cottony fluff helps wolves living in snowy places like Montana, U.S.A., keep warm, but coastal wolves' habitat is so mild that they don't need the extra layer.

A wolf's sense of smell is about a hundred times more sensitive than a human's.

SEA SIZE

About the size of a German shepherd, coastal wolves are about 20 percent smaller than grey wolves living in North American forests. Scientists think it could be because these seafood eaters don't need the extra strength. After all, coastal wolves are wrestling otters, not gigantic moose like their grey wolf cousins. "They aren't chasing massive prey, so they don't need the large body size to take them down," Darimont says.

SWIMMING TEAM CHAMPS

One small island usually isn't big enough for coastal wolves to find and eat the three kilograms (7 lb) of food they need each day. So the canines doggy-paddle from island to island in search of more food. "They swim between islands like we walk on sidewalks," conservationist Ian McAllister says. And these wolves really are super swimmers. Scientists have spotted them on nearly every one of the thousand islands and rocky outcrops in the area, McAllister says, sometimes swimming up to 12 kilometres (7.5 miles) between each strip of land.

3

Some coastal wolves can get 90 percent of their diet from the sea.

4

5

SPLASHY SURPRISE

Grey wolves that live in open habitats like the tundra often hunt by chasing big, hoofed animals across a wide plain, Darimont says. But that style of hunting doesn't work on a coast that's full of thick rainforest or tiny islands too small to run across. Instead, they often sneak up on prey — then pounce. "The seals haul out of the ocean to get away from killer whales," McAllister says. "But on land, they're not safe from ambushing wolves."

SEAFOOD, PLEASE!

What's to eat? Coastal wolves use their powerful sense of smell to find whatever snacks the ocean served up that day. They might dig in the sand for crabs and clams, feast on fish eggs stuck to kelp or sneak up on larger animals like sunbathing seals or otters.

Others get their fill of fish just from salmon. "They wait in the shallows where the salmons' backsides are poking out, then snap up the tastiest-looking fish they can find," Darimont says. A coastal wolf might scarf down 10 salmon in one morning. Talk about fish breath!

HOW TO SPEAK GORILLA

A YOUNG MOUNTAIN GORILLA IN THE DEMOCRATIC REPUBLIC OF THE CONGO REACHES FOR A CAMERA.

Discover five surprising ways these apes communicate.

Keepers entering the gorilla enclosure at the Columbus Zoo and Aquarium in Ohio, U.S.A., often hear a noise that sounds like a babbling human. But it's just Mac, a western lowland gorilla. The ape greets his carers by making long, low grumbling sounds, gorilla-speak for "Hi, there!" When keepers exit the area in the evening, he makes a similar sound as if to say "Good night."

Mac isn't just making noise. Gorillas like him have things to say. And if you pick up a little gorilla language, you just might understand them.

"Apes are excellent communicators," Columbus Zoo curator Audra Meinelt says. And sound isn't the only way gorillas 'talk'. They use movements and even body odour to get their point across. It's no wonder experts think gorillas are among the most advanced animal communicators after humans. Check out these five amazing stories.

1 "What's in it for me?"

Nia, a western lowland gorilla, was excited when she discovered a new 'toy' — a plastic cup — had been added to her habitat at the Columbus Zoo. When zookeepers came to replace the cup with another toy, Nia wouldn't give it up. So Nia's keepers offered her a treat as a reward. Nia gave up the cup — and realised that things she finds in her habitat can be valuable. The next time Nia found a cup in her space, the gorilla broke it into several pieces and only gave the keepers one piece at a time ... in exchange for a treat after every piece!

Other gorillas at the zoo caught on to Nia's trick. "They'll hold out an item they think we might want, but not all the way," zookeeper Heather Carpenter says. "If we try to get it, they'll pull it back like, 'Not so fast!' Their actions are telling us that they'll give us what we want — but only when we offer something *they* want."

A WESTERN LOWLAND GORILLA GOOFS OFF IN ITS ZOO ENCLOSURE.

3 "Follow me."

Kighoma the eastern lowland gorilla is the leader of his troop in the Democratic Republic of the Congo, a country in Africa. It's easy to spot the gorilla in charge, according to Sonya Kahlenberg of the Gorilla Rehabilitation and Conservation Education Center. Adult male leaders are identified by the silver fur on their back. (They're called, well, silverbacks.) And they're often belching!

"It sounds like *na-oom*, kind of like a throat clearing. It means, 'I'm over here,'" Kahlenberg says. "And whenever Kighoma is ready to move, he'll make that grumbling sound and the other gorillas know to follow him."

2 "Help!"

Anthropologist Kelly Stewart wanted to see how the wild mountain gorillas she was observing would react to her new gorilla T-shirt. But when she opened her jacket to reveal the shirt to a young female, Simba, the gorilla screamed — a sound that means "I'm scared!" in young gorillas. And *that* told the older troop members that Simba needed help. The group's leader, Uncle Bert, barrelled towards Stewart with a deep roar. Stewart quickly covered her top and stepped away from Simba, who stopped screaming. Uncle Bert backed off once Simba was quiet — the little gorilla was okay now that the unfamiliar 'gorilla' had gone. "I never wore that T-shirt again!" Stewart says.

A SILVERBACK MOUNTAIN GORILLA IN RWANDA LEADS HIS TROOP.

A GORILLA GETS A WHIFF OF SOMETHING GROSS.

4 "I'm not happy."

When zookeepers at the Dallas Zoo in Texas, U.S.A., smell a sport sock–like odour, they know it's time to do an extra check on the gorillas. The smell comes from the male apes' armpits, and it may mean that a squirrel has entered their exhibit, or that the males aren't getting along. Either way, the stink signifies that something's not quite right.

5 "You've got this!"

Fasha the wild mountain gorilla had got her foot caught in a poacher's trap in the forests of Rwanda, Africa. She escaped, but couldn't keep up with her troop. But Icyororo the gorilla wasn't leaving her friend behind. Arms linked, they made their way through the forest. Every few minutes Icyororo turned and patted Fasha as if to say, "We're almost there."

When the pals crossed a river together, Icyororo gave Fasha a hug, demonstrating gorillas' amazing ability to encourage their loved ones.

You can do this!

SUPER SNAKES

Snakes are masters of disguise, skilled hunters and champion eaters. More than 3,000 species of these reptiles slither around the world. Check out these surprising facts about snakes.

AMAZON TREE BOA

AFRICAN SAW-SCALED VIPER

SNAKES SMELL WITH THEIR TONGUES.

Smell that mouse? A snake uses its tongue to help it smell. It flicks its long, forked tongue to pick up chemical molecules from the air, ground or water. The tongue carries the smelly molecules back to two small openings — called the Jacobson's organ — in the roof of the snake's mouth. Cells in the Jacobson's organ analyse the scent. Mmm, lunch!

SNAKE VENOM CAN KILL.

By sinking two hollow, pointy fangs into their prey, many snakes inject venom to paralyse or kill victims before devouring them. Africa's puff adder is thought to be one of the world's deadliest snakes. Up to 1.8 metres (6 ft) long and weighing as much as 6 kilograms (13 lb), the puff adder strikes fast. Its venom can cause severe pain, tissue damage and even death in humans. It's a snake to be respected ... from a distance.

PUFF ADDER

SNAKES CHANGE THEIR SKIN.

Snakes literally grow out of their skin. Every few months, most start rubbing against the ground or tree branches. Starting at the mouth, a snake slithers out of its too-tight skin. Like a sock, the skin comes off inside out. Voilà — the snake has a fresh, shiny look. Nice makeover.

GOLDEN TREE SNAKE

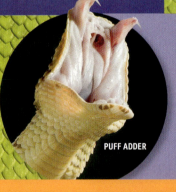

DIONE RAT SNAKE

CONSTRICTORS GIVE WICKED HUGS.

Boas, anacondas, pythons and other snakes called constrictors are amazing squeezers. This kind of snake wraps its muscular body around a victim and squeezes until the animal suffocates. The twisted talent comes from muscles attached to 200 or more vertebrae in a snake's backbone. (Humans are born with only 33 vertebrae.)

5 COOL REASONS TO LOVE BATS

1 FLIP, FLAP AND FLY
Bats are the only mammals that can truly fly. A bat's wings are basically folds of skin stretched between extra-long finger and hand bones.

2 VALUABLE DROPPINGS
Bat droppings, called guano, are super rich in nitrogen, a main ingredient in plant food. The ancient Inca of South America protected bats as a valuable source of fertiliser for their crops. Guano is still used in farming today.

3 MARVELLOUS MOSQUITO MUNCHERS
Many bats are born bug-eaters, filling their bellies with moths, mosquitoes and other winged insects. The brown bat gulps down as many as a thousand mosquito-sized insects in an hour. Each night the bats from one Texas, U.S.A., cave consume about 181 tonnes (197 tons) of bugs, many of them crop-eating pests. That's about the weight of six fully loaded cement trucks.

4 EXTREME FLIGHT
Hoary bats migrate up to 1,609 kilometres (1,000 miles) south from Canada each autumn. Mexican free-tailed bats often fly up to 5 kilometres (3 miles) high, where tailwinds help speed them along at more than 97 kilometres an hour (60 mph).

5 SUPERMUM STRENGTH
A newborn bat may weigh as much as a third of its mother's weight, yet the mum can hold her baby while clinging by her toes to a crack in a cave's ceiling.

Going Batty

LITTLE BROWN BAT
'Little' is right — a brown bat weighs about as much as two small coins!

SHORT-TAILED FRUIT BAT
After just one night of dining, this bat can scatter up to 60,000 undigested seeds — crucial to rainforest plant growth.

COMMON VAMPIRE BAT
Vampires' main diet is the blood of cows and horses. Rarely do they take a bite out of humans.

WHITE TENT BATS
These fruit-eaters often create 'tents' to roost in. They make bites in a large leaf so it folds over itself. Then the bats snuggle under.

FLYING FOX
There are about 60 species of bats called flying foxes (above). This kind sometimes roosts in a 'camp' of up to a million individuals.

VELVETY FREE-TAILED BAT
This bat fills its cheek pouches with insects in midair, and then chews and swallows them later.

PALLID BAT
Using big ears to listen for rustlings, a pallid bat locates and grabs its prey from the ground.

DESERT LONG-EARED BAT
Sonar emitted by this kind of bat echoes off prey, signaling where its meal lies.

OLD WORLD LEAF-NOSED BAT
Complex nose structures for hunting gave this bat its name.

Bet You Didn't Know!

Bat Spit May Save Lives
A substance in the saliva of vampire bats could help victims of strokes survive, according to researchers at Monash University in Melbourne, Australia. Strokes happen when a blood clot blocks blood flow to the brain. An anticlotting substance in bat spit makes blood flow freely, so a bat can continue to feed. The researchers think the same substance may be able to dissolve blood clots in stroke patients. Fortunately, the substance would be contained in medicine, and bats would not be required to bite patients!

6 Tips Every Polar

Life in the frozen wilds of the Arctic Circle isn't exactly easy, even if you're a polar bear, the world's largest land-dwelling predator. To withstand the subzero temperatures, snow-covered landscapes and day after day without sun, you're going to need to put all 680 kilograms (1,500 lb) of your muscle, bone and body fat to good use. If you were a polar bear, here's what you'd need to know to survive on the Arctic ice.

1 Walk, Don't Run … or Better Yet, Sit Still.

When walking or running, a polar bear expends more than twice the energy used by most other mammals. Want to save energy? Don't move at all. If you do run, make it a short trip. After an eight-kilometre (5-mile) run, even young bears in good shape can become overheated.

2 Barefoot … *hmm* … *Bear*foot Is Best.

Ever wonder why your paws are so big? On an adult, they're huge — up to 30 centimetres (12 in) across. Working like snowshoes, they spread weight across the snow and ice, keeping you from sinking. That way your paws don't make any crunching noises, which could warn prey that 'Bigfoot' is on the way.

3 Don't Let Cubs Become Polar Bear Snacks.

It's a harsh fact of Arctic life that adult males sometimes kill and eat polar bear cubs, so mother bears are very protective. Most will chase away male polar bears much bigger than they are. Male bears are not the only threats from which mums defend their cubs. Some brave mothers will rear up on their hind legs to leap at hovering helicopters!

Bear Should Know

4 Fat's Where It's At.

Because you live in the cold Arctic climate, having a layer of fat is a good thing. That fat, called blubber, works like a fleece jacket — it insulates your body from the frosty air and near-freezing water. When food is scarce, your 10-centimetre (4-in)-thick blubber gives you energy and helps keep you afloat when you swim because fat weighs less than water.

5 Neatness Counts. So Does Drying Off.

A clean bear is a warm bear. That's because dirty, matted fur doesn't hold body heat like clean fur does. After eating, spend up to 15 minutes cleaning yourself — licking your chest, paws and muzzle with your long tongue. In summertime, take baths straight after you eat. Then dry yourself by shaking off excess moisture or using snow like a thick, fluffy towel to rub away the water.

6 Always Wear White.

You may have noticed that the hairs in your thick fur coat aren't really white. Each is transparent with a hollow core that reflects light. This helps you to blend in with your surroundings — a neat trick, especially while you're hunting wary seals. Good thing wearing white is always stylish for polar bears.

HOW TO
SPEAK
DOG

C'MON! CATCH ME IF YOU CAN!

Watch a group of dogs playing in the park. These pups don't know each other, yet within a few minutes of meeting, they'll start playing a doggie game. As they wrestle and chase, it's obvious they're 'talking'. But instead of words, they're using body language. Learning to 'listen' to your pup's body language will help you get closer to your pet. Check out what your dog may be trying to tell you through these five behaviours.

THE PLAY-BOW

The play-bow means your pup is ready for fun with another dog. She'll crouch down with her 'elbows' almost touching the ground, her tail waving madly and her rump in the air. After holding this pose for a few seconds, she'll take off running, checking over her shoulder to make sure the other dog is following. When her new playmate comes bounding after her, the two dogs will race and chase. If one dog bangs into the other too hard, it'll do a quick play-bow to say, "Oops!" So the next time your dog play-bows, let the games begin!

A dog's tail should never be pulled. Pulling it could dislocate the bones and cause nerve damage. Then the tail won't move anymore.

THE SHOWY TAIL

A dog strutting around with his tail held high is showing he's in charge. This works even better if the dog has a tail that's easy to see. Maybe that's why wolves have big bushy tails, and why many dogs have tails with lighter-coloured hair on the underside. The light colour shows when their tails go up, a perfect signal flag.

Check out this book!

THE BEGGING STARE

That sweet little beggar staring directly at you while you eat isn't starving. He's controlling you. A staring dog is communicating with you. Outside, he might be telling you that he's the boss so you'd better not come too close. But at the dinner table, he's probably begging for a scrap. And if you sneak him a bite, he might think he's got you well trained — and taking orders from *him!* So ignore a staring, begging dog. Make sure that nobody else feeds him from the table, either. Eventually the pooch will realise *you're* in charge and that begging doesn't work. Next time you tell him to go and lie down, he might just do it.

Scientists say dogs are four times more likely to steal food when they think you're not looking.

A dog can make about 100 different facial expressions.

THE BUTT-SNIFF

Dogs sure have a weird way of saying hello. Instead of shaking paws, they sniff each other's rear ends! One dog lets the other sniff him. Then they switch positions. Why? Dogs identify friends by the way they smell, not by looks. It's the anal glands — located in a pooch's bottom — that give each pup a signature scent. To a dog, another pup's personal smell carries as much data as an ID card. This information tells if a dog is healthy or sick, young or old and even what he ate for dinner.

THE BELLY-UP

Time for a belly rub! That's what it looks like a dog is saying when she rolls onto her back with her front legs bent and her belly exposed. When you start rubbing, sometimes one hind leg will kick, and she'll look super content. The kicking leg is just a reflex — kind of like what happens when the doctor taps your knee with a rubber hammer. But the real meaning of this dog's position is submission and trust. She's saying that you're in charge, and she's okay with that.

5 Silly Pet Tricks

JUST CALL ME STEPH FURRY.

BINI THE BUN

Rabbit Plays Basketball
1

Los Angeles, California, U.S.A.

Before he goes to bed at night, Bini the Holland lop tries to make a slam dunk. If the rabbit misses, he grabs the rebound and tries again. "He won't go to sleep until he makes a basket," owner Shai Lighter says. Bini started shooting hoops on his own — sort of. One night, Lighter saw the rabbit dropping the same ball inside a box over and over again. So he bought Bini a miniature basketball hoop and rewarded the slam dunks with the animal's preferred treat: oat seeds. In addition to playing basketball, Bini also loves helping Lighter with chores. "He knows how to use a mini vacuum cleaner."

Most Holland lops enjoy playing with cat toys.

THIS IS JUST HOW I ROLL.

Pug Coasts on Skateboard
Washington, D.C., U.S.A.

2

Jumping on his skateboard, Mr. Butts pushes off with a paw, and then zips past his favourite bakery. "Mr. Butts has about a 20 percent chance of being distracted by a pastry," owner Justin Siemaszko says. If he's not, the pup is usually rewarded with bread after he shows off some sweet boarding moves. And he'll sneeze to let his owners know if he hasn't had his baked goods fast enough after hopping off the board. "The bigger the sneeze, the bigger his disapproval," Siemaszko says. To train for the trick, Siemaszko and his wife, Beth, first taught Mr. Butts to sit and stay on the board while it wasn't moving. Later, they upped the difficulty by practising while the board was rolling, starting with only two of the pug's feet on the board. "Once he could push off successfully, he started boarding by himself," Siemaszko says. Mr. Butts's favourite spot to zoom past? The Washington Monument on D.C.'s National Mall!

Some pugs in ancient China had their own mini palaces and bodyguards.

3

Pig Makes Art
Franschhoek, South Africa

Pigcasso, the 456-kilogram (1,000-lb) rescue pig, doesn't take her art too seriously — she prefers to dance while she paints. "She tosses her head and flaps her ears," says Joanne Lefson, the founder of Farm Sanctuary SA, where Pigcasso lives. The pig first learned to paint after she picked up a stray paintbrush with her mouth. Noticing the pig's fascination, Lefson set up a canvas and prepped a brush with paint to see what Pigcasso would do. "She started painting on it almost right away," Lefson says. When art time is over, Pigcasso dramatically tosses the brush into the air. That's not the only unusual thing this artist does. Says Lefson, "When the painting is completely done, she dips her nose in beetroot ink and 'signs' the artwork for a finishing touch."

I BET THIS WILL BE WORTH A MILLION POUNDS ONE DAY.

Pigs prefer to sleep nose-to-nose.

I'M BASICALLY FLYING!

A guinea pig's teeth never stop growing.

BOW BEFORE YOUR ONE TRUE RULER.

4

Guinea Pig Clears Hurdles
Austin, Texas, U.S.A.

Rolly the guinea pig jumps like a champion show pony. But unlike a pony, Rolly jumps over little bars stuck into toilet-paper-roll tubes — and she sometimes squeaks while soaring. Owner Malia Canann taught her pet the trick by encouraging Rolly to follow bits of lettuce over small hurdles she placed close to the ground. As Rolly learned, Canann increased the height of the hurdles. Now her jumps are as high as a toilet-paper-roll tube!

5

Cat Strikes Pose
Dana Point, California, U.S.A.

Touchdown! Why does this cat throw her paws up in the air like a referee? Because she's super pumped about lapping up a bit of coconut oil. Keys the cat stood on her hind legs and placed her paws in the air for the first time a few years ago while trying to get her owner out of bed. Peter Mares thought the move was cute and rewarded Keys with a little coconut oil. The cat's been doing the move ever since. But what if Mares doesn't have any coconut oil? "She'll work for a little bit of ice cream," he says.

Prehistoric TIMELINE

HUMANS HAVE WALKED on Earth for some 200,000 years, a mere blip in the planet's 4.5-billion-year history. A lot has happened during that time. Earth formed and oxygen levels rose in the millions of years of the Precambrian time. The productive Paleozoic era gave rise to hard-shelled organisms, vertebrates, amphibians and reptiles.

Dinosaurs ruled Earth in the mighty Mesozoic. And 66 million years after dinosaurs became extinct, modern humans emerged in the Cenozoic era. From the first tiny molluscs to the dinosaur giants of the Jurassic and beyond, Earth has seen a lot of transformation.

THE PRECAMBRIAN TIME

4.5 billion to 542 million years ago

- Earth (and other planets) formed from gas and dust left over from a giant cloud that collapsed to form the sun. The giant cloud's collapse was triggered when nearby stars exploded.
- Low levels of oxygen made Earth a suffocating place.
- Early life-forms appeared.

THE PALEOZOIC ERA

542 million to 252 million years ago

- The first insects and other animals appeared on land.
- 450 million years ago (mya), the ancestors of sharks began to swim in the oceans.
- 430 mya, plants began to take root on land.
- More than 360 mya, amphibians emerged from the water.
- Slowly, the major landmasses began to come together, creating Pangaea, a single supercontinent.
- By 300 mya, reptiles had begun to dominate the land.

What Killed the Dinosaurs?

It's a mystery that's boggled the minds of scientists for centuries: What happened to the dinosaurs? Although various theories have bounced around, a recent study confirms that the most likely culprit is an asteroid or comet that created a giant crater. Researchers say that the impact set off a series of natural disasters like tsunamis, earthquakes and temperature swings that plagued the dinosaurs' ecosystem and disrupted their food chain. This, paired with intense volcanic eruptions that caused drastic climate changes, is thought to be why half of the world's species — including the dinosaurs — died in a mass extinction.

DINO TIMES

THE MESOZOIC ERA

251 million to 65 million years ago

The Mesozoic era, or the age of the reptiles, consisted of three consecutive time periods (shown below). This is when the first dinosaurs began to appear. They would reign supreme for more than 150 million years.

TRIASSIC PERIOD

251 million to 201 million years ago

- The first mammals appeared. They were rodent-sized.
- The first dinosaur appeared.
- Ferns were the dominant plants on land.
- The giant supercontinent of Pangaea began breaking up towards the end of the Triassic.

JURASSIC PERIOD

201 million to 145 million years ago

- Giant dinosaurs dominated the land.
- Pangaea continued its breakup, and oceans formed in the spaces between the drifting landmasses, allowing sea life, including sharks and marine crocodiles, to thrive.
- Conifer trees spread across the land.

CRETACEOUS PERIOD

145 million to 66 million years ago

- The modern continents developed.
- The largest dinosaurs developed.
- Flowering plants spread across the landscape.
- Mammals flourished, and giant pterosaurs ruled the skies over small birds.
- Temperatures grew more extreme. Dinosaurs lived in deserts, swamps and forests from the Antarctic to the Arctic.

THE CENOZOIC ERA — TERTIARY PERIOD

65 million to 2.6 million years ago

- Following the dinosaur extinction, mammals rose as the dominant species.
- Birds continued to flourish.
- Volcanic activity was widespread.
- Temperatures began to cool, eventually ending in an ice age.
- The period ended with land bridges forming, which allowed plants and animals to spread to new areas.

DINO Classification

Classifying dinosaurs and all other living things can be a complicated matter, so scientists have devised a system to help with the process. Dinosaurs are put into groups based on a very large range of characteristics.

Scientists put dinosaurs into two major groups: the bird-hipped ornithischians and the lizard-hipped saurischians.

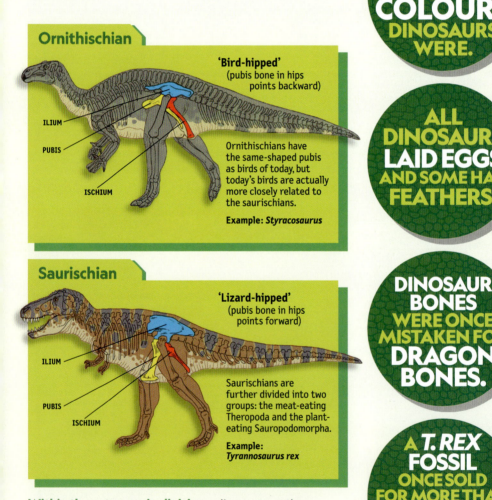

Ornithischian

ILIUM

PUBIS

ISCHIUM

'Bird-hipped'
(pubis bone in hips points backward)

Ornithischians have the same-shaped pubis as birds of today, but today's birds are actually more closely related to the saurischians.

Example: *Styracosaurus*

Saurischian

ILIUM

PUBIS

ISCHIUM

'Lizard-hipped'
(pubis bone in hips points forward)

Saurischians are further divided into two groups: the meat-eating Theropoda and the plant-eating Sauropodomorpha.

Example:
Tyrannosaurus rex

Within these two main divisions, dinosaurs are then separated into orders and then families, such as Stegosauria. Like other members of the Stegosauria, *Stegosaurus* had spines and plates along the back, neck and tail.

NO ONE **KNOWS** WHAT **COLOURS** DINOSAURS WERE.

ALL DINOSAURS LAID EGGS AND SOME HAD **FEATHERS.**

DINOSAUR BONES WERE ONCE MISTAKEN FOR **DRAGON BONES.**

A *T. REX* **FOSSIL** ONCE SOLD FOR MORE THAN **EIGHT MILLION DOLLARS.**

③ NEWLY DISCOVERED DINOS

Humans have been searching for—and discovering—dinosaur remains for hundreds of years. In that time, at least 1,000 species of dinos have been found all over the world, and thousands more may still be out there waiting to be unearthed. Recent discoveries include *Dineobellator notohesperus*, a feathered meat-eating raptor with razor-sharp teeth and claws.

1 *Dineobellator notohesperus* (Saurischian)

Name Meaning: Navajo warrior from the Southwest

Length: 2 metres (7 ft), not including tail

Time Range: Late Cretaceous

Where: New Mexico, U.S.A.

2 *Wulong bohaiensis* (Saurischian)

Name Meaning: Dancing dragon

Length: About the size of a crow

Time Range: Early Cretaceous

Where: Liaoning Province, China

3 *Allosaurus jimmadseni* (Saurischian)

Name Meaning: Jim Madsen's different reptile

Length: 8–9 metres (26–29 ft)

Time Range: Late Jurassic

Where: Utah, U.S.A.

DINO DEFENCES

Scientists don't know for sure whether plant-eating dinos used their amazing attributes to battle their carnivorous cousins, but these herbivores were armed with some pretty wicked ways they could have used to defend themselves.

ARMOUR: *GASTONIA*
(GAS-TONE-EE-AH)

Prickly *Gastonia* was covered in heavy defensive armour. To protect it from the strong jaws of meat-eaters, it had four horns on its head, thick layers of bone shielding its brain, rows of spikes sticking out from its back and a tail with triangular blades running along each side.

SPIKES: *KENTROSAURUS*
(KEN-TROH-SORE-US)

Stand back! This cousin of *Stegosaurus* had paired spikes along its tail, which it could swing at attackers with great speed. One paleontologist estimated that *Kentrosaurus* could have swung its treacherous tail fast enough to shatter bones!

CLUB TAIL:
ANKYLOSAURUS
(AN-KYE-LOH-SORE-US)

Steer clear! *Ankylosaurus* possessed a heavy, knobby tail that it could have used to whack attackers. It may not have totally protected the tanklike late Cretaceous dino from a determined *T. rex*, but a serious swing could have generated enough force to do some real damage to its rival reptile.

WHIP TAIL:
DIPLODOCUS
(DIH-PLOD-UH-KUS)

Some scientists think this late Jurassic giant's tail — about half the length of its 27-metre (90-ft) body — could have been used like a whip and swished at high speeds, creating a loud noise that would send potential predators running.

HORNS:
TRICERATOPS
(TRI-SERR-UH-TOPS)

There's no evidence *Triceratops* ever used its horns to combat late Cretaceous snack-craving carnivores. But scientists do believe the famous three-horned creature used its frills and horns in battle with other members of its species.

QUIZ WHIZ

Explore just how much you know about animals with this quiz!

Write your answers on a piece of paper. Then check them below.

1 How did a hippo in Masai Mara National Reserve in Kenya help other animals?
- **a.** by taking in their babies
- **b.** by giving them extra food
- **c.** by providing them with shelter
- **d.** by helping them cross the river

2 After eating, a polar bear will spend up to 15 minutes doing what?
- **a.** cleaning its fur
- **b.** taking a nap
- **c.** flossing
- **d.** looking for its next meal

3 True or false? Apes are excellent communicators.

4 When hunting for food, peacock mantis shrimp _____.
- **a.** form a bubble of vapour
- **b.** unleash a powerful punch
- **c.** use their limbs to hold down prey
- **d.** all of the above

5 What does it mean if a dog does a play-bow?
- **a.** he's in charge
- **b.** he wants to play
- **c.** he's hungry
- **d.** he's scared

Not **STUMPED** yet? Check out the *NATIONAL GEOGRAPHIC KIDS QUIZ WHIZ* collection for more crazy **ANIMAL** questions!

ANSWERS: 1. d; 2. a; 3. True; 4. d; 5. b

HOMEWORK HELP

Wildly Good Animal Reports

Seahorse

Your teacher wants a written report on the seahorse. Not to worry. Use these organisational tools so you can stay afloat while writing a report.

STEPS TO SUCCESS: Your report will follow the format of a descriptive or expository essay (see page 197 for 'How to Write a Perfect Essay') and should consist of a main idea, followed by supporting details and a conclusion. Use this basic structure for each paragraph, as well as the whole report, and you'll be on the right track.

1. Introduction
State your **main idea.**
Seahorses are fascinating fishes with many unique characteristics.

2. Body
Provide **supporting points** for your main idea.
Seahorses are very small fishes.
Seahorses are named for their head shape.
Seahorses display behaviour that is rare among almost all other animals on Earth.

Then **expand** on those points with further description, explanation or discussion.
Seahorses are very small fishes.
Seahorses are about the size of an M&M at birth, and most adult seahorses would fit in a teacup.
Seahorses are named for their head shape.
With long, tube-like snouts, seahorses are named for their resemblance to horses.
A group of seahorses is called a herd.
Seahorses display behaviour that is rare among almost all other animals on Earth.
Unlike most other fish, seahorses stay with one mate their entire lives. They are also among the only species in which dads, not mums, give birth to the babies.

3. Conclusion
Wrap it up with a **summary** of your whole paper.
Because of their unique shape and unusual behaviour, seahorses are among the most fascinating and easily distinguishable animals in the sea.

KEY INFORMATION

Here are some things you should consider including in your writing:

What does your animal look like?
What other species is it related to?
How does it move?
Where does it live?
What does it eat?
What are its predators?
How long does it live?
Is it endangered?
Why do you find it interesting?

SEPARATE FACT FROM FICTION: Your animal may have been featured in a movie or in myths and legends. Compare and contrast how the animal has been portrayed with how it behaves in reality. For example, penguins can't dance the way they do in *Happy Feet*.

PROOFREAD AND REVISE: As you would do with any essay, when you've finished, check for misspellings, grammatical mistakes and punctuation errors. It often helps to have someone else proofread your work, too, as he or she may catch things you have missed. Also, look for ways to make your sentences and paragraphs even better. Add more descriptive language, choosing just the right verbs, adverbs and adjectives to make your writing come alive.

BE CREATIVE: Use visual aids to make your report come to life. Include an animal photo file with interesting images found in magazines or printed from websites. Or draw your own! You can also build a miniature animal habitat scene. Use creativity to help communicate your passion for the subject.

THE FINAL RESULT: Put it all together in one final, polished draft. Make it neat and clean, and remember to cite your references.

SCIENCE and TECHNOLOGY

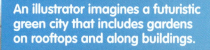

An illustrator imagines a futuristic green city that includes gardens on rooftops and along buildings.

10 FASCINATING FACTS ABOUT PHONES AND OTHER DEVICES

In the **Mobile Phone Throwing World Championships,** held in Finland, contestants hurled old phones for sport.

The average **MOBILE PHONE** contains more than **£1.00** worth of **GOLD.**

A HOME in Somerville, Massachusetts, U.S.A., was the **FIRST to have a telephone line** some **145 YEARS AGO.**

Five billion people — or more than 64 percent of the world's population — **own a mobile device.**

After receiving the patent for the first **TELEPHONE** in 1876, Alexander Graham Bell recommended answering by saying **"AHOY."**

INVENTED IN 1992, THE **FIRST SMARTPHONE** WAS NAMED **'SIMON'** AND WEIGHED ABOUT AS MUCH AS A **CAN OF SOUP.**

Emojis were first introduced on an early version of a smartphone in the late 1990s in Japan.

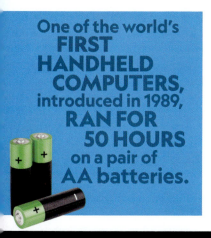

One of the world's **FIRST HANDHELD COMPUTERS,** introduced in 1989, **RAN FOR 50 HOURS** on a pair of **AA batteries.**

To keep new products secret, **APPLE** gives them code names such as **'PURPLE'** for the **iPhone** and **'GIZMO'** for the **Apple Watch.**

There are **NO PHONES** on the International Space Station.

5 COOL INVENTIONS

SUPERSMART GADGETS, ACCESSORIES AND VEHICLES THAT COULD CHANGE YOUR LIFE.

1 BIKE TAKES FLIGHT

The Speeder has a seat and handlebars just like a motorcycle, but this contraption travels to a place you could never reach on a regular bike — **the sky!** Just press a button to take off. Four **turbojet engines** on the bike's front and back launch it off the ground. Steer the handlebars to move the craft **through the air.** Weighing about 104 kilograms (230 lb), the bike won't require a pilot's licence to fly. Although still being tested, the Speeder is expected to reach speeds of **96.6 kilometres an hour (60 mph) and climb up to 4,572 metres (15,000 ft).** Talk about getting a lift!

2 SOLAR-POWERED TENT

Normally you'd be out of luck if your smartphone battery drained while you were camping — but this time you're sleeping in a **Bang Bang solar-powered tent.** The brightly coloured four-person tent comes with a **solar panel** that soaks up sunlight all day. This creates enough energy to charge a lithium battery bank inside the tent. All you have to do is **connect your gadget** to the battery bank and charge away. Now you'll always have plenty of juice in your phone to have that **dance party under the stars.**

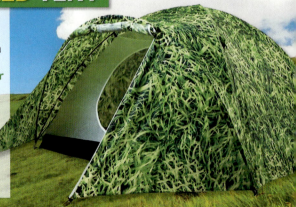

❸ DOG WATER FOUNTAIN

Your dog can sit, fetch and play dead, but can it **drink from a water fountain?** That trick is simple for your pet with the **Pawcet,** which lets thirsty dogs get a fresh drink whenever they want with **the touch of a paw.** Just hook up the Pawcet to your garden hose, and all your pup has to do is **step on the platform** to drink. Now that's something that'll really get your dog's tail wagging.

❹ BIRD PHOTO BOOTH

Snap pictures of hungry **blue tits** or **goldfinches** with the **Bird Photo Booth.** Simply pop your phone in the enclosure in this **bird feeder,** then sneak into your house and **watch the birds chow down** in real time from a live feed on your computer tablet. See the perfect shot? Click away as you get the **ultimate up-close pics** of your **garden birds.** But these aren't ordinary snaps: The Bird Photo Booth's **high-quality lens** lets your phone take images that'll rival those of a real-life wildlife photographer. **Say "tweet!"**

WESTERN SCRUB-JAY

❺ JET-POWERED SURFBOARD

Surf's up! But the big waves are crashing *so* far away from the shore. No need to exhaust yourself paddling to them — just hop on a **WaveJet,** a **jet-propelled surfboard,** to reach the swells without breaking a sweat. Powered by a pair of **battery-operated engines** at the base of the board, simply hit a switch on a **wristband** to pick up your speed to **16 kilometres an hour (10 mph),** about five times the average person's paddling speed. Not a surfer? The removable engine pod can be attached to **stand-up paddleboards, boogie boards** and **kayaks,** so you'll get a boost however you hit the water.

History's Greatest Hits

GEORGE WASHINGTON CARVER'S quest for knowledge made him a world-famous scientist and inventor. Find out about the groundbreaking life of this American hero.

START

Around 1864

George Washington Carver is born into slavery on a farm in Missouri, U.S.A. When slavery is abolished in 1865, his former owners, Moses and Susan Carver, decide to raise the orphaned George as their son.

1891 to 1896

Carver becomes the first Black student accepted at Iowa State University, where he studies agriculture, the science of farming.

SPUD SPRAY

MASHED MOSQUITOES

1896

Carver becomes a teacher at Tuskegee University in Alabama, U.S.A. He invents hundreds of products, including new kinds of paints and insecticides (chemicals used to kill insects).

PEANUT POWER

1906

Discovering more than 300 ways to use peanut plants, Carver turns the nuts into glue, medicine and paper. He shares his knowledge with farmers. (Fun fact: Carver did not invent peanut butter.)

No, Teddy. I said more water, not less.

Whoops.

1915

Carver becomes famous for his farming tips, and even advises the former U.S. president Theodore Roosevelt on agricultural matters.

1943

By the end of his career, Carver is a symbol of the important contributions of African Americans and inspires people all over, no matter what their skin colour is.

ACCIDENTS Happen

BUT SOMETIMES THEY RESULT IN AMAZING DISCOVERIES.

THE INVENTION: THE POPSICLE

THE MOMENT OF 'OOPS': Overnight freezing

THE DETAILS: When 11-year-old Frank Epperson left a glass of powdered soda mix overnight on his porch in Oakland, California, U.S.A., in 1905, he made snack history. The next morning, he discovered that his drink had frozen after an unusually cold night, the mixing stick still propped up in the glass. Hoping to salvage his soda after failing to pull it out of the glass, Epperson ran the cup under warm water. Pop! The primitive Popsicle slid out, complete with the stirrer stick as a handle. Twenty years later, Epperson patented his idea, calling it the Popsicle.

THE INVENTION: THE SLINKY

THE MOMENT OF 'OOPS': Falling objects

THE DETAILS: In 1943, engineer Richard James was at his desk in Pittsburgh, Pennsylvania, U.S.A., when a box of shipbuilding supplies in a nearby shelf suddenly tipped over. Startled, James looked up from his work. In the middle of everything falling, he noticed a metal spring slink to the ground. As he watched it walk over itself down some books stacked on the ground, he was struck with an idea: It might make a great toy! The Slinky — named by James's wife, Betty — was an instant hit, with the first 400 selling out in 90 minutes.

HOW TO FACE FAILURE

Some people might hate hearing the word 'failure'. But we say it's not so bad. Follow these tips to make failure fantastic.

FAILURE IS THE BEST TEACHER.

Embrace the teaching power of messing up. Fill in your teammates on your embarrassment on the football pitch. They'll learn how to avoid making the same mistake themselves.

SUCCESS IS NOTHING WITHOUT FAILURE.

When you fell off your bike, you weren't a failure unless you stayed on the ground. But you hopped back on the seat and kept trying. Failing first makes success feel extra sweet!

FAILURE STINGS — AND THAT'S OKAY!

Don't ignore a flunked test or a missed catch because they're painful. Do better next time by studying harder and practising more. But most importantly, just move on.

FUTURE WORLD:

What will restaurants be like decades from now? "You can expect a lot of changes in terms of using technology to grow and order our meals," says Paul Takhistov, a food scientist at Rutgers University in New Brunswick, New Jersey, U.S.A. "We'll also be able to personalise our food more." Check out what's cooking at this restaurant of the future.

HUNGRY? PRESS PRINT

A quick finger scan at your table shows that you're low on certain nutrients. Just press a button, and a 3D printer uses pureed food cartridges to 'print' lasagne that's packed with specific vitamins that your body needs. "Healthy food isn't one size fits all," Takhistov says. "We have different bodies, so we need different nutrients." These printers will also increase efficiency, allowing chefs to quickly print personalised food for large crowds.

FOOD-IN-A-BOX

Some of the lettuce in this kitchen is sad. Or rather, one of the lettuce emojis on the giant computer screens is frowning. That's because the chef didn't use the right recipe of sunlight, water and nutrients to get the real-life leafy plant inside a box behind the screen to grow. So she taps the touch screen to make the temperature cooler, and the lettuce's frown turns upside down on the fridge-shaped 'box farm'. Without planting seeds in soil, this restaurant can grow all the fruits and vegetables it needs. "Anybody can be a farmer," says Hildreth England, a senior strategist at the Massachusetts Institute of Technology. "If you live in Iceland, you can grow strawberries that taste as if they're from Mexico."

WASTE NOT

Researchers are currently working on ways to convert human waste into nutrients. Whether you're eating on Earth or during a space vacation, in the future some of your food will probably have recycled ingredients.

Food

GROW UP

What will happen to farms in the future? Some will be *much* taller. Cities will continue to expand as the human population climbs to nine billion people, leaving less land to farm. Agriculture is likely to be housed in towering vertical skyscrapers situated in these cities. Luckily, indoor farms typically use less water, and plants seem to grow faster in these environments.

GET SMART

To order with ease and keep germs from spreading at your favourite restaurant, you tap the table to open a digital menu and choose from freshly grown salads and 3D-printed creations. An alarm lets you know when your food is waiting in the cubby at one side of the table — just lift the door and take your meal. Forgot something? A robot server will stop by to see if you need anything else.

HUNTING FOR HOLOGRAMS

Let's go fishing ... in the kitchen? The catch of the day is a 3D hologram that the chef hooks in midair. One day people will stock their kitchens by gathering ingredients in a virtual world. Simply pick a berry from a digital bush or choose a cut of beef from a cow on a virtual farm. After you've finished foraging, the hologram setup sends details to a local market that delivers your order. Scientists working on this program hope to connect people to their food sources and make shopping more fun.

FUTURE WORLD:

A buzzer goes off, marking the start of a race. Your heart is pounding — not that you can hear it over the sound of revving engines. Your car weaves through the other vehicles, making its way to the front of the pack. Peering through the windscreen, you see the finish line ahead. Your car crosses first! The crowd roars.

You aren't actually in the car. But thanks to a pair of smartglasses you're wearing in the stands, you experienced exactly what the real driver did on the course.

"In the future, advanced technology will enable us to feel as if we're part of the event," says Aymeric Castaing, founder of Umanimation, a future-tech media company. Take a peek at more ways we'll be entertained by 2060 and beyond — but first, check out two terms to know.

1. Augmented reality (AR): Technology that layers computer-generated images onto things in the real world (like in Pokémon GO)

2. Virtual reality (VR): A computer-generated experience that makes you feel as if you're inside a totally different world

SUPER STADIUMS

Didn't see that catch? No worries: In the future, 3D holograms could appear in midair above the field to show replays of sports moments. For some events, you'll even get a seat in a flying pod that can put you close to the action. (The pod even flies you home afterwards!) Meanwhile, say goodbye to long lines for food or team jerseys. Through an app, flying drones will deliver anything you order right to your seat.

GAME ON

A colourful alien zooms directly towards you, attempting to knock you aside with its spaceship. You put your hands in front of you, blocking the alien with a powerful force field. A crowd cheers your dramatic victory.

To the group assembled in front of you in the park, it looks like you just took down an alien spaceship — thanks to VR goggles and a suit with motion sensors. Everything you saw through your goggles was projected onto a video screen at a virtual gaming playground. There, the audience can watch and cheer as you go up against the aliens. They can also wear headsets and feel as if they're in outer space, too!

Entertainment

MUSEUMS TO GO

Museums of the future will blend real life with AR and VR. For example, you can check out a sculpture at an art museum with AR glasses, getting details about the artist and style. Then, using your VR headset, you can draw your own masterpiece inspired by what you saw. Not feeling creative? "Using your in-home VR headset and a 3D printer, you can create what you saw in the museum in your bedroom," Castaing says. It's like taking the museum home with you — sort of.

THE BIG SCREEN

There won't be a bad seat in the house at cinemas in the future. Films will surround the audience with 3D screens in every direction ... including the floor and ceiling. You'll feel like you're underwater at the latest ocean adventure blockbuster. Plus, robots will deliver the snacks you've ordered from your seat's tablet directly to your rotating chair.

DROID BEATS

Ready to rock out to your favourite band? Whether it's pop-star robots or a robot orchestra conductor, future music may be in non-human hands. And audiences won't just hear music played by robots — they'll be able to see it. AR glasses will allow audiences to see which notes are coming out of the instruments in front of them. "AR glasses could even enable beginning musicians to take their lessons on the go," Castaing says. "The glasses could essentially become their teacher."

WHAT IS LIFE?

This seems like such an easy question to answer. Everybody knows that singing birds are alive and rocks are not. But when we start studying bacteria and other microscopic creatures, things get more complicated.

SO WHAT EXACTLY IS LIFE?

Most scientists agree that something is alive if it can reproduce, grow in size to become more complex in structure, take in nutrients to survive, give off waste products and respond to external stimuli, such as increased sunlight or changes in temperature.

KINDS OF LIFE

Biologists classify living organisms by how they get their energy. Organisms such as algae, green plants and some bacteria use sunlight as an energy source. Animals (like humans), fungi and some single-celled microscopic organisms called Archaea use chemicals to provide energy. When we eat food, chemical reactions within our digestive system turn our food into fuel.

Living things inhabit land, sea and air. In fact, life also thrives deep beneath the oceans, embedded in rocks kilometres below Earth's crust, in ice and in other extreme environments. The life-forms that thrive in these challenging environments are called extremophiles. Some of these draw directly upon the chemicals surrounding them for energy. Because these are very different forms of life than what we're used to, we may not think of them as alive, but they are.

HOW IT ALL WORKS

To understand how a living organism works, it helps to look at one example of its simplest form — the single-celled bacterium called *Streptococcus*. There are many kinds of these tiny organisms, and some are responsible for human illnesses. What makes us sick or uncomfortable are the toxins the bacteria give off in our bodies.

A single *Streptococcus* bacterium is so small that at least 500 of them could fit on the dot above this letter *i*. These bacteria are some of the simplest forms of life we know. They have no moving parts, no lungs, no brain, no heart, no liver and no leaves or fruit. Yet this life-form reproduces. It grows in size by producing long-chain structures, takes in nutrients and gives off waste products. This tiny life-form is alive, just as you are alive.

What makes something alive is a question scientists grapple with when they study viruses, such as the ones that cause the common cold and smallpox. They can grow and reproduce within host cells, such as those that make up your body. Because viruses lack cells and cannot metabolise nutrients for energy or reproduce without a host, scientists ask if they are indeed alive. And don't go looking for them without a strong microscope — viruses are a hundred times smaller than bacteria.

Scientists think life began on Earth 4.1 to 3.9 billion years ago, but no fossils exist from that time. The earliest fossils ever found are from the primitive life that existed 3.6 billion years ago. Other life-forms, some of which are shown below, soon followed. Scientists continue to study how life evolved on Earth and whether it is possible that life exists on other planets.

MICROSCOPIC ORGANISMS

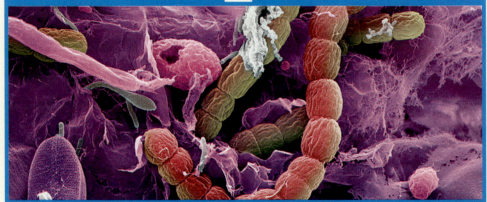

The Three Domains of Life

Biologists divide all living organisms into three domains, or groups: Bacteria, Archaea and Eukarya. Archaea and Bacteria cells do not have nuclei—cellular parts that are essential to reproduction and other cell functions—but they are different from each other in many ways. Because human cells have a nucleus, we belong to the Eukarya domain.

1 BACTERIA

DOMAIN BACTERIA: These single-celled microorganisms are found almost everywhere in the world. Bacteria are small and do not have nuclei. They can be shaped like rods, spirals or spheres. Some of them are helpful to humans, and some are harmful.

2 ARCHAEA

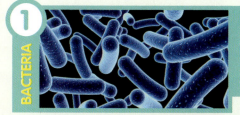

DOMAIN ARCHAEA: These single-celled microorganisms are often found in extremely hostile environments. Like Bacteria, Archaea do not have nuclei, but they have some genes in common with Eukarya. For this reason, scientists think the Archaea living today most closely resemble the earliest forms of life on Earth.

3 EUKARYA

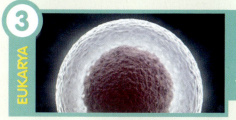

DOMAIN EUKARYA: This diverse group of life-forms is more complicated than Bacteria and Archaea, as Eukarya have one or more cells with nuclei. These are the tiny cells that make up your whole body. Eukarya are divided into four groups: fungi, protists, plants and animals.

FYI

WHAT IS A DOMAIN? Scientifically speaking, a domain is a major taxonomic division into which natural objects are classified (see page 38 for 'What Is Taxonomy'?).

FUNGI

KINGDOM FUNGI Mainly multicellular organisms, fungi cannot make their own food. Mushrooms and yeast are fungi.

PROTISTS

PROTISTS Once considered a kingdom, this group is a 'grab bag' that includes unicellular and multicellular organisms of great variety.

PLANTS

KINGDOM PLANTAE Plants are multi-cellular, and many can make their own food using photosynthesis (see page 102 for 'Photosynthesis').

ANIMALS

KINGDOM ANIMALIA Most animals, which are multicellular, have their own organ systems. Animals do not make their own food.

HOW DOES YOUR GARDEN GROW?

The plant kingdom is about 400,000 species strong, growing all over the world: on top of mountains, in the sea, in freezing temperatures — everywhere. Without plants, life on Earth would not be able to survive. Plants provide food and oxygen for animals, including humans.

Plants have three distinct characteristics:

1. Most have chlorophyll (a green pigment that makes photosynthesis work and turns sunlight into energy), while some are parasitic. Parasitic plants don't make their own food — they take it from other plants.
2. Plants cannot change their location on their own.
3. Their cell walls are made from a stiff material called cellulose.

Photosynthesis

Plants are lucky — most don't have to hunt or shop for food. Most use the sun to produce their own food. In a process called photosynthesis, a plant's chloroplast (the part of the plant where the chemical chlorophyll is located) captures the sun's energy and combines it with carbon dioxide from the air and nutrient-rich water from the ground to produce a sugar called glucose.

Plants burn the glucose for energy to help them grow. As a waste product, plants emit oxygen, which humans and other animals need to breathe. When we breathe, we exhale carbon dioxide, which the plants then use for more photosynthesis — it's all a big, finely tuned system. So the next time you pass a lonely houseplant, give it thanks for helping you live.

SOIL STATS

Look around your garden and you'll see lots of living things: pretty flowers, chirping birds and more.

Dig around in the soil and you'll find up to

30
EARTHWORMS

per .09 square metre (1 sq ft). They break down organic matter in the soil.

But did you know there's a whole living world hidden in the soil beneath your feet? Next time you dig in the soil, think about these fascinating facts!

4 GRAMS (1 tsp)
OF SOIL CONTAINS:

3 METRES
(9 ft) OF FUNGI STRANDS

100
TINY SOIL INSECTS

HUNDREDS
OF CILIATES AND NEMATODES

There can be as much as

1,814
KILOGRAMS

(4,000 lb) of plant roots in every 4,047 square metres (1 acre) of soil.

UP TO
1 BILLION
BACTERIA

SEVERAL
THOUSAND
FLAGELLATES AND AMOEBAS

Your Amazing Body!

YOUR SKIN SHEDS AND REGROWS ABOUT ONCE A MONTH.

The human body is a complicated mass of systems — nine systems, to be exact. Each system has a unique and critical purpose in the body, and we wouldn't be able to survive without all of them.

The **NERVOUS** system controls the body.

The **MUSCULAR** system makes movement possible.

The **SKELETAL** system supports the body.

The **CIRCULATORY** system moves blood throughout the body.

The **RESPIRATORY** system provides the body with oxygen.

The **DIGESTIVE** system breaks down food into nutrients and gets rid of waste.

The **IMMUNE** system protects the body against disease and infection.

The **ENDOCRINE** system regulates the body's functions.

The **REPRODUCTIVE** system enables people to produce offspring.

Weird but true!

YOUR **BRAIN** CAN HOLD **100 TIMES** MORE INFORMATION THAN AN AVERAGE **COMPUTER.**

A speck of **blood** contains about **5 million red** blood cells.

Your hands and wrists contain 26 percent of the bones in your body.

LOOK OUT!

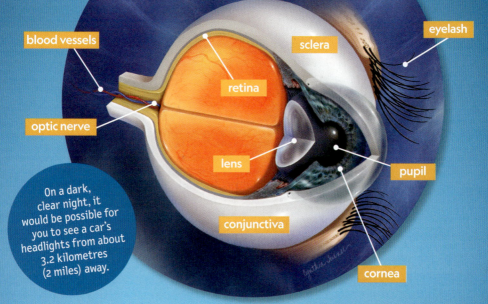

blood vessels

sclera

eyelash

retina

optic nerve

lens

pupil

conjunctiva

cornea

On a dark, clear night, it would be possible for you to see a car's headlights from about 3.2 kilometres (2 miles) away.

Your eyes are two of the most amazing organs in your body.

These small, squishy, fluid-filled balls have almost three-quarters of your body's sensory receptors. They're like two supersmart cameras, but more complex.

So how do you see the world around you? It begins when you open the protective cover of your eyelid and let in the light. Light enters your eye through the window of your cornea and passes through the aqueous humour, a watery fluid that nourishes the eye tissue. It enters the black circle in the iris (the coloured part of your eye), called the pupil. Because people need to be able to see in both bright and low light, muscles in the iris automatically make the pupil smaller when the light is strong and wider when the light is dim. Light then travels to the lens, whose muscles adjust it to be able to see objects both near and far. Then the light goes through the vitreous humour (a clear jelly-like substance) to the retina. The retina, a layer of about 126 million light-sensitive cells, lines the back of your eyeball. When these cells absorb the light, they transform it into electrical signals that are sent along the optic nerve to the brain. The brain then makes sense of what you are seeing.

A TOPSY-TURVY WORLD

Turn this over in your mind: You're looking at the world topsy-turvy, and you don't even know it. Like a camera lens, your lens focuses light, creates an image and turns it upside down.

Yep, when your lens focuses light inside your eye, it flips the image so it lands on your retina upside down. But your brain knows to flip the image automatically to match your reality. But what if your reality suddenly

CAMERA LENS

changed? A well-known experiment in the mid-20th century in which a person wore special light-inverting goggles showed that his brain actually adjusted to the new, inverted world by eventually seeing the reversed view as normal! It is thought that newborn babies see the world upside down for a short while, until their brains learn how to turn things right side up.

WHY can't
I eat peanuts or pet a fluffy dog without
FEELING ICKY?

Sounds like you have an allergy, and you're not alone! As many as 30 percent of grown-ups and 40 percent of kids suffer from allergies. Allergic reactions include itching, sneezing, coughing, a runny nose, vomiting, rashes and shortness of breath. They happen when your body's immune system—which normally fights germs—treats something harmless, like food or a particular medicine, like it's a dangerous invader. Once it detects one of these intruders, called an allergen, your immune system goes into high alert. It creates antibodies to repel the intruder, causing the tissues around the allergen to become inflamed or swollen, which can make it hard for you to breathe. Extreme reactions can even result in a potentially deadly full-body response known as anaphylactic shock.

AWFUL
allergens

PEANUTS
One of the most common food allergens, along with shellfish.

PET DANDER
Tiny flakes of shed fur and feathers can make your eyes water and your nose go *ah-choo!*

DUST MITES
Millions of these microscopic arachnids live in your house, feasting on your dead skin cells. Cleaning stirs up clouds of mite shells and their micro-poop.

PENICILLIN
Antibiotics like penicillin kill bacteria that make us sick, but they can do more harm than good for patients allergic to them.

POLLEN
Plants project this fine powdery substance into the breeze to fertilise other plants. It can irritate the nasal passages of allergy sufferers, causing sneezing and watery eyes—a condition commonly called hay fever.

Why do
we have allergies?

Stories of allergies go back to ancient Egypt, yet their causes largely remain a mystery. Not everyone has allergies. Some form in childhood. Some happen later in life. And sometimes they go away as you get older. You may inherit a likelihood of having allergies from your parents but usually not their particular allergies.

Scientists suspect humans evolved with these extreme and mysterious immune reactions to combat genuinely deadly threats, such as parasitic worms or other toxins. And though doctors are doubtful they can ever cure allergies, they've come up with many ways to test for them and provide medications that treat the symptoms.

The majority of food allergies are caused by 'the Big 8' — milk, eggs, fish, shellfish, tree nuts, peanuts, wheat and soy.

WHY can't I USE
my left hand as well as my right one
(or the other way around)?

About nine out of ten of you reading this book will turn its pages with your right hand —

the same hand you use to write a note or chuck a fastball. About 90 percent of humans are right-handed, meaning their right hand is their dominant hand. The other 10 percent are left-handed. Activities that feel natural with the dominant hand are awkward or difficult with the other one. Ever try to sign your name with your nondominant hand? Not so easy!

Cave paintings going back more than 5,000 years show humans favouring their right or left hands according to the same nine-to-one ratio we see today. And the same goes for the stone tools our evolutionary ancestors used 1.5 million years ago: Studies show a similar dominance of the right hand long before the human species, *Homo sapiens,* appeared on the fossil record.

ARE YOU A 'mixed-hander'?

What about people who can use their nondominant hand almost as well as their dominant? They're called mixed-handers. (Scientists don't like using the term 'ambidextrous', which implies neither hand is dominant.) About one percent of people are elite lefties/righties. Are you? Grab a piece of paper and find out!

So **why** is one hand dominant?

Scientists have discovered a sequence of genes linked to hand dominance, making it a trait that's passed along to children just like hair colour or dimples. These traits determine how our brains are wired. How? The brain is split into two symmetrical halves known as hemispheres. In about 90 percent of people, the left side of the brain processes language skills. These people are typically right-handed. People born with genes for left-handedness—about 10 percent of the population—typically have brains that process speech on the right side.

So whichever side of the brain controls speech usually corresponds with a dominant hand on the opposite side. Because the left side of the brain controls the right side of the body and vice versa, scientists suspect that the evolution of our dominant hand is somehow connected to the development of our language capabilities. Humans can have a dominant eye, foot and ear, too—but scientists aren't quite sure why. That's just one of many reasons the human brain is considered the most complex object in the universe.

107

MICROORGANISMS AND YOU

BACTERIA

FUNGUS

VIRUS

Images are not to scale.

Every 6.5 square centimetres (1 sq in) of your skin hosts about **six million bacteria.**

PROTOZOA CAN BE TRANSMITTED BY MOSQUITOES

Some microorganisms (tiny living things) can make your body sick. They are too small to see with the naked eye. These creatures — bacteria, viruses, fungi and protozoa — are what you may know as germs.

Bacteria are microscopic organisms that live nearly everywhere on Earth, including on and in the human body. 'Good' bacteria help our digestive systems work properly. Harmful bacteria can cause illnesses, including ear infections and tonsillitis.

A virus, like a cold or the flu, needs to live inside another living thing (a host) to survive; then it can grow and multiply throughout the host's body.

Fungi get their food from the plants, animals or people they live on. Some fungi can get on your body and cause skin diseases such as ringworm.

Protozoa are single-celled organisms that can spread disease to humans through contaminated water and dirty living conditions. Protozoa can cause infections such as malaria, which occurs when a person is bitten by an infected mosquito.

ADD IT UP

So you know that you have bacteria on your skin and in your body. But do you know how many? One hundred trillion — that's 100,000,000,000,000! Most are harmless and some are pretty friendly, keeping more dangerous bacteria at bay, protecting you from some skin infections and helping your cuts heal.

GERM **SHOWDOWN**

Scientists in Wales studied three greeting styles to determine which was the cleanest. Find out which one has the upper hand.

HANDSHAKE

AN AVERAGE HANDSHAKE TRANSFERRED **MORE THAN 5 TIMES AS MUCH BACTERIA** AS A FIST BUMP. (A STRONG HANDSHAKE TRANSFERRED **10 TIMES** AS MUCH.)

HIGH FIVE

A HIGH FIVE PASSED **TWICE AS MANY** GERMS AS A FIST BUMP.

FIST BUMP

WINNER:

FIST BUMPS HAVE THE **LEAST SKIN-TO-SKIN CONTACT** OF THE GREETINGS, WHICH MAKES IT LESS LIKELY FOR MICROBES TO JUMP **FROM ONE HAND TO ANOTHER.**

THE SCIENCE OF
SPOOKY

HOW THESE CREEPY THINGS AFFECT YOUR BRAIN

What's that strange noise in the night? Is it the wind? Or something else?

"When you encounter something scary, your brain releases chemicals," psychologist Martin Antony says. "These chemicals make our hearts race, so we breathe faster and sweat. Your nervous system is preparing your body to either fight a threat or run away from it." Scientists call this the 'fight-or-flight' response.

So which so-called spookiness makes us feel this way—and why? Discover what puts the *eek!* in these five freaky things.

THE FEAR: SPIDERS

SCIENTIFIC NAME: Arachnophobia

SPOOKY SCIENCE: Humans have been afraid of spiders since our ancient human ancestors thought they carried deadly diseases. "Today, we know that's not true," psychology professor Kyle Rexer says. "But a lot of people still have incorrect ideas about how dangerous spiders are." Although some spiders *can* be deadly, most are not. In fact, humans actually benefit from the existence of spiders. By eating disease-carrying critters such as mosquitoes and cockroaches, these arachnids act as a form of pest control. Plus, scientists are currently studying spider venom in the hope that it can one day be used in medicines to manage pain or cure illnesses.

THE FEAR: CLOWNS

SCIENTIFIC NAME: Coulrophobia

SPOOKY SCIENCE: One way we decide if a person is friend or foe is by evaluating their facial expressions. Clowns — with their makeup, wigs and fake noses — are hard to read, which is what makes them scary to some people. "It's hard to tell how a clown is feeling," psychology professor Frank McAndrew says. "So we think, If clowns can hide their emotions, what else might they be hiding?"

FIGHT THE FRIGHT

It's natural to avoid things that scare us. "But to get over your fears — whether you're afraid of spiders, clowns, the dark or, well, anything — you have to *focus* on them instead of avoid them," Rexer says. He shares some useful tips to help you manage your fears.

THE FEAR: HEIGHTS
SCIENTIFIC NAME: Acrophobia

SPOOKY SCIENCE: When you're standing on solid ground, your eyes work with your inner ears to help you stay balanced. But if you're standing, say, at the edge of a cliff, your sense of balance can get out of whack. "Your inner ear is saying you're surrounded by solid ground, but your eyes are saying, 'Nope,'" inner-ear specialist Dennis Fitzgerald says. Your brain is getting mixed signals, which can cause vertigo, or dizziness that makes heights feel scary.

THE FEAR: DARKNESS
SCIENTIFIC NAME: Nyctophobia

SPOOKY SCIENCE: As with other phobias, humans developed a fear of the dark to avoid danger. Our ancestors had to be extra cautious at night to protect themselves against things like animal predators and human invaders. (This was before electric lighting!) "Many people still have that fear of the dark today," Antony says. "It's a fear of the unknown."

THE FEAR: SMALL SPACES
SCIENTIFIC NAME: Claustrophobia

SPOOKY SCIENCE: Maybe you've been stuck in an elevator before and thought it was no big deal. For some people, though, just the fear of being stuck can cause them to take the stairs. "Small spaces might cause some people to worry about running out of oxygen, or never being able to get out — no matter how unlikely that is," Antony says. "To increase our chances of survival, people have evolved to avoid being trapped. For some, that could be anywhere."

- Expose yourself to things that you're afraid of in a way that you feel safe. For example, if you fear public speaking, try practising in front of a mirror first, and then give the speech to a small group of trusted friends.

- If you feel anxious, place one or both of your hands on your stomach and focus on breathing slowly and deeply. Regulating your breathing will help you feel calmer and can lessen your sense of panic.

- Don't be too hard on yourself! Everyone's afraid of *something*. Just make sure it doesn't stop you from living your life. Talk to an adult if it feels like too much to handle on your own.

QUIZ WHIZ

Test your science and technology knowledge by taking this quiz!

Write your answers on a piece of paper. Then check them below.

1 In the future, customised 3D-printed food may include which special ingredient?

a. vitamins specific to our bodies' needs
b. extra sugar
c. invisible broccoli
d. freeze-dried ice cream

2 **True or false?** About 90 percent of humans are left-handed.

3 One teaspoon of _____ contains 3 metres (9 ft) of fungi strands.

a. pasta sauce
b. pond water
c. sand
d. soil

4 What is the scientific name for the fear of the dark?

a. coulrophobia
b. claustrophobia
c. nyctophobia
d. arachnophobia

5 **True or false?** Scientists study microscopic organisms on Earth to see if it's possible that life exists on other planets.

Not **STUMPED** yet? Check out the *NATIONAL GEOGRAPHIC KIDS QUIZ WHIZ* collection for more crazy **SCIENCE AND TECHNOLOGY** questions!

ANSWERS: 1. a; 2. False. 90 percent of people are right-handed.; 3. d; 4. c; 5. True

HOMEWORK HELP

This Is How It's Done!

Sometimes, the most complicated problems are solved with step-by-step directions. These 'how-to' instructions are also known as a process analysis essay. Although scientists and engineers use this tool to program robots and write computer code, you also use process analysis every day, from following a recipe to putting together a new toy or gadget. Here's how to write a basic process analysis essay.

Step 1: Choose Your Topic Sentence

Pick a clear and concise topic sentence that describes what you're writing about. Be sure to explain to the readers why the task is important — and how many steps there are to complete it.

Step 2: List Materials

Do you need specific ingredients or equipment to complete your process? Mention these right away so the readers will have all they need to do this activity.

Step 3: Write Your Directions

Your directions should be clear and easy to follow. Assume that you are explaining the process for the first time, and define any unfamiliar terms. List your steps in the exact order the readers will need to follow to complete the activity. Try to keep your essay limited to no more than six steps.

Step 4: Restate Your Main Idea

Your closing idea should revisit your topic sentence, drawing a conclusion relating to the importance of the subject.

EXAMPLE OF A PROCESS ANALYSIS ESSAY

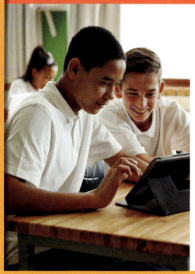

Downloading an app is a simple way to enhance your tablet. Today, I'd like to show you how to search for and add an app to your tablet. First, you will need a tablet with the ability to access the internet. You'll also want to ask a parent for permission before you download anything onto your tablet. Next, select the specific app you're seeking by going to the app store on your tablet and entering the app's name into the search bar. Once you find the app you're seeking, select 'download' and wait for the app to load. When you see that the app has fully loaded, tap on the icon and you will be able to access it. Now you can enjoy your app and have more fun with your tablet.

A woman in Venice, Italy, poses in a traditional mask and costume during Carnival — an annual festival celebrated before the Christian season of Lent.

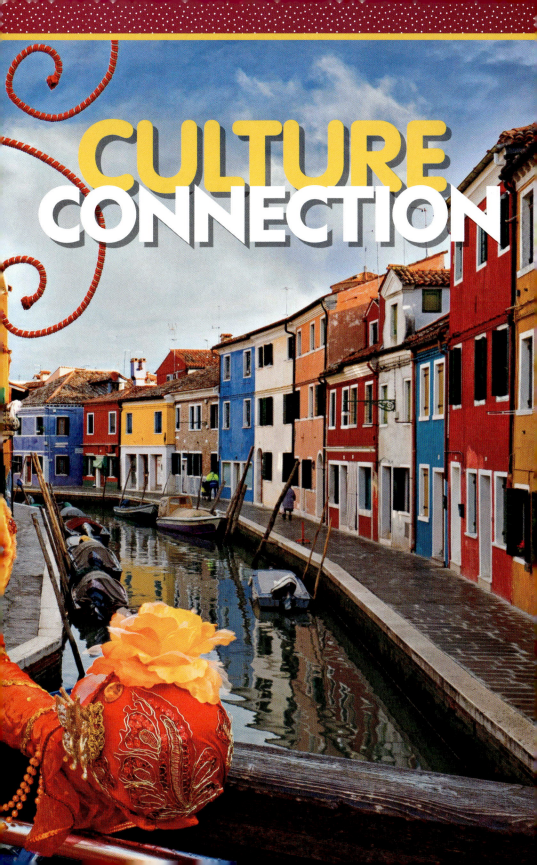

CULTURE CONNECTION

CELEBRATIONS

UP HELLY AA
25 January

This annual daylong festival celebrating the history of Shetland, Scotland, involves costume-clad participants marching through town with torches and the burning of a full-scale replica of a Viking longship.

CHINESE NEW YEAR
1 February

Also called Lunar New Year, this holiday marks the new year according to the lunar calendar. Families celebrate with parades, feasts and fireworks. Young people may receive gifts of money in red envelopes.

QINGMING FESTIVAL
5 April

Also known as Grave Sweeping Day, this Chinese celebration calls on people to return to the graves of their loved ones. There, they tidy up the graves, as well as light firecrackers, burn fake money and leave food as an offering to the spirits.

RAMADAN AND EID AL-FITR
2 April* – 1 May**

A Muslim holiday, Ramadan is a month long, ending in the Eid al-Fitr celebration. Observers fast during this month—eating only after sunset. People pray for forgiveness and hope to purify themselves through observance.

EASTER
17 April [+]

A Christian holiday that honours the resurrection of Jesus Christ, Easter is celebrated by giving out chocolate eggs or animals, and having outdoor Easter egg hunts.

LEI DAY
1 May

Celebrating the 'aloha spirit' in Hawaii, this day is all about the leis, or the traditional flower garland worn as a necklace or a crown. Events include hula shows, lei making and craft shows.

Around the World

ROSH HASHANAH
25* – 27 September

A Jewish holiday marking the beginning of a new year on the Hebrew calendar. Celebrations include prayer, ritual foods and a day of rest.

DIWALI
24 – 28 October

To symbolise the inner light that protects against spiritual darkness, people light their homes with clay lamps for India's largest and most important holiday.

HANUKKAH
18* – 26 December

This Jewish holiday is eight days long. It commemorates the rededication of the Temple in Jerusalem. Hanukkah celebrations include the lighting of menorah candles for eight days and the exchange of gifts.

CHRISTMAS DAY
25 December

A Christian holiday marking the birth of Jesus Christ, Christmas is usually celebrated by decorating trees, exchanging presents and having festive gatherings.

*Begins at sundown.
**Dates may vary slightly by location.
† Orthodox Easter is 24 April.

2022 CALENDAR

JANUARY
S	M	T	W	T	F	S
						1
2	3	4	5	6	7	8
9	10	11	12	13	14	15
16	17	18	19	20	21	22
23	24	25	26	27	28	29
30	31					

FEBRUARY
S	M	T	W	T	F	S
		1	2	3	4	5
6	7	8	9	10	11	12
13	14	15	16	17	18	19
20	21	22	23	24	25	26
27	28					

MARCH
S	M	T	W	T	F	S
		1	2	3	4	5
6	7	8	9	10	11	12
13	14	15	16	17	18	19
20	21	22	23	24	25	26
27	28	29	30	31		

APRIL
S	M	T	W	T	F	S
					1	2
3	4	5	6	7	8	9
10	11	12	13	14	15	16
17	18	19	20	21	22	23
24	25	26	27	28	29	30

MAY
S	M	T	W	T	F	S
1	2	3	4	5	6	7
7	8	9	10	11	12	13
14	15	16	17	18	19	20
21	22	23	24	25	26	27
28	29	30	31			

JUNE
S	M	T	W	T	F	S
			1	2	3	4
5	6	7	8	9	10	11
12	13	14	15	16	17	18
19	20	21	22	23	24	25
26	27	28	29	30		

JULY
S	M	T	W	T	F	S
					1	2
3	4	5	6	7	8	9
10	11	12	13	14	15	16
17	18	19	20	21	22	23
24	25	26	27	28	29	30
31						

AUGUST
S	M	T	W	T	F	S
	1	2	3	4	5	6
7	8	9	10	11	12	13
14	15	16	17	18	19	20
21	22	23	24	25	26	27
28	29	30	31			

SEPTEMBER
S	M	T	W	T	F	S
				1	2	3
4	5	6	7	8	9	10
11	12	13	14	15	16	17
18	19	20	21	22	23	24
25	26	27	28	29	30	

OCTOBER
S	M	T	W	T	F	S
						1
2	3	4	5	6	7	8
9	10	11	12	13	14	15
16	17	18	19	20	21	22
23	24	25	26	27	28	29
30	31					

NOVEMBER
S	M	T	W	T	F	S
		1	2	3	4	5
6	7	8	9	10	11	12
13	14	15	16	17	18	19
20	21	22	23	24	25	26
27	28	29	30			

DECEMBER
S	M	T	W	T	F	S
				1	2	3
4	5	6	7	8	9	10
11	12	13	14	15	16	17
18	19	20	21	22	23	24
25	26	27	28	29	30	31

Bet You Didn't Know!

8 New Year Celebrations Across the Globe

1 **Giant water fights IN THAILAND** ring in the new year in early spring.

2 **IN IRAN,** festivities kick off with the **arrival of spring** and last 13 days.

3 Kids in **BELGIUM** **write letters** to their parents and godparents and read them aloud on New Year's Day.

4 **IN LONDON,** New Year's revellers have been showered with **edible banana confetti** and **peach-flavoured snow** at midnight.

5 Residents in **SCOTLAND** **open** their front doors before midnight on New Year's Eve to let the **old year out** and the **new year in.**

6 New Year **IN ETHIOPIA** happens in **September,** which is the end of the rainy season.

7 More than 2,000 **CANADIANS** **take an icy plunge** at Vancouver's Polar Bear Swim each New Year's Day.

8 **IN THE UNITED STATES,** the Creek tribe's new year starts **in midsummer,** after the **corn ripens.**

What's Your Chinese Horoscope?
Locate your birth year to find out.

In Chinese astrology, the zodiac runs on a 12-year cycle, based on the lunar calendar. Each year corresponds to one of 12 animals, each representing one of 12 personality types. Read on to find out which animal year you were born in and what that might say about you.

RAT
1972, '84, '96, 2008, '20
Say cheese! You're attractive, charming and creative. When you get angry, you can have really sharp teeth!

RABBIT

1975, '87, '99, 2011, '23
Your ambition and talent make you jump at opportunity. You also keep your ears open for gossip.

HORSE
1966, '78, '90, 2002, '14
Being happy is your *mane* goal. And though you're clever and hardworking, your teacher may tell you off for horsing around.

ROOSTER
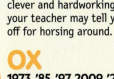
1969, '81, '93, 2005, '17
You crow about your adventures, but inside you're really shy. You're thoughtful, capable, brave and talented.

OX
1973, '85, '97, 2009, '21
You're smart, patient and as strong as an ... well, you know what. Though you're a leader, you never brag.

DRAGON
1976, '88, 2000, '12
You're on fire! Health, energy, honesty and bravery make you a living legend.

SHEEP
1967, '79, '91, 2003, '15
Gentle as a lamb, you're also artistic, compassionate and wise. You're often shy.

DOG

1970, '82, '94, 2006, '18
Often the leader of the pack, you're loyal and honest. You can also keep a secret.

TIGER
1974, '86, '98, 2010, '22
You may be a nice person, but no one should ever enter your room without asking—you might attack!

SNAKE

1977, '89, 2001, '13
You may not speak often, but you're very clever. You always seem to have a stash of cash.

MONKEY
1968, '80, '92, 2004, '16
No 'monkey see, monkey do' for you. You're a clever problem-solver with an excellent memory.

PIG

1971, '83, '95, 2007, '19
Even though you're courageous, honest and kind, you never hog all the attention.

Try This! GINGERBREAD HOUSES

YOU WILL NEED

- 1 CAN READY-MADE VANILLA ICING
- 1/4 TEASPOON CREAM OF TARTAR
- CARDBOARD
- RECTANGULAR GINGER BISCUITS
- SERRATED KNIFE (ASK FOR AN ADULT'S HELP)
- ASSORTED SWEETS, PRETZELS AND BISCUITS, INCLUDING SQUARE TOFFEES (NOT SHOWN)
- DESICCATED COCONUT

WHAT TO DO

MIX THE 'GLUE': Icing will hold each biscuit building together. Combine the vanilla icing with the cream of tartar. To apply the icing, squeeze it out of a sealed freezer bag with a hole cut in one corner.

BUILD THE HOUSE:

BASE Cut a piece of cardboard that's big enough to hold the scene.

WALLS The front and back walls are each made of a whole biscuit turned horizontally. Ask a parent to create the two remaining sides. For each, use a serrated knife to gently saw the top of a whole biscuit into a peak (inset, above). Run a thin line of icing along the bottom edge and sides of the biscuits. 'Glue' them together in a rectangle on top of the cardboard. Prop up the walls while you work.

PEAKED ROOF Run icing along the tops of the walls. Place two whole biscuits — turned horizontally — on top of the sides, using icing to hold them in place. Let the icing set overnight.

WAGON USE RECTANGULAR BISCUITS FOR THE BOTTOM AND HALF A BISCUIT FOR THE BACK. 'GLUE' THE PIECES IN PLACE. ADD PRETZEL WHEELS AND A TOFFEE UNDER THE WAGON FOR SUPPORT.

SILO CUT OFF THE TOPS OF TWO CAKE ICE-CREAM CONES, THEN ICE THE OPEN ENDS TOGETHER. STICK ON COLOURFUL LIQUORICE AND TOP WITH A FOIL MUFFIN CASE.

SNOWMAN SKEWER TWO MARSHMALLOWS ONTO A PRETZEL STICK. USE GUMDROPS FOR THE HAT, EYES AND NOSE; PRETZELS FOR THE ARMS; AND STRING LIQUORICE FOR A SCARF.

Fun Winter Gift Idea

Snow Globes

YOU WILL NEED
- SMALL JAR WITH A LID (A BABY FOOD JAR WORKS WELL.)
- SANDPAPER
- INSTANT-BONDING GLUE (FOLLOW DIRECTIONS ON THE TUBE AND USE WITH ADULT SUPERVISION.)
- PLASTIC ANIMAL OR FIGURINE THAT FITS IN THE JAR
- NAIL POLISH REMOVER
- BABY OIL
- SMALL HANDFUL OF WHITE GLITTER

WHAT TO DO

Turn the jar's lid upside down. Use sandpaper to scuff the inside of the lid. Glue the bottom of the figurine to the centre of the lid. (Nail polish remover cleans glue off skin and surfaces.) Let dry for four hours. Fill the jar with baby oil. Add glitter. To seal, put glue around the rim of the jar. Close the lid tightly and dry for four hours. Turn the jar over, and let it snow!

DOGHOUSE Follow the steps on the left for the gingerbread house, but use small biscuits for all sides and the roof.

BARN Use rectangular biscuits for the barn's roof and sides. For the front and back, cut a peak in a whole biscuit (inset, above left).

DECORATIONS 'Glue' on your favourite treats to create doors, rooftops, trees and anything else you can imagine. Let everything set overnight. Cover the cardboard base with desiccated coconut to finish your snowy scene.

DOG 'GLUE' TWO GUMDROPS TOGETHER TO FORM THE BODY. STICK ON PIECES OF GUMDROPS FOR THE EARS, NOSE AND TAIL.

121

10 WOW-WORTHY WAYS TO GET AROUND

In Madeira, Portugal, you can take a **10-minute toboggan ride down a curvy road** in the capital city.

Consisting of just two stations, continental Europe's oldest underground line in Istanbul, Turkey, transports passengers **UP or DOWN** a steep hill.

A **HABEL-HABEL** IS A MOTORCYCLE USED IN THE PHILIPPINES WITH AN **EXTRA-LONG SEAT** THAT CAN CARRY **FOUR TO FIVE PEOPLE.**

IN THAILAND, TAXIS COME IN THE FORM OF **TUK-TUKS —** THREE-WHEELED CARS WITH OPEN SIDES AND A COVERED TOP.

Stretching **9,289 kilometres** (5,772 miles) and passing through **seven time zones,** the **TRANS-SIBERIAN RAILWAY** is the **longest train route** in the world.

Residents in Lapland, Finland — which has about the same number of reindeer as people — take sled rides to get from here to there.

TO GET FROM PLACE TO PLACE IN PAKISTAN, YOU CAN **RIDE A TANGAH,** a chauffeured wagon pulled by one or two horses.

Roosevelt Island in New York City is accessible by a tramway that travels 76 metres (250 ft) above the East River.

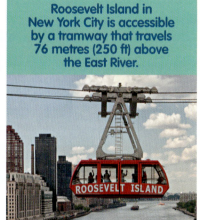

VISITORS TO THE COLUMBIA ICEFIELD IN JASPER, ALBERTA, CANADA, CLIMB ONTO A GIANT VEHICLE THAT'S **PART SCHOOL BUS, PART MONSTER TRUCK.**

To go between Greek islands, visitors can take a **hydrofoil,** a high-speed ferry that skims the water.

123

MONEY AROUND THE WORLD!

The Southern Cross constellation appears on **Brazilian coins.**

ACCORDING to some **PEOPLE, CANADA'S $100 BANKNOTE** gives off the scent of **MAPLE SYRUP.**

A British businessman created his own currency —named the **PUFFIN**— for an island he owned off of England.

IN FEBRUARY 2015, SCUBA DIVERS OFF ISRAEL FOUND MORE THAN **2,600 GOLD COINS** DATING BACK AS FAR AS THE NINTH CENTURY.

A **JANITOR** at a **GERMAN LIBRARY** found and turned in a **BOX OF RARE COINS** thought to be worth **HUNDREDS OF THOUSANDS OF POUNDS.**

Botswana's currency is named **PULA,** meaning **'RAIN',** which is **VALUABLE** in this **ARID NATION.**

ANCIENT GREEKS believed that **PLACING A COIN IN A DEAD PERSON'S MOUTH** would pay for the ferry ride to the afterlife.

COINS CREATED IN **1616** FOR WHAT IS NOW **BERMUDA** WERE NICKNAMED **'HOGGIES'** BECAUSE THEY HAD IMAGES OF **HOGS** ON THEM.

More than **$5 TRILLION** in **MONOPOLY MONEY** has been printed since 1935.

IN INDIA, the **SLANG TERM** for **100,000 RUPEES IS** *PETI,* OR **SUITCASE.** You might need one to carry that much money!

KING TUT APPEARS ON THE EGYPTIAN 1-POUND COIN.

A BRITISH ARTIST MADE A DRESS OUT OF USED **BANKNOTES** FROM AROUND THE **WORLD.**

MONEY TIP! CLIP COUPONS FOR YOUR PARENTS. Ask if they'll put the money they save into your piggy bank.

125

CHEW ON THIS

QUESADILLAS!

The quesadilla you order at a restaurant can be filled with lots of things, but the traditional treat from Mexico is almost sure to have one ingredient: cheese. Think of a quesadilla — or, roughly translated, 'little cheesy thing' in Spanish — as a twist on a toasted cheese sandwich that you can add other ingredients to.

Astronauts take **TORTILLAS** into space because they produce fewer crumbs than bread.

COURGETTE gets its name from the French word for squash.

Eating **MONTEREY JACK CHEESE** may help prevent tooth decay.

The spicy flavour of a **JALAPEÑO** is concentrated near its seeds.

One ear of **CORN** produces about 600 kernels.

MAKE YOUR OWN QUESADILLAS

Get a parent's help to heat up this cheesy dish.

1 Preheat the oven to 200°C (400°F). In a frying pan, heat 45 millilitres (3 tbsp) of olive oil over medium heat.

2 Cut 1 courgette in half lengthwise and thinly slice the halves crosswise.

3 Add courgette and 240 millilitres (8 fl oz) of frozen corn kernels to the pan. Cook, stirring occasionally, for 6 minutes.

4 Brush one side of 4 tortillas with olive oil. Lay 2 of the tortillas, oiled side down, on a baking sheet.

5 Place half of the vegetable filling on each tortilla, and sprinkle each with 115 grams (4 oz) of grated Monterey Jack cheese.

6 Place the remaining 2 tortillas on top, with their oiled side up.

7 Bake for 5 minutes, and then flip. Continue baking until cheese has melted, for about 5 more minutes.

8 Cut each quesadilla into wedges and top with a handful of sliced jalapeños.

CANDY APPLES!

Legend has it that a shop owner just wanted to sell more cinnamon-flavoured candies. Instead, he sparked a candy apple craze! After dipping some apples into the melted red sweets, the man displayed the fruit in his window. He then discovered that customers didn't want just the cinnamon candy—they wanted the whole treat, apple and all. Soon he was selling thousands of candy apples a year.

COCONUTS were once so valued that their shells were sometimes mounted and painted in gold.

CARAMEL, butterscotch and toffee share most of the same ingredients but are cooked at different temperatures.

One **PISTACHIO** tree can produce about 50,000 nuts every two years.

CANDY CORN was sold as a summertime treat in 1950s U.S.A.

Pilgrims on the *Mayflower* took **APPLE** seeds from England to the United States.

MAKE YOUR OWN TOFFEE APPLES

Get a parent's help to create some fun fruit.

1 Wash and dry 6 apples and remove the stems. Stick a wooden skewer in the stem end of each apple. (You can also use ice pop sticks.)

2 Unwrap and place 40 individual toffees in a microwave-safe bowl with 30 millilitres (2 tbsp) of milk.

3 Microwave the mixture for 2 minutes, stirring once. Allow the toffee to cool.

4 Roll each apple in the toffee, twirling to make sure the apple is completely coated.

5 Place the apples on a baking sheet covered with parchment paper. Sprinkle the apples with your favourite topping—such as pistachios or candy corn—and allow them to set.

SAVING
Languages At Risk

Today, there are more than 7,000 languages spoken on Earth. But by 2100, more than half of those may disappear. In fact, experts say one language dies every two weeks, due to the increasing dominance of larger languages such as English, Spanish and Mandarin.

So what can be done to keep dialects from disappearing altogether? To start, several National Geographic explorers have embarked on various projects around the planet. Together, they are part of the race to save some of the world's most threatened languages, as well as to protect and preserve the cultures they belong to. Here are some of the explorers' stories.

The Explorer: Tam Thi Ton
The Language: Bahnar

The Work: By gathering folklore like riddles and comics, Ton is creating bilingual learning materials for elementary students to teach them Bahnar, the language of an ethnic group living in Vietnam's Central Highlands.

TON IN A BAHNAR CLASSROOM

NARAYANAN SHARES STORIES FROM THE FIELD AT NATIONAL GEOGRAPHIC'S HEADQUARTERS IN WASHINGTON, D.C., U.S.A.

The Explorer: Sandhya Narayanan
The Languages: Quechua and Aymara

The Work: By immersing herself in the indigenous languages of the Andean region along the Peru-Bolivia border, Narayanan aims to understand how interactions between indigenous groups affect language over time.

The Explorer: K. David Harrison
The Language: Koro-Aka

The Work: Harrison led an expedition to India which identified Koro-Aka, a language that was completely new to science. He is also vice president of the Living Tongues Institute for Endangered Languages, dedicated to raising awareness and revitalising small languages.

HARRISON DOING AN INTERVIEW

The Explorer: Susan Barfield
The Language: Mapudungun

The Work: Barfield shines a light on the language of the Mapuche people of Southern Chile with her trilingual children's book, *El Copihue*. The book is based on a Mapuche folktale and is illustrated by Mapuche students.

BARFIELD PRESENTS AN OFFERING DURING A BOOK BLESSING CEREMONY.

PERLIN INTERVIEWS A VILLAGE LEADER.

The Explorer: Ross Perlin
The Language: Seke

The Work: In an effort to preserve the Seke language of northern Nepal, Perlin has been working closely with speakers both in their villages and in New York, where many now live, including young speakers determined to document their own language.

The Explorer: Lal Rapacha
The Language: Kiranti-Kõits

The Work: As the founder and director of the Research Institute for Kiratology in Kathmandu, Nepal, Rapacha carries out research on the lesser-known languages of indigenous Himalayan people, including Kiranti-Kõits, his endangered mother tongue.

RAPACHA WORKING IN THE FIELD IN NEPAL

MYTHOLOGY

GREEK

EGYPTIAN

The ancient Greeks believed that many gods and goddesses ruled the universe. According to this mythology, the Olympians lived high atop Greece's Mount Olympus. Each of these 12 main gods and goddesses had a unique personality that corresponded to particular aspects of life, such as love or death.

THE OLYMPIANS

Aphrodite was the goddess of love and beauty.

Apollo, Zeus's son, was the god of the sun, music and healing. Artemis was his twin.

Ares, Zeus's son, was the god of war.

Artemis, Zeus's daughter and Apollo's twin, was the goddess of the hunt and of childbirth.

Athena, born from the forehead of Zeus, was the goddess of wisdom and crafts.

Demeter was the goddess of fertility and nature.

Hades, Zeus's brother, was the god of the underworld and the dead.

Hephaestus, the son of Hera, was the god of fire.

Hera, the wife and older sister of Zeus, was the goddess of women and marriage.

Hermes, Zeus's son, was the messenger of the gods.

Poseidon, the brother of Zeus, was the god of the seas and earthquakes.

Zeus was the most powerful of the gods and the top Olympian. He wielded a thunderbolt and was the god of the sky and thunder.

Egyptian mythology is based on a creation myth that tells of an egg that appeared on the ocean. When the egg hatched, out came Ra, the sun god. As a result, ancient Egyptians became worshippers of the sun and of the nine original deities, most of whom were the children and grandchildren of Ra.

THE NINE DEITIES

Geb, son of Shu and Tefnut, was the god of the earth.

Isis (Ast), daughter of Geb and Nut, was the goddess of fertility and motherhood.

Nephthys (Nebet-Hut), daughter of Geb and Nut, was protector of the dead.

Nut, daughter of Shu and Tefnut, was the goddess of the sky.

Osiris (Usir), son of Geb and Nut, was the god of the afterlife.

Ra (Re), the sun god, is generally viewed as the creator. He represents life and health.

Seth (Set), son of Geb and Nut, was the god of the desert and chaos.

Shu, son of Ra, was the god of air.

Tefnut, daughter of Ra, was the goddess of rain.

All cultures around the world have unique legends and traditions that have been passed down over generations. Many myths refer to gods or supernatural heroes who are responsible for occurrences in the world. For example, Norse mythology tells of the red-bearded Thor, the god of thunder, who is responsible for creating lightning and thunderstorms. And many creation myths, especially those from some of North America's native cultures, tell of an earth-diver represented as an animal that brings a piece of sand or mud up from the deep sea. From this tiny piece of earth, the entire world takes shape.

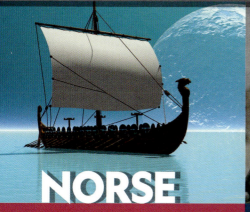

NORSE

ROMAN

Norse mythology originated in Scandinavia, in northern Europe. It was complete with gods and goddesses who lived in a heavenly place called Asgard that could be reached only by crossing a rainbow bridge.

Although Norse mythology is lesser known, we use it every day. Most days of the week are named after Norse gods, including some of these major deities.

NORSE GODS

Balder was the god of light and beauty.

Freya was the goddess of love, beauty and fertility.

Frigg, for whom Friday was named, was the queen of Asgard. She was the goddess of marriage, motherhood and the home.

Heimdall was the watchman of the rainbow bridge and the guardian of the gods.

Hel, the daughter of Loki, was the goddess of death.

Loki, a shape-shifter, was a trickster who helped the gods — and caused them problems.

Skadi was the goddess of winter and of the hunt. She is often represented as the 'Snow Queen'.

Thor, for whom Thursday was named, was the god of thunder and lightning.

Tyr, for whom Tuesday was named, was the god of the sky and war.

Wodan, for whom Wednesday was named, was the god of war, wisdom, death and magic.

Much of Roman mythology was adopted from Greek mythology, but the Romans also developed a lot of original myths as well. The gods of Roman mythology lived everywhere, and each had a role to play. There were thousands of Roman gods, but here are a few of the stars of Roman myths.

ANCIENT ROMAN GODS

Ceres was the goddess of the harvest and motherly love.

Diana, daughter of Jupiter, was the goddess of hunting and the moon.

Juno, Jupiter's wife, was the goddess of women and fertility.

Jupiter, the patron of Rome and master of the gods, was the god of the sky.

Mars, the son of Jupiter and Juno, was the god of war.

Mercury, the son of Jupiter, was the messenger of the gods and the god of travellers.

Minerva was the goddess of wisdom, learning and the arts and crafts.

Neptune, the brother of Jupiter, was the god of the sea.

Venus was the goddess of love and beauty.

Vesta was the goddess of fire and the hearth. She was one of the most important of the Roman deities.

GREEK MYTHS

POSEIDON: GOD OF THE SEAS

Poseidon—along with his brother Hades and his sisters, Hestia, Demeter and Hera—was swallowed at birth by his father, Cronus. Then a sixth child, Zeus, who was never swallowed, and thus had never known humiliation, freed them. Poseidon sized things up: Zeus was a force to be reckoned with—he was the guy to follow.

For 10 long years, the six brothers and sisters fought their father and aunts and uncles—the mighty Titans. It was a nasty war, but what war isn't? Poseidon gritted his teeth and did his part. He was no coward, after all. But now and then there was a lull in the battle, perhaps because Zeus got distracted or because the Titans needed a rest. Who knew? Whatever the case, Poseidon was grateful, and in those moments he took refuge in visiting Pontus, the ancient god of all the waters, the partner to his grandmother Gaia, Mother Earth, and his grandfather Uranus, Father Heaven. He swam in Pontus's waters, and despite how badly his life had gone so far, despite all the long years of savage war, he was happy.

Best of all, Poseidon found a friend in Nereus. He loved the watery depths as much as Poseidon did. Together they plunged to the corals and sponges that lived along the seabed. They rode on the backs of turtles. They flapped their arms like the rays they followed and then let their arms hang in the water, moving at the whim of the currents.

But then it was back to war ... until the glorious moment when the hundred-handed sons of Gaia joined the battle on Zeus's side, and then the Cyclopes gave Zeus the thunderbolt and Hades the helmet that made him invisible and Poseidon the trident. It worked, that

POSEIDON, GOD OF THE SEAS, WITH HIS TRIDENT

TREASURY OF GREEK MYTHOLOGY

CLASSIC STORIES OF GODS, GODDESSES, HEROES & MONSTERS

BY DONNA JO NAPOLI • ILLUSTRATIONS BY CHRISTINA BALIT

CHECK OUT THIS BOOK!

With his hair flying out behind him, he swam the seas in search of those who might need help. And when he wasn't patrolling, he let himself be absorbed in the watery mysteries.

That's when he discovered the finest mystery ever. She was the daughter of the sea god Phorcys and the sea goddess Ceto. That heritage made her the perfect wife in Poseidon's eyes. She was one of three sisters, called the Gorgons. The other two sisters were immortal, like the gods. But Medusa, as she was called, was mortal.

Poseidon found her mortality that much more alluring. How amazing to know someone vulnerable. He put his arms out and let the serpents of her hair swarm around them. Good! Those serpents could bite and poison—good protection. He gingerly touched the wings that jutted from her shoulder blades. Good! Those wings could carry her far from an attacker. He stroked her scales. Very good! They were harder than armour. And most assuring of all, she had a special power: Anything mortal that looked directly at her face would turn instantly to stone.

And so Poseidon felt almost safe in loving Medusa. They revelled together comfortably in his sea kingdom. At least for a while ...

trident. Poseidon struck it on the ground and the entire Earth shook. The Olympian gods won.

Zeus appointed Poseidon ruler of the seas. Poseidon knew his brother felt the seas were an inferior realm. Ha! Nothing could've pleased Poseidon more.

THE MORTAL MEDUSA EMBRACES HER HUSBAND, POSEIDON.

133

World Religions

Around the world, religion takes many forms. Some belief systems, such as Christianity, Islam and Judaism, are monotheistic, meaning that followers believe in just one supreme being. Others, like Hinduism, Shintoism and most native belief systems, are polytheistic, meaning that many of their followers believe in multiple gods.

All of the major religions have their origins in Asia, but they have spread around the world. Christianity, with the largest number of followers, has three divisions — Roman Catholic, Eastern Orthodox and Protestant. Islam, with about one-fifth of all believers, has two main divisions — Sunni and Shiite. Hinduism and Buddhism account for almost another one-fifth of believers. Judaism, dating back some 4,000 years, has more than 13 million followers, less than one percent of all believers.

CHRISTIANITY

Based on the teachings of Jesus Christ, a Jew born about 2,000 years ago in the area of modern-day Israel, Christianity has spread worldwide and actively seeks converts. Followers in Switzerland (above) participate in an Easter season procession with lanterns and crosses.

BUDDHISM

Founded about 2,400 years ago in northern India by the Hindu prince Gautama Buddha, Buddhism spread throughout East and Southeast Asia. Buddhist temples have statues, such as the Mihintale Buddha (above) in Sri Lanka.

HINDUISM

Dating back more than 4,000 years, Hinduism is practised mainly in India. Hindus follow sacred texts known as the Vedas and believe in reincarnation. During the festival of Navratri, which honours the goddess Durga, the Garba dance is performed (above).

Novice Monks

Members of the Wild Boars youth football team were rescued from a flooded Thai cave in July 2018. A few weeks later, 11 of the boys were ordained as novice Buddhist monks and spent nine days in a monastery. This act honoured Saman Gunan, a Thai Navy SEAL who died while rescuing them.

ISLAM

Muslims believe that the Quran, Islam's sacred book, records the words of Allah (God) as revealed to the Prophet Muhammad beginning around A.D. 610. Believers (above) circle the Kaaba in the Haram Mosque in Mecca, Saudi Arabia, the spiritual centre of the faith.

JUDAISM

The traditions, laws and beliefs of Judaism date back to Abraham (the patriarch) and the Torah (the first five books of the Old Testament). Followers pray before the Western Wall (above), which stands below Islam's Dome of the Rock in Jerusalem.

QUIZ WHIZ

How vast is your knowledge about the world around you? Quiz yourself!

Write your answers on a piece of paper. Then check them below.

1 Some people think that Canada's $100 banknote gives off the scent of _____.

a. roses
b. bubble gum
c. maple syrup
d. licorice

2 Lapland, Finland, has about the same number of _____ as people.

a. roosters
b. rats
c. rabbits
d. reindeer

3 Which animal is represented in Chinese astrology?

a. tiger
b. dragon
c. snake
d. all of the above

4 In Hawaii, _____ is a holiday celebrating the 'aloha spirit'.

5 **True or false?** The ancient Romans believed in thousands of gods.

Not **STUMPED** yet? Check out the *NATIONAL GEOGRAPHIC KIDS QUIZ WHIZ* collection for more crazy **CULTURE** questions!

ANSWERS: 1. c; 2. d; 3. d; 4. Lei Day; 5. True. Some of the popular gods include Diana, Jupiter and Mars.

HOMEWORK HELP

Explore a New Culture

STAMPS OF BRAZIL

YOU'RE A STUDENT, but you're also a citizen of the world. Writing a report on a foreign nation or your own country is a great way to better understand and appreciate how different people live. Pick the country of your ancestors, one that's been in the news or one that you'd like to visit one day.

CURRENCY AND COINS OF BRAZIL

Passport to Success

A country report follows the format of an expository essay because you're 'exposing' information about the country you choose.

The following step-by-step tips will help you with this monumental task.

FLAG OF BRAZIL

1 **RESEARCH.** Gathering information is the most important step in writing a good country report. Look to internet sources, encyclopedias, books, magazine and newspaper articles and other sources to find important and interesting details about your subject.

2 **ORGANISE YOUR NOTES.** Put the information you have gathered into a rough outline. For example, sort everything you have found about the country's system of government, climate, etc.

3 **WRITE IT UP.** Follow the basic structure of good writing: introduction, body and conclusion. Remember that each paragraph should have a topic sentence that is then supported by facts and details. Incorporate the information from your notes, but make sure it's in your own words. And make your writing flow with good transitions and descriptive language.

4 **ADD VISUALS.** Include maps, diagrams, photos and other visual aids.

5 **PROOFREAD AND REVISE.** Correct any mistakes, and polish your language. Do your best!

6 **CITE YOUR SOURCES.** Be sure to keep a record of your sources.

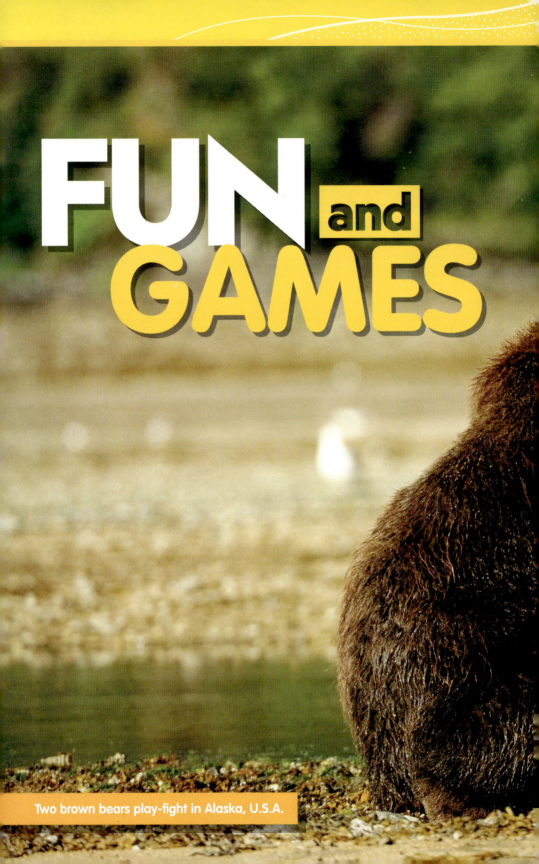

FUN and GAMES

Two brown bears play-fight in Alaska, U.S.A.

GREEN SCENE

You're the newly elected mayor of this busy city. The first order of business? Transform it into the greenest town in the world. Start by finding 15 pieces of litter from the list below. Then locate eight blue recycling bins and two green compost bins to clean up the city.

ANSWERS ON PAGE 338

1. cardboard box
2. crumpled-up paper
3. drink can
4. paper cup
5. phone book
6. cereal box
7. newspapers
8. half-eaten apple
9. egg carton
10. paper bag
11. banana peel
12. glass bottle
13. magazine
14. takeaway box
15. milk carton

WHAT IN THE WORLD?

RING TOSS

These images show close-up and faraway views of items with ring shapes. On a separate sheet of paper, unscramble the letters to identify what's in each picture.

ANSWERS ON PAGE 338

SLAKLTBBAE TNE

LAUH-OPOH

LNPEIPEAP

RETE KTNRU

TODHNGUU

YKE IGNR

MWGIISMN GIRN

ODDRRATBA

UNRAST

FIND THE HIDDEN ANIMALS

Animals often blend in with their environments for protection. Find each animal listed below in one of the pictures. On a separate sheet of paper, write the letter of the correct picture and the animal's name.

ANSWERS ON PAGE 338

1. American alligator
2. grey tree frog
3. eastern screech owl
4. black-tailed deer
5. black rhino
6. feather star shrimp

CRITTER CHAT

I'M A LEAN, GREEN, BUG-EATING MACHINE!

If animals used social media, what would they say?
Follow this red-eyed tree frog's day as it updates its feed.

Red-Eyed Tree Frog

LIVES IN: Southern Mexico and Central America
SCREEN NAME FabFrog
FRIENDS

KEEL-BILLED TOUCAN	CENTRAL AMERICAN AGOUTI	KINKAJOU
BananaBeak	ForestFriend	KinkaWoo

START

7:20 p.m.

 FabFrog: New profile pic alert! How do I look?

 BananaBeak: Uh, like a snack. But I've found a different treat, so you can chill out ... for now.

ForestFriend: Hey @BananaBeak, where's that tree you're tasting from? I'll munch up whatever fruit you drop. 🙂

 KinkaWoo: Now *I'm* in the mood for something sweet. Anybody seen a beehive? #AskingForMyTongue

10 p.m.

 FabFrog: Thanks to my suction-cup toes, I'm totally an acrobat—er, acro-*frog!*

 KinkaWoo: That looks like a lot of work when you could just *hang* out. Tails are for winners.

 BananaBeak: You're all just annoyed you're stuck to the trees. I'm a sky princess. 😎

 ForestFriend: The forest floor is good enough for me. I like my home so much I rub my butt all over it so it smells like me. #Normal

 FabFrog: That's so gross, even for me— and I ooze smelly slime.

5 a.m.

 FabFrog: Now you see me— now you don't. #PerfectCamouflage

ForestFriend: Are we playing hide-and-seek? I'm pretty great at disappear-ing in the brush.

 KinkaWoo: Oh, that reminds me ... I've got to go and find my hide-and-sleep tree hole. See y'all tomorrow!

 FabFrog: PSYCH! I was only hiding to jump out and ambush a moth. #Crunchy

 BananaBeak: Whoa—you've got some serious leaping skills. And I thought *I* was the only one that could fly!

FUNNY FILL-IN

Ask a friend to give you words to fill in the blanks in this story and write them on a separate sheet of paper. Then read the story out loud and fill in the words for a laugh.

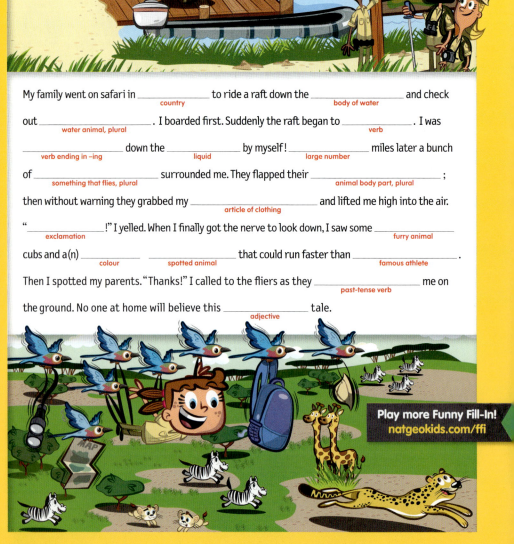

My family went on safari in _____ to ride a raft down the _____ and check

country   *body of water*

out _____ . I boarded first. Suddenly the raft began to _____ . I was

water animal, plural   *verb*

_____ down the _____ by myself! _____ miles later a bunch

verb ending in –ing   *liquid*   *large number*

of _____ surrounded me. They flapped their _____ ;

something that flies, plural   *animal body part, plural*

then without warning they grabbed my _____ and lifted me high into the air.

article of clothing

"_____!" I yelled. When I finally got the nerve to look down, I saw some _____

exclamation   *furry animal*

cubs and a(n) _____ _____ that could run faster than _____ .

colour   *spotted animal*   *famous athlete*

Then I spotted my parents. "Thanks!" I called to the fliers as they _____ me on

past-tense verb

the ground. No one at home will believe this _____ tale.

adjective

Play more Funny Fill-In!
natgeokids.com/ffi

144

WHAT IN THE WORLD?

OVER THE RAINBOW

These photographs show close-up views of rainbow-coloured objects. On a separate sheet of paper, unscramble the letters to identify what's in each picture.

ANSWERS ON PAGE 338

APNTI EST

KSOCS

POLPLIOL

TRAORP

AKEC

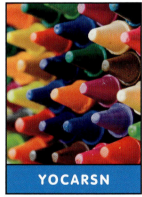

YOCARSN

KSSRNLEPI

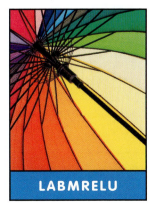

LABMRELU

NKISYL

145

LAUGH OUT LOUD

"YOUR MUM SENT ME UP SO YOU WON'T BE LATE FOR SCHOOL AGAIN!"

"DIDN'T I TELL YOU TO CLEAN OFF YOUR BELLY BEFORE SNACK TIME?"

"IT'S JUST UNTIL THE BRACES COME OFF."

"AW, MUM. DO I REALLY HAVE TO GO TO SCHOOL TODAY?"

Just Joking

CROCODILE

KNOCK, KNOCK.

Who's there?
Dinosaur.
Dinosaur who?
Dinosaur because he fell down!

Q What happened when 500 hares got loose in the centre of town?

A The police had to comb the area.

Q What do you call a very popular perfume?

A A best smeller.

TONGUE TWISTER Say this fast three times:
Six slick sightseers click.

FUNNY FILL-IN

Ask a friend to give you words to fill in the blanks in this story and write them on a separate sheet of paper. Then read the story out loud and fill in the words for a laugh.

My friends and I _____ (past-tense verb) a machine that can _____ (verb) stuff. But before we could show it off,

we had to _____ (verb) it. I put a(n) _____ (noun) on a table and _____ (past-tense verb) a button. Then there was

a(n) _____ (adjective) blast. Suddenly I saw green strips towering above me. It was grass — we

_____ (adverb ending in -ly) _____ (past-tense verb) ourselves! We heard a noise. I turned and saw a(n) _____ (noun)

with eight eyes. My friend quickly scaled a nearby _____ (something in nature) , while the rest of us tied our

_____ (article of clothing, plural) together to make a rope. Our friend pulled us to safety, with the creature

_____ (verb ending in -ing) towards us. A(n) _____ (flying animal) picked us up from there, dropping us on top of our machine.

We gathered together and _____ (past-tense verb) on the button. I opened my _____ (body part, plural) . I was

_____ (adjective) enough to see into my house! Our big adventure had come to a close.

WHAT IN THE WORLD?

WILD STYLE

These images show close-up views of African animals. On a separate sheet of paper, unscramble the letters to identify what's in each picture.

ANSWERS ON PAGE 338

AREBZ

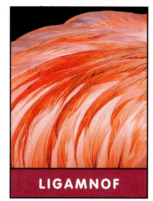

LIGAMNOF

FAEIRGF

AHLNEPET

ALMDILNR

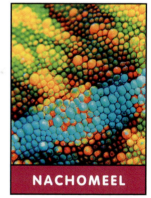

NACHOMEEL

DELRPOA

TRSEITOO

RIFACNA IDLW OGD

FIND THE HIDDEN ANIMALS

Animals often blend in with their environments for protection. Find each animal listed below in one of the pictures. On a separate sheet of paper, write the letter of the correct picture and the animal's name.

ANSWERS ON PAGE 338

1. crabs
2. hare
3. alligator
4. praying mantis
5. seal
6. frogfish

Ask a friend to give you words to fill in the blanks in this story and write them on a separate sheet of paper. Then read the story out loud and fill in the words for a laugh.

CAR WASH! DONATIONS ACCEPTED

This weekend, my mother, sister and I _____ our _____ _____
                                      past-tense verb   adjective   type of transportation

to a car wash. As a(n) _____ waved us in, we heard a(n) _____ . A huge
                        type of job   funny sound

_____ was _____ cars! "_____!" we yelled. Using its
  animal   verb ending in –ing   exclamation

_____ , it wiped the back of the _____ in front of us. _____ dripped
  body part   noun   something gross

from a(n) _____ strapped to its hoof as it sprayed _____ with its trunk. Then the
            noun   noun

creature _____ the cars with its ears. Everyone was covered in _____ .
          past-tense verb   type of liquid

Who knows where that _____ came from—but our car has never
                       same animal

been so _____ !
          adjective

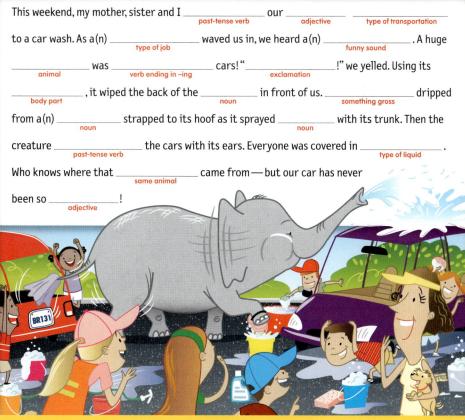

151

WHAT IN THE WORLD?

POSITIVELY PURPLE

These images show close-up views of purple objects. On a separate sheet of paper, unscramble the letters to identify what's in each picture.

ANSWERS ON PAGE 338

UMLSP

ANYR

AES NAF

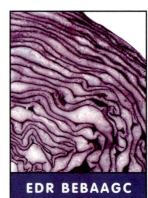

LCOHASEE

FRSAHSIT

EDR BEBAAGC

ARYOSCN

DCRHOI

TMHESATY

SIGNS OF THE TIMES

Seeing isn't always believing. Two of these funny signs are not real. Can you figure out which two are fake?
ANSWERS ON PAGE 338

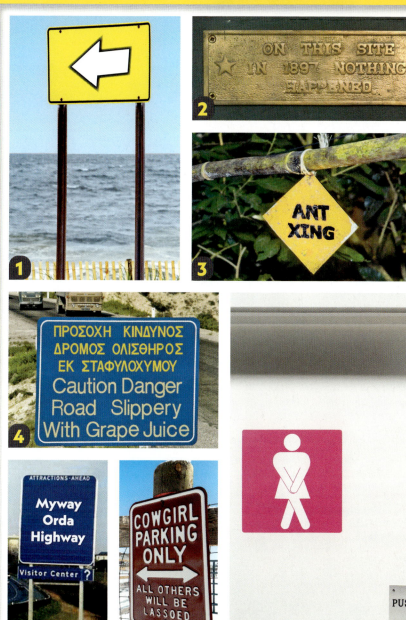

1.

2. ON THIS SITE IN 1897 NOTHING HAPPENED

3. ANT XING

4. ΠΡΟΣΟΧΗ ΚΙΝΔΥΝΟΣ ΔΡΟΜΟΣ ΟΛΙΣΘΗΡΟΣ ΕΚ ΣΤΑΦΥΛΟΧΥΜΟΥ
Caution Danger Road Slippery With Grape Juice

5. ATTRACTIONS · AHEAD
Myway Orda Highway
Visitor Center ?

6. COWGIRL PARKING ONLY ALL OTHERS WILL BE LASSOED

7. PUSH

Just Joking

DACHSHUND

KNOCK, KNOCK.
Who's there?
Howl.
Howl who?
Howl you feeling today?

Q How did the flea get from one dog to the other?

A It itchhiked.

Q What did the dog bring on her camping trip?

A A pup-up tent.

Q What's the biggest problem with corgi jokes?

A They're too short.

Check out this book!

Just Joking DOGS

FUNNY FILL-IN

Ask a friend to give you words to fill in the blanks in this story and write them on a separate sheet of paper. Then read the story out loud and fill in the words for a laugh.

Play more Funny Fill-In!
natgeokids.com/ffi

_____ and I have a winter tradition. Every year we put on all the jumpers we can find,
*friend's name*

pack sandwiches and a thermos of _____ and go hiking in the mountains. All that changed when
*liquid*

my family moved to _____, where it's always _____ °C! But we had to follow our
*warm place* _*large number*_

tradition. So this year we put on our _____, packed _____ soup and
*type of warm clothing, plural* _*something gross*_

hired a(n) _____. We _____ up a tall _____ until we could see all
*type of transportation* _*past-tense verb*_ _*noun*_

the way to _____. We _____ our _____ onto our
*faraway city* _*past-tense verb*_ _*type of athletic equipment, plural*_

_____ and, with a(n) _____, pushed ourselves down. We were moving faster than
*body part, plural* _*sound*_

a(n) _____, and _____ were _____ our faces. "_____!"
*animal* _*something small, plural*_ _*verb ending in -ing*_ _*exclamation*_

we yelled. It was a total blast until we realised our ride was right where we left it—way up at the top.

155

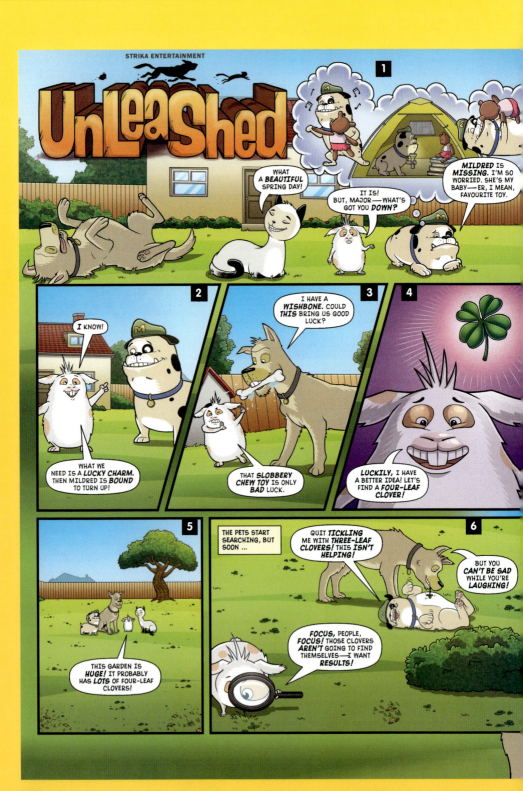

Macrophotography provides a close-up look at bismuth crystals.

SPACE and EARTH

A LOOK INSIDE

The distance from Earth's surface to its centre is 6,437 kilometres (4,000 miles) at the Equator. There are four layers: a thin, rigid crust; the rocky mantle; the outer core, which is a layer of molten iron; and finally the inner core, which is believed to be mostly solid iron.

The **CRUST** includes tectonic plates, landmasses and the ocean. Its average thickness varies from 8 to 40 kilometres (5 to 25 miles).

The **MANTLE** is about 2,900 kilometres (1,800 miles) of hot, thick, solid rock.

The **OUTER CORE** is liquid molten rock made mostly of iron and nickel.

The **INNER CORE** is a solid centre made mostly of iron and nickel.

What if you could dig to the other side of Earth?

Got a magma-proof suit and a magical drill that can cut through any surface? Then you're ready to dig through 12,714 kilometres (7,900 miles) to Earth's other side. But first you'd need to drill about 40 kilometres (25 miles) through the planet's ultra-tough crust to its mantle. The heat and pressure at the mantle are intense enough to turn carbon into diamonds — and to, um, crush you. If you were able to survive, you'd still have to bore another 2,897 kilometres (1,800 miles) to hit Earth's Mars-size core that can reach 6093°C (11,000°F). Now just keep drilling through the core and then the mantle and crust on the opposite side until you resurface on the planet's other side. But exit your tunnel fast. A hole dug through Earth would close quickly as surrounding rock filled in the empty space. The closing of the tunnel might cause small earthquakes, and your path home would definitely be blocked. Happy digging!

ROCK STARS

Rocks and minerals are everywhere on Earth! And it can be a challenge to tell one from the other. So what's the difference between a rock and a mineral? A rock is a naturally occurring solid object made mostly from minerals. Minerals are solid, nonliving substances that occur in nature — and the basic components of most rocks. Rocks can be made of just one mineral or, like granite, of many minerals. But not all rocks are made of minerals: Coal comes from plant material, while amber is formed from ancient tree resin.

Igneous

Named for the Greek word meaning 'from fire', igneous rocks form when hot, molten liquid called magma cools. Pools of magma form deep underground and slowly work their way to Earth's surface. If they make it all the way, the liquid rock erupts and is called lava. As the layers of lava build up, they form a mountain called a volcano. Typical igneous rocks include obsidian, basalt and pumice, which is so chock-full of gas bubbles that it actually floats in water.

ANDESITE

GRANITE PORPHYRY

Metamorphic

Metamorphic rocks are the masters of change! These rocks were once igneous or sedimentary, but thanks to intense heat and pressure deep within Earth, they have undergone a total transformation from their original form. These rocks never truly melt; instead, the heat twists and bends them until their shapes substantially change. Metamorphic rocks include slate as well as marble, which is used for buildings, monuments and sculptures.

MICA SCHIST

BANDED GNEISS

Sedimentary

When wind, water and ice constantly wear away and weather rocks, smaller pieces called sediment are left behind. These are sedimentary rocks, also known as gravel, sand, silt and clay. As water flows downhill, it carries the sedimentary grains into lakes and oceans, where they are deposited. As the loose sediment piles up, the grains eventually get compacted or cemented back together again. The result is new sedimentary rock. Sandstone, gypsum, limestone and shale are sedimentary rocks that have formed this way.

LIMESTONE

HALITE

Identifying Minerals

With so many different minerals in the world, it can be a challenge to tell one from another. Fortunately, each mineral has physical characteristics that geologists and amateur rock collectors use to tell them apart. Check out the physical characteristics below: colour, lustre, streak, cleavage, fracture and hardness.

Colour

When you look at a mineral, the first thing you see is its colour. In some minerals, this is a key factor because their colours are almost always the same. For example, azurite, below, is always blue. But in other cases, impurities can change the natural colour of a mineral. For instance, fluorite, above, can be green, red, violet and other colours as well. The change makes it a challenge to identify by colour alone.

FLUORITE

AZURITE

Lustre

'Lustre' refers to the way light reflects from the surface of a mineral. Does a mineral appear metallic, like gold or silver? Or is it pearly like orpiment, or brilliant like diamond? 'Earthy', 'glassy', 'silky' and 'dull' are a few other terms used to describe lustre.

ORPIMENT

DIAMOND

Streak

The 'streak' is the colour of the mineral's powder. When minerals are ground into powder, they often have a different colour than when they are in crystal form. For example, the mineral pyrite usually looks gold, but when it is rubbed against a ceramic tile called a 'streak plate', the mark it leaves is black.

PYRITE

Cleavage

'Cleavage' describes the way a mineral breaks. Because the structure of a specific mineral is always the same, it tends to break in the same pattern. Not all minerals have cleavage, but the minerals that do, like this microcline, break evenly in one or more directions. These minerals are usually described as having 'perfect cleavage'. But if the break isn't smooth and clean, cleavage can be considered 'good' or 'poor'.

MICROCLINE

GOLD

Fracture

Some minerals, such as gold, do not break with cleavage. Instead, geologists say that they 'fracture'. There are different types of fractures, and, depending on the mineral, the fracture may be described as jagged, splintery, even or uneven.

Hardness

The level of ease or difficulty with which a mineral can be scratched refers to its 'hardness'. Hardness is measured using a special chart called the Mohs Hardness Scale. The Mohs scale goes from 1 to 10. Softer minerals, which appear on the lower end of the scale, can be scratched by the harder minerals on the upper end of the scale.

RATING	MINERAL NAME	EXAMPLES
1	TALC	BAR OF SOAP
2	GYPSUM	FINGERNAIL
3	CALCITE	COPPER PENNY
4	FLUORITE	SOFT IRON NAIL
5	APATITE	STEEL POCKETKNIFE BLADE
6	ORTHOCLASE	WINDOW GLASS
7	QUARTZ	HARDENED STEEL FILE
8	TOPAZ	TOPAZ
9	CORUNDUM	RUBY, SAPPHIRE
10	DIAMOND	DIAMOND

HOW TO MAKE A
DIAMOND

These sparkly gems have been treasured for thousands of years, but geologists still aren't exactly sure how diamonds formed on Earth. Here's how scientists think natural diamonds are made.

1 FIND CARBON BURIED

^{6}C

161 KILOMETRES
(100 miles)
BELOW EARTH'S SURFACE.

2 HEAT TO ABOUT
1204°C
(2200°F)
IN EARTH'S MANTLE.

3 SQUEEZE UNDER HIGH PRESSURE OF
50,973
KILOGRAMS PER SQUARE CENTIMETRE
(725,000 lb per sq in)

The largest rough diamond was discovered in **1905** and weighed **635 GRAMS** (1.4 lb).

4 WAIT
1–3 BILLION YEARS
(THAT'S ALMOST 75 PERCENT OF THE AGE OF EARTH!)

5
CUT RAW STONE INTO THE CLASSIC DIAMOND SHAPE WITH

58 FACETS.

EVERY MINERAL HAS ITS OWN SPECIAL CRYSTAL SHAPE, CALLED ITS HABIT.

Mineral crystals usually begin as a liquid. As the liquid cools or evaporates, the atoms in the liquid begin to join together to form the crystal. Large well-formed crystals will only grow if the conditions are right.

THESE AMETHYST CRYSTALS GREW SLOWLY FROM A LIQUID STATE.

Salt of the Earth

In this experiment you can try your hand at growing two different types of crystals using some simple salt solutions. **Here's what you'll need:**

2 small (250 ml) disposable clear plastic cups	Container of table salt	Container of Epsom salts (available at most pharmacies)	Hot water	Permanent marker	Magnifying glass

1 Use the marker to label one cup 'plain salt' and the other 'Epsom salts'. Fill each cup about half-way with hot water.

2 Stir in 25 to 30 millilitres (5 or 6 tsp) of table salt into the cup labelled 'plain salt' so that all the salt dissolves. Use a different teaspoon to do the same with the Epsom salts in the other cup.

3 Place both cups in a safe location, and allow the water to evaporate completely. It should take about a week or so.

4 After the water has completely evaporated from each cup, carefully observe the crystals that have formed on the bottom of each cup by using the magnifying glass.

You will see that the crystal habit of the table salt is little cubes, while the Epsom salt appears to be long needlelike prisms. You can experiment further by mixing different amounts of the two salts together to see what types of crystals they produce.

TABLE SALT

EPSOM SALT

A HOT TOPIC

WHAT GOES ON
INSIDE A STEAMING, BREWING VOLCANO?

If you could look inside a volcano, you'd see something that looks like a long pipe, called a conduit. It leads from inside the magma chamber under the crust up to a vent, or opening, at the top of the mountain. Some conduits have branches that shoot off to the side, called fissures.

When pressure builds from gasses inside the volcano, the gasses must find an escape, and they head up towards the surface! An eruption occurs when lava, gasses, ash and rocks explode out of the vent.

CRATER

VENT

CONDUIT

FISSURE

MAGMA CHAMBER

HARDENED LAVA AND ASH LAYERS

TYPES OF VOLCANOES

CINDER CONE VOLCANO
Eve Cone, Canada

Cinder cone volcanoes look like an upside-down bowl. They spew cinder and hot ash. Some of these volcanoes smoke and erupt for years at a time.

COMPOSITE VOLCANO
Licancábur, Chile

Composite volcanoes, or stratovolcanoes, form as lava, ash and cinder from previous eruptions harden and build up over time. These volcanoes spit out pyroclastic flows, or thick explosions of hot ash that travel at hundreds of kilometres an hour.

SHIELD VOLCANO
Mauna Loa, Hawaii, U.S.A.

The gentle, broad slopes of a shield volcano look like an ancient warrior's shield. Its eruptions are often slower. Lava splatters and bubbles rather than shooting forcefully into the air.

LAVA DOME VOLCANO
Mount St. Helens, Washington, U.S.A.

Dome volcanoes have steep sides. Hardened lava often plugs the vent at the top of a dome volcano. Pressure builds beneath the surface until the top blows.

RING OF FIRE

Although volcanoes are found on every continent, most are located along an arc known as the Ring of Fire. This area, which forms a horseshoe shape in the Pacific

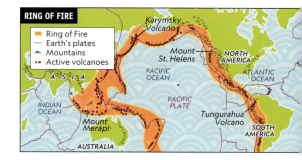

RING OF FIRE
- Ring of Fire
- Earth's plates
- Mountains
- Active volcanoes

Karymsky Volcano
Mount St. Helens
NORTH AMERICA
ASIA
PACIFIC OCEAN
ATLANTIC OCEAN
PACIFIC PLATE
INDIAN OCEAN
Tungurahua Volcano
Mount Merapi
SOUTH AMERICA
AUSTRALIA

Ocean, stretches some 40,000 kilometres (24,900 miles). Several of the large, rigid plates that make up Earth's surface are found here, and they are prone to shifting towards each other and colliding. The result? Volcanic eruptions and earthquakes—and plenty of them. In fact, the Ring of Fire hosts 90 percent of the world's recorded earthquakes and about 75 percent of active volcanoes. Turn the page for more hot facts about the Ring of Fire!

10 HOT THINGS ABOUT THE RING OF FIRE

With **more than a dozen recorded eruptions** since 1519, Popocatépetl in Mexico is among the **most dangerous volcanoes** in the Ring of Fire.

MOST OF THE 450-PLUS VOLCANOES FOUND ALONG THE RING OF FIRE ARE LOCATED **UNDERWATER.**

Part of the **RING OF FIRE,** Russia's **KAMCHATKA PENINSULA** contains more than **150 VOLCANOES,** about 30 of which are active.

EXPERTS THINK THE RING OF FIRE STARTED TO FORM SOME 100 MILLION YEARS AGO — DURING THE **CRETACEOUS PERIOD** WHEN DINOSAURS WERE WIDESPREAD.

The world's **strongest earthquake** to date — **Chile's Valdivia earthquake** in 1960 — resulted from activity along the Ring of Fire.

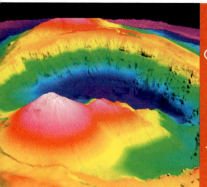

A DEEP-SEA ROBOT USED **SONAR** TO CREATE A COLOURFUL PHOTO OF THE **UNDERWATER BROTHERS VOLCANO,** SUBMERGED ABOUT 1,600 METRES (1 MILE) DEEP IN THE PACIFIC OCEAN.

The Ring of Fire is home to the Mariana Trench. At **11 KILOMETRES** (7 miles) deep, it's the **deepest part** of any of the world's oceans.

The **Ring of Fire** is **not an actual ring —** rather it is in the **shape of a horseshoe.**

LAVA GULLS that live on the Galápagos Islands, which are located on the Ring of Fire, have **DARK PLUMAGE** to blend in with the **DARK VOLCANIC ROCK.**

ABOUT **10 PERCENT** OF THE WORLD'S VOLCANIC ACTIVITY OCCURS IN **JAPAN,** WHICH LIES ALONG THE WESTERN EDGE OF THE RING OF FIRE.

A Universe of Galaxies

5 COOL FACTS TO RECORD

When astronauts first journeyed beyond Earth's orbit in 1968, they looked back to their home planet. The big-picture view of our place in space changed the astronauts' lives—and perhaps humanity. If you could leave the universe and similarly look back, what would you see? Remarkably, scientists are mapping this massive area. They see ... bubbles. Not actual soap bubbles, of course, but a structure that looks like a pan full of them. Like bubble walls, thin surfaces curve around empty spaces in an elegantly simple structure. Zoom in to see that these surfaces are groups of galaxies. Zoom in further to find one galaxy, with an ordinary star—our sun—orbited by an ordinary planet—Earth. How extraordinary.

DIGITAL TRAVELLER!

Take a simulated flight through our universe, thanks to the data collected by the Sloan Digital Sky Survey. Search the internet for 'APOD flight through universe sdss'. Sit back and enjoy the ride!

2 DARK MATTER

The universe holds a mysterious source of gravity that cannot be properly explained. This unseen matter—the ghostly dark ring in this composite Hubble telescope photo—seems to pull on galaxy clusters, drawing galaxies towards it. But what is this strange stuff? It's not giant black holes, planets, stars or anti-matter. These would show themselves indirectly. For now, astronomers call this source of gravity 'dark matter'.

1 GALAXY CLUSTERS AND SUPERCLUSTERS

Gravity pulls things together—gas in stars, stars in galaxies. Galaxies gather, too, sometimes by the thousands, forming galaxy clusters and superclusters with tremendously superheated gas. This gas can be as hot as 100 million degrees Celsius (180 million degrees Fahrenheit), filling space between them. These clusters hide a secret. The gravity among the galaxies isn't enough to bring them together. The source of the extra gravity is a dark secret.

3 IT STARTED WHEN ...
The Big Bang

Long ago, the universe was compressed: It was hotter, smaller, denser than now, and completely uniform—almost. Extremely minor unevenness led to a powerful energy release that astronomers call the big bang. In a blip of time, the universe expanded tremendously. The first particles formed. Atoms, galaxies, forces and light ... all developed from this. Today's great filaments (see fact 4) may be organised where those first uneven patches existed.

4 FILAMENTS AND SHEETS
Bubbles of Space

What is the universe like at its grandest scale? The biggest big-picture view is jaw-dropping. Clusters and superclusters of galaxies—red and yellow areas in this illustration—along with dark matter, string together to form structures that are millions and billions of light-years long. These so-called walls, sheets or filaments surround vast voids, or 'bubbles', of nearly empty space—the blue areas. The universe has a structure, nonrandom and unexpected.

5 COLLISION ZONE

Saying that galaxies form clusters and superclusters is like saying two football teams simply meet. During a game, there's a lot of action and energy. Similarly, as clusters and superclusters form, there's lots going on—as evidenced by the super-high-energy x-rays that are detected (pink in this colourised image).

PLANETS

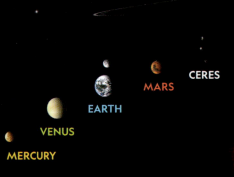

CERES

MARS

EARTH

VENUS

MERCURY

JUPITER

SUN

MERCURY

Average distance from the sun:
   57,900,000 kilometres (35,980,000 miles)
Position from the sun in orbit: 1st
Equatorial diameter:
   4,878 kilometres (3,030 miles)
Length of day: 59 Earth days
Length of year: 88 Earth days
Known moons: 0
Fun fact: On Mercury, the sun appears to rise and set twice a day.

VENUS

Average distance from the sun:
   108,200,000 kilometres (67,230,000 miles)
Position from the sun in orbit: 2nd
Equatorial diameter:
   12,100 kilometres (7,520 miles)
Length of day: 243 Earth days
Length of year: 224.7 Earth days
Known moons: 0
Fun fact: The surface pressure on Venus is so strong that it could melt lead and crush a submarine.

EARTH

Average distance from the sun:
   149,600,000 kilometres (93,000,000 miles)
Position from the sun in orbit: 3rd
Equatorial diameter:
   12,750 kilometres (7,900 miles)
Length of day: 24 hours
Length of year: 365 days
Known moons: 1
Fun fact: Scientists believe a 'mini moon' — most likely a small asteroid — recently circled Earth.

MARS

Average distance from the sun:
   227,936,000 kilometres (141,633,000 miles)
Position from the sun in orbit: 4th
Equatorial diameter:
   6,794 kilometres (4,221 miles)
Length of day: 25 Earth hours
Length of year: 1.9 Earth years
Known moons: 2
Fun fact: Some dust storms on Mars may last for several months.

This artwork shows the eight planets and five dwarf planets in our solar system. The relative sizes and positions of the planets are shown but not the relative distances between them.

SATURN

URANUS

NEPTUNE

PLUTO

HAUMEA

MAKEMAKE

ERIS

JUPITER
Average distance from the sun:
778,412,000 kilometres (483,682,000 miles)
Position from the sun in orbit: 6th
Equatorial diameter:
142,980 kilometres (88,840 miles)
Length of day: 9.9 Earth hours
Length of year: 11.9 Earth years
Known moons: 79*
Fun fact: A rover is expected to enter Jupiter's orbit in 2029.

SATURN
Average distance from the sun:
1,433,600,000 kilometres (890,800,000 miles)
Position from the sun in orbit: 7th
Equatorial diameter:
120,540 kilometres (74,900 miles)
Length of day: 10.7 Earth hours
Length of year: 29.5 Earth years
Known moons: 82*
Fun fact: Some of the chunks of rock and ice that make up Saturn's rings are as big as a mountain.

URANUS
Average distance from the sun:
2,871,000,000 kilometres (1,784,000,000 miles)
Position from the sun in orbit: 8th
Equatorial diameter:
51,120 kilometres (31,760 miles)
Length of day: 17.2 Earth hours
Length of year: 84 Earth years
Known moons: 27
Fun fact: Winds on Uranus can be 7.5 times stronger than hurricane winds on Earth.

NEPTUNE
Average distance from the sun:
4,498,000,000 kilometres (2,795,000,000 miles)
Position from the sun in orbit: 9th
Equatorial diameter:
49,528 kilometres (30,775 miles)
Length of day: 16 Earth hours
Length of year: 164.8 Earth years
Known moons: 14
Fun fact: Neptune may have oceans of liquid diamond.

*Includes provisional moons, which await confirmation and naming from the International Astronomical Union.

For information about dwarf planets, see page 174.

173

DWARF PLANETS

Haumea

Eris

Pluto

Thanks to advanced technology,

astronomers have been spotting many never-before-seen celestial bodies with their telescopes. One new discovery? A population of icy objects orbiting the sun beyond Pluto. The largest, like Pluto itself, are classified as dwarf planets. Smaller than the moon but still massive enough to pull themselves into a ball, dwarf planets nevertheless lack the gravitational 'oomph' to clear their neighbourhood of other sizable objects. So, although larger, more massive planets pretty much have their orbits to themselves, dwarf planets orbit the sun in swarms that include other dwarf planets as well as smaller chunks of rock or ice.

So far, astronomers have identified five dwarf planets: Ceres, Pluto, Haumea, Makemake and Eris. There are also three newly discovered dwarf planets that will need additional study before they are named. Astronomers are observing hundreds of newly found objects in the frigid outer solar system. As time and technology advance, the family of known dwarf planets will surely continue to grow.

CERES
Position from the sun in orbit: 5th
Length of day: 9.1 Earth hours
Length of year: 4.6 Earth years
Known moons: 0

PLUTO
Position from the sun in orbit: 10th
Length of day: 6.4 Earth days
Length of year: 248 Earth years
Known moons: 5

HAUMEA
Position from the sun in orbit: 11th
Length of day: 3.9 Earth hours
Length of year: 282 Earth years
Known moons: 2

MAKEMAKE
Position from the sun in orbit: 12th
Length of day: 22.5 Earth hours
Length of year: 305 Earth years
Known moons: 1*

ERIS
Position from the sun in orbit: 13th
Length of day: 25.9 Earth hours
Length of year: 561 Earth years
Known moons: 1

*Includes provisional moons, which await confirmation and naming from the International Astronomical Union.

Bet You Didn't Know!

9 marvellous facts about Mars

1 MARS has 2 small MOONS.

2 A YEAR ON MARS lasts nearly twice as long as one on Earth.

3 The average TEMPERATURE on Mars is **-63°C** (-81°F).

4 You could JUMP 3 TIMES HIGHER on Mars than on Earth.

5 It takes 6 to 11 MONTHS for a spacecraft to TRAVEL from Earth to Mars.

6 By the 2040s, astronauts might VISIT MARS.

7 From Mars's surface, the SKY is the colour of BUTTERSCOTCH.

8 One VOLCANO on Mars is about 3 TIMES TALLER than Mount Everest.

9 Mars is nicknamed THE RED PLANET because it's covered in RED DUST.

BLACK HOLES

BLACK HOLE →

A black hole really seems like a hole in space. Most black holes form when the core of a massive star collapses, falling into oblivion. A black hole has a stronger gravitational pull than anything else in the known universe. It's like a bottomless pit, swallowing anything that gets close enough to it to be pulled in. It's black because it pulls in light. Black holes come in different sizes. The smallest known black hole has a mass about three times that of the sun. The biggest one scientists have found so far has a mass about three billion times greater than the sun's. Really big black holes at the centres of galaxies probably form by swallowing enormous amounts of gas over time. In 2019, scientists released the first image of a black hole's silhouette (left). The image, previously thought impossible to record, was captured using a network of telescopes.

SKY DREAMS

The Plough, also called the Big Dipper, is part of the constellation commonly known as the Great Bear.

LONG AGO, people looking at the sky noticed that some stars made shapes and patterns. By playing join the dots, they imagined people and animals in the sky. Their legendary heroes and monsters were pictured in the stars.

Today, we call the star patterns identified by the ancient Greeks and Romans 'constellations'. There are 88 constellations in all. Some are only visible when you're north of the Equator, and some only when you're south of it.

In the 16th-century age of exploration, European ocean voyagers began visiting southern lands, and they named the constellations that are visible in the Southern Hemisphere, such as the Southern Cross. Astronomers used the star observations of these navigators to fill in the blank spots on their celestial maps.

Constellations aren't fixed in the sky. The star arrangement that makes up each one would look different from another location in the universe. Constellations also change over time because every star we see is moving through space. Over thousands of years, the stars in the Plough, which is part of the larger constellation Ursa Major (the Great Bear), will move so far apart that the recognisable pattern will disappear.

Sky Calendar 2022

Jupiter

Leonid meteor shower

Supermoon

• 3-4 JANUARY
QUADRANTIDS METEOR SHOWER PEAK. Featuring up to 40 meteors an hour, it is the first meteor shower of every new year.

• 6-7 MAY
ETA AQUARIDS METEOR SHOWER PEAK. View about 30 to 60 meteors an hour.

• 15-16 MAY
TOTAL LUNAR ECLIPSE. Look for the moon to darken and then take on a deep red colour as it passes completely through Earth's umbra — or dark shadow. It will be visible in North America, Greenland, parts of western Europe, western Africa and the Atlantic Ocean.

• 14 JUNE
SUPERMOON, FULL MOON. The moon will be full and at a close approach to Earth, and likely to appear bigger and brighter than usual. Look for two more supermoons on July 13 and August 11.

• 12-13 AUGUST
PERSEID METEOR SHOWER PEAK. One of the best — see up to 90 meteors an hour! Best viewing is in the direction of the constellation Perseus.

• 14 AUGUST
SATURN AT OPPOSITION. This is your best chance to view the ringed planet in 2022.

• 27 AUGUST
MERCURY AT GREATEST EASTERN ELONGATION. Visible low in the western sky just after sunset, Mercury will be at its highest point above the horizon.

• 26 SEPTEMBER
JUPITER AT OPPOSITION. This is your best chance to view Jupiter in 2022. The gas giant will appear bright in the sky and be visible throughout the night. Got a pair of binoculars? You may be able to spot Jupiter's four largest moons as well.

• 21-22 OCTOBER
ORIONID METEOR SHOWER PEAK. View up to 20 meteors an hour. Look towards the constellation Orion for the best show.

• 8 NOVEMBER
TOTAL LUNAR ECLIPSE. The second total lunar eclipse of 2022 will be visible from Australia, Japan, eastern Russia, the Pacific Ocean and some areas of western and central North America.

• 13-14 DECEMBER
GEMINID METEOR SHOWER PEAK. A spectacular show — see up to 120 multicoloured meteors an hour!

• 2022—VARIOUS DATES
VIEW THE INTERNATIONAL SPACE STATION (ISS). Visit https://spotthestation.nasa.gov to find out when the ISS will be flying over your neighbourhood.

Dates may vary slightly depending on your location. Check with a local planetarium for the best viewing times in your area.

177

QUIZ WHIZ

Is your space and Earth knowledge out of this world? Take this quiz!

Write your answers on a piece of paper. Then check them below.

1 **True or false?** Salt is a type of crystal.

2 **How many moons does Mars have?**
a. 2   c. 6
b. 4   d. 12

3 **Fill in the blank.**
The world's strongest _____ resulted from activity along the Ring of Fire.

4 **True or false?** The gas in galaxy clusters can be as hot as 100 million degrees Celsius (180 million degrees Fahrenheit).

5 **A deep-sea robot used sonar to create a colourful photo of what underwater object?**
a. a trench
b. a ridge
c. a volcano
d. a coral reef

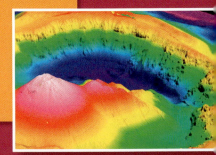

Not **STUMPED** yet? Check out the *NATIONAL GEOGRAPHIC KIDS QUIZ WHIZ* book collection for more crazy **SPACE AND EARTH** questions!

ANSWERS: 1. True; **2.** a; **3.** earthquake; **4.** True; **5.** c.

HOMEWORK HELP

ACE YOUR SCIENCE PROJECT

You can learn a lot about science from books, but to really experience it firsthand, you need to get into the lab and 'do' some science. Whether you're taking part in a science fair or just want to learn more on your own, there are many scientific projects you can do. So put on your goggles and lab coat, and start experimenting.

Most likely, the topic of the project will be up to you. So remember to choose something that you're interested in.

THE BASIS OF ALL SCIENTIFIC INVESTIGATION AND DISCOVERY IS THE SCIENTIFIC METHOD. CONDUCT YOUR EXPERIMENT USING THESE STEPS:

Observation/Research — Ask a question or identify a problem.

Hypothesis — Once you've asked a question, do some thinking and come up with some possible answers.

Experimentation — How can you determine if your hypothesis is correct? You test it. You perform an experiment. Make sure the experiment you design will produce an answer to your question.

Analysis — Gather your results, and use a consistent process to carefully measure the results.

Conclusion — Do the results support your hypothesis?

Report Your Findings — Communicate your results in the form of an essay that summarises your entire experiment.

Bonus!

Take your project one step further. Your school may have an annual science day, but there are also other science competitions you could take part in. Compete with other students for awards and prizes.

EXPERIMENT DESIGN
There are three types of experiments you can do.

MODEL KIT — a display, such as an 'erupting volcano' model. Simple and to the point.

DEMONSTRATION — shows the scientific principles in action, such as a tornado in a wind tunnel.

INVESTIGATION — the tip-top science project. This kind demonstrates proper scientific experimentation and uses the scientific method to reveal answers to questions.

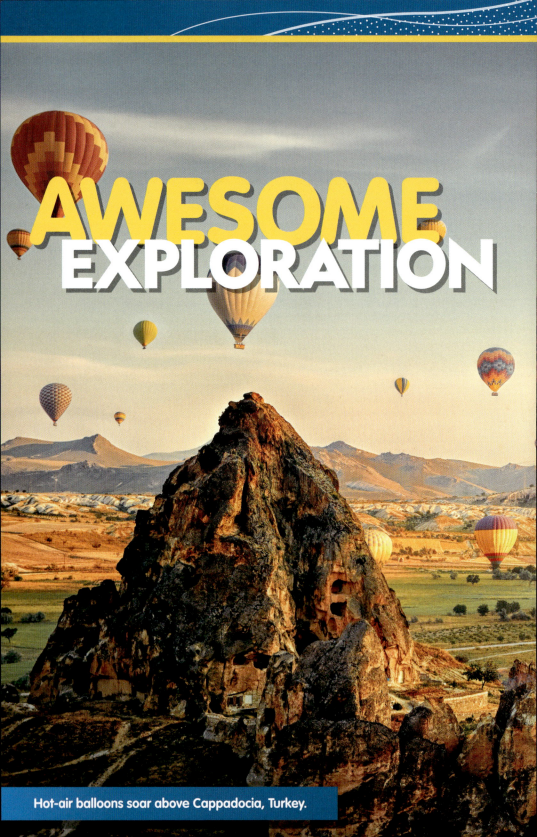

AWESOME
EXPLORATION

Hot-air balloons soar above Cappadocia, Turkey.

As a marine scientist, National Geographic Explorer Salomé Buglass has spent countless hours studying the unique ecology of Ecuador's Galápagos Islands. Here, she reveals some intriguing things about her research there.

10 COOL FACTS ABOUT THE GALÁPAGOS ISLANDS

"IT'S FAIRLY COMMON TO SPOT A **GIANT TORTOISE** CROSSING THE ROAD OR A **MARINE IGUANA** SNEAKING INTO THE SUPERMARKET."

"When I have free time from work, I GO SURFING. I have to dodge turtles especially, or their hard shells will break my board!"

"Blue-footed boobies are everywhere. When they're diving for food, they travel at speeds up to **97 kilometres an hour** (60 mph)."

"The **Galápagos penguins** are so adorable. They **mate for life,** and I like to look for my favourite couple."

"There is a **GREAT RESPECT FOR WILDLIFE** on the islands. We know to stay away from animals and **NOT PET OR FEED THEM.** We appreciate and admire nature from a distance."

"To study the oceans, we use robots with cameras, called **remotely operated vehicle (ROV),** to explore as far as **180 metres** (590 ft) **below the water's surface."**

"Living on the Galápagos Islands is a unique experience. **Only a few locals can own a car,** SO EVERYONE RIDES BIKES."

"It's not unusual to spot some **whitetip reef sharks** basking in shallow water among mangroves."

"During a recent trip, we discovered **AN UNKNOWN SPECIES OF KELP. Finding this kind of kelp** in the tropical part of the world is like **finding A POLAR BEAR IN MIAMI!"**

"**DARWIN** and **WOLF ISLANDS** have one of the **HIGHEST DENSITIES OF SHARKS IN THE WORLD.** I've swum among hundreds and hundreds of hammerhead sharks."

DARE TO EXPLORE

From listening to animals to reading the stars, three National Geographic explorers share secrets about communicating with the world.

"Don't be afraid to take things apart. Play with them, see how they work and experiment on your own."

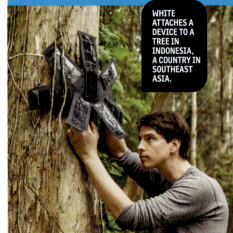

WHITE PREPARES TO MOUNT A LISTENING DEVICE TO A TREE THAT WILL HELP NAB ILLEGAL LOGGERS ON THE GROUND.

THE ENGINEER

Topher White attaches recycled mobile phones to trees in remote rainforests around the world, hoping to pick up the sounds of illegal loggers. He describes trying to work while being swarmed by bees.

"Even though the forests can be home to illegal loggers, sometimes what's going on in the treetops is scarier than what's on the ground. One time I was installing a phone and bees kept landing on me. Eventually I was completely covered with them! But I had to finish the job, even if it meant getting a *lot* of bee stings.

"The phones I place each have an app that turns the phone into a listening device. They capture all the sounds of the rainforest. Listening to this noise can help us pick out the sounds of things like chain saws and logging trucks. If we can pinpoint the sounds of illegal logging, we can instantly send alerts to local authorities and tribes, who are then able to stop illegal loggers on the spot. In a way, the trees are telling us when they need help."

WANT TO BE AN ENGINEER?

STUDY	Mathematics, physics
WATCH	The documentary series *The Trials of Life*
READ	*The Wild Trees* by Richard Preston

WHITE ATTACHES A DEVICE TO A TREE IN INDONESIA, A COUNTRY IN SOUTHEAST ASIA.

FROM LEFT: ASTRONOMERS HALEY FICA, MUNAZZA ALAM AND SARA CAMNASIO STAND IN FRONT OF A 6.4-METRE (21-FT)-WIDE TELESCOPE IN CHILE.

THE ASTRONOMER

Munazza Alam searches the sky for a planet that humans could live on one day. She discusses her hunt for what she calls the 'Earth twin'.

"I spend a lot of my nights at observatories atop mountain ranges, using high-resolution telescopes that are sometimes the size of a school bus. I'm observing faraway planets outside our solar system called exoplanets. By analysing these exoplanets, I hope to discover if any of them have atmospheres similar to Earth that people could one day survive in. You could say I'm searching for Earth's twin. An 'Earth twin' would be a rocky planet with temperatures that would support liquid water. We haven't found one yet, but I do think we're getting closer. The more we study the stars and their planets, the more we can understand what they're like. As an astronomer, it's my job to keep examining the sky in the hopes that it'll reveal new things about our galaxy and beyond."

"If you have a curiosity, don't let that flame go out. Never let go of that enthusiasm, because it will inspire you forever."

WANT TO BE AN ASTRONOMER?

STUDY	Physics, astronomy
WATCH	*Zathura: A Space Adventure*
READ	*The Magic School Bus: Lost in the Solar System* by Joanna Cole

THE VETERINARIAN

Jan Pol has helped nearly 500,000 animal patients in his 50 years as a veterinarian. His many amazing stories make it hard to choose just one, but here he recalls two supercute tales: a pair of injured hounds and a sick kitten.

"Dogs will chase anything that moves — including porcupines. One time two coonhounds came into the vet clinic with hundreds of porcupine quills stuck in their muzzles. Ouch! If we didn't remove the pointy spines, they could cause an infection that would make the dogs ill. So we sedated the pups and plucked the quills out one by one. They went back to their owner just fine, but dogs never learn their lesson — next time they meet a porcupine, I'm sure they'll be back!

"I believe that every pet has the right to a good life."

"Another time a family brought in this stray kitten with a very infected eye. The family didn't want to give up on the kitten, so I wouldn't either. But I wasn't sure what was wrong until I started the surgery.

"I almost couldn't believe it — a huge insect larva was growing in the kitten's eye! We had to remove the eye, but the kitten was completely fine without it. Even better: The stray kitten found a home with the family who brought it in."

WANT TO BE A VETERINARIAN?

STUDY	Mathematics, biology
WATCH	*Beethoven*
READ	*All Creatures Great and Small* by James Herriot

DR. POL TREATS JUST ABOUT ANYTHING: HORSES, DOGS — EVEN HEDGEHOGS!

Keep Earth WILD

A National Geographic photographer gives you a behind-the-scenes look at his quest to save animals.

Joel Sartore has squealed like a pig, protected his camera from a parakeet and suffered through a stink attack — all to help save animals through photography. "I hope people will look these animals in their eyes and then be inspired to protect them," says Sartore, a National Geographic photographer.

Sartore is on a mission to take pictures of more than 15,000 animal species living in captivity through his project, the National Geographic Photo Ark. During each photo shoot, he works with zookeepers, aquarists and wildlife rehabbers to keep his subjects safe and comfortable. But things can still get a little, well, wild! Read on for some of Sartore's most memorable moments.

Moment of **SNOOZE**

GIANT PANDAS, *native to China*

Zoo Atlanta, Atlanta, Georgia, U.S.A.

These giant pandas were just a few months old when I put the football-size twins in a small, white photo tent and snapped a few pics as they tumbled on top of each other. But the youngsters were tiring out, and I knew I was losing my chance to get a memorable photo before they drifted off to sleep. One cub put his head on the back of the other, and I managed to capture an awesome shot just seconds before the two cubs fell asleep.

> Some arctic fox dens are 300 years old.

Moment of **HA**

ARCTIC FOX, *native to the Arctic regions of Eurasia, North America, Greenland and Iceland*

Great Bend Brit Spaugh Zoo, Great Bend, Kansas, U.S.A.

Todd the arctic fox wanted to sniff everything, but he was moving too quickly for me to get a good picture. I needed to do something surprising to get his attention, so I squealed like a pig! The weird sound made the fox stop, sit down and tilt his head as if he were thinking, What's the matter with you? Good thing I was fast, because the pig noise only worked once. The next time I squealed, Todd completely ignored me.

More **WILDNESS!**

Photo Ark spotlights all kinds of animals. Meet some of Joel Sartore's strangest subjects.

BUDGETT'S FROG

ORANGE SPOTTED FILEFISH

MEDITERRANEAN RED BUG

NORTH AMERICAN PORCUPINE

Sartore uses black or white backgrounds because he wants the focus to be on the animals. That way a mouse is as important as an elephant.

Newborn giant pandas are about the size of newborn kittens.

A single colony of grey-headed flying foxes can include a million bats.

Giraffes sometimes use their tongues to clean their ears.

Moment of YAY

GREY-HEADED FLYING FOX, *native to southeastern Australia*

Australian Bat Clinic, Advancetown, Australia

"When I arrived at the clinic, I was amazed to see all sorts of bats just hanging from laundry racks all over the rescue centre. They sleepily watched me as I walked through the room and asked a staff member for a friendly flying fox to photograph. She scooped up a sweet bat and placed its feet on a wire rack in front of my backdrop. The calm bat didn't seem to mind being in front of the camera. The best part? This clinic rehabilitates bats that have torn their wings, and my subject was eventually released back into the wild."

Moment of YUM

RETICULATED GIRAFFE, *native to Africa*

Gladys Porter Zoo, Brownsville, Texas, U.S.A.

"You definitely can't make a giraffe do anything it doesn't want to do. So to get this animal to be part of our photo shoot, we combined the activity with one of the giraffe's favourite things: lunch. We hung the huge black backdrop from the rafters in the part of the giraffe's enclosure where it gets fed. The giraffe ambled in, not minding me at all. For about 10 minutes, while the animal munched on bamboo leaves, I could take all the pictures I wanted. But as soon as lunch was over, the giraffe walked out, and our photo shoot was done."

187

SECRETS OF THE

DARING SCIENTISTS SEARCH FOR

A bizarre world lies under the sparkling Atlantic Ocean off the islands of the Bahamas, a world few have seen. Here, a system of superdeep underwater caves called blue holes contains odd-looking creatures, six-storey-high rock formations and even ancient human remains. Scuba-diving scientists must dodge whirlpools and squeeze through narrow tunnels to study blue holes — but their risky expeditions uncover amazing secrets.

FANGED CRUSTACEAN

WEIRD WATER

NEON PINK CAVE WATER!

Dive about nine metres (30 ft) into some blue holes, and the water turns pink. It looks nice — but it's poisonous. Because of a weak current here, rainwater and salt water mix in a way that traps a layer of toxic gas where pink bacteria thrive. To avoid getting ill, divers do not linger here.

In other blue holes, ocean tides can whip up whirlpools that look like giant bathtub drains. Scientists must circle carefully, or else risk being sucked in.

CREATURE FEATURE

Farther down, the caves become dark and twisty. Anthropologist and National Geographic Explorer Kenny Broad and his team have found many odd species here, including a tiny, transparent crustacean that is venomous (above).

Blue holes also contain fossils of animals — even birds. During the last ice age, these areas were dry and made perfect perches for the fliers. In one watery cave, a 12,000-year-old owl's nest was found surrounded by lizard bones — leftovers from the owl's meals.

BLUE HOLES

CLUES ABOUT UNDERWATER CAVES.

HOW BLUE HOLES FORMED

During past ice ages — the most recent about 18,000 years ago — water levels dropped and new land was exposed. Rain ate away at the land, forming holes that became deep caves. The caves filled with water after sea levels rose again. The deepest known blue hole is about 200 metres (660 ft) deep.

BONE-CHILLING DISCOVERY

The most amazing find in the blue holes? Human skeletons. Scientists were able to trace the remains back 1,400 years to the time of the Lucayans — the first people believed to live in the Bahamas. No one is sure how the bones ended up in the submerged caves. But the team thinks the Lucayans might have used these areas as burial sites for their dead. With more investigation, the mystery of the skeletons may soon be solved. But scientists believe that other secrets are waiting to be uncovered in blue holes. "There are hundreds left that no human has seen," Broad says. "It's a whole other world for exploration."

A BLUE HOLE OFF BELIZE

SURVIVAL STORY

ORANGUTAN
TO THE RESCUE

After getting lost in the rainforest, National Geographic Explorer Agustín Fuentes received some very unlikely help. Read on to find out how Fuentes found his way home.

All Agustín Fuentes wanted to do was find the rare maroon leaf monkey. He'd been spending some time at Camp Leakey, an orangutan research camp on Borneo, a large, mountainous island in Southeast Asia, and he got the urge to take a day trip into the dense rainforest to seek one out. So he packed up his compass, head torch and small backpack, and off he went.

After four hours of following marked trails, Fuentes thought he caught a glimpse of a maroon leaf monkey. But then it scampered away into the rainforest. He had a decision to make: Should he stay on the trails and hope to see the monkey again? Or should he follow it?

"I took a risk and went off trail," Fuentes says.

Bad move. Forty-five minutes later, Fuentes found himself deep in the rainforest, with no maroon leaf monkey in sight. He used his compass to guess as to which direction he was heading and kept walking.

"Another 30 minutes passed, and I began to get a little nervous," says Fuentes. "Darkness was coming on quickly."

Fuentes tried to find comfort in the fact that he was in a place where another human had likely never been. As he looked around the rainforest, there was so much to admire.

"At one point, I spotted a shimmering metallic blue pool in an opening. I moved closer, and the blue image vibrated. Suddenly, hundreds of blue butterflies took flight before me," he says. "They had been feasting on wild pig droppings on the ground a few feet away."

Pulling out his compass, Fuentes headed south, thinking he'd eventually hit the river, if not a trail first. It paid off. After about 20 minutes, he saw an unmarked trail. Seconds later, he heard a rustling. He shone his head torch towards the sound. It was an orangutan! And not just any orangutan: Fuentes recognised right away that she was one of the apes being rehabilitated at camp.

"We looked at each other, and she held out her hand to me," he says. "Then she led me, hand in hand, to camp. Just like me, she was heading back for the evening."

Extreme Job!

There's not much normal about John Stevenson's job. A volcanologist, Stevenson evaluates eruptions, follows lava flow and travels to remote locations to learn more about volcanoes. Read on for more details on his risky but rewarding career.

TESTING NEW RESEARCH EQUIPMENT

SCIENCE-MINDED "As a kid, I really liked science and nature, and in college I pursued chemical engineering but studied geology as well. Having a background in all of the sciences gave me a better understanding of the bigger picture, from volcano monitoring to understanding eruptions."

BIG DIG "I once spent ten days collecting pumice and ash samples from a 4,200-year-old eruption in Iceland. We'd dig in the soil until we found the layer of ash that we wanted, then spend up to two hours photographing and taking samples. At night, we'd find a nice spot by a stream, eat dinner and camp out."

DANGER IN THE AIR "Being exposed to the edge of a lava flow can be dangerous. The air is hot and can be thick with poisonous sulfur dioxide gas. Once, while working at the active Bárðarbunga volcano in Iceland, we had to wear gas masks and use an electronic gas meter as dust swirled around us."

RAINING ASH "When I worked at Volcán de Colima in Mexico, we camped a few miles from the crater. One night, I woke up to a whooshing sound. This quickly changed to a *patter-patter-patter* that sounded like heavy rain falling on the tent. When I put my hand out to feel the rain, it was covered in coarse grey sand. The volcano had erupted, and ash was raining down on us. We quickly packed up our stuff and headed to a safer spot."

JOB PERKS "I get to play with fun gadgets in cool locations. If I didn't have to work, I would still go hiking and camping and play with gadgets and computers in my spare time anyway. I enjoy trying to solve the problems of getting the right data and finding a way to process it so that it can tell us about how the world works."

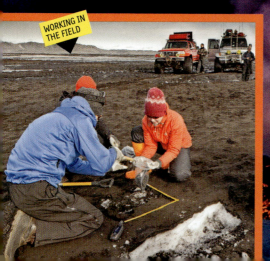

WORKING IN THE FIELD

Bet You Didn't Know!

8 deep facts about caves

1 Certain ice caves in Iceland are filled with hot springs.

2 1,000-year-old popcorn was found in a cave in Utah, U.S.A.

3 The world's largest cave — Son Doong in Vietnam — was discovered in 1990 by a local man seeking shelter from a storm.

4 Speleology is the study of caves.

5 A cave in American Fork Canyon was used as a dance hall during World War II.

A girl stands at the entrance of a cave in the French Alps.

6 Experts believe only about 1% of Earth's caves have been discovered.

7 Ancient cave paintings in Australia show an almost 2.4-metre-tall (8-ft) bird.

8 In 2018, a 346-kilometre (215-mi) underwater cave was discovered near Tulum, Mexico.

HOW TO
SURVIVE A
KILLER BEE ATTACK!

1 Buzz Off

Killer bees — or Africanised honeybees — attack only when their hive is being threatened. If you see several bees buzzing near you, a hive is probably close by. Heed their 'back off' attitude and slowly walk away.

2 Don't Join the Swat Team

Your first instinct might be to start swatting and slapping the bees. But that just makes the buzzers angry. Loud noises have the same effect, so don't start screaming, either. Just get away.

3 Don't Play Hide-and-Seek

Hives are often near water, but don't even think about outlasting the bees underwater. They'll hover and attack when you come up for air, even if you try to swim for it.

4 Run Like the Wind

Killer bees will chase you, but they'll give up when you're far enough away from the hive (usually about 183 metres [200 yd]). Take off running and don't stop until the buzzing does.

5 Create a Cover-Up

Killer bees often go for the face and throat, which are the most dangerous places to be stung. While you're on the run, protect your face and neck with your hands, or pull your shirt over your head.

HOW TO
SURVIVE A
BEE STING!

1. De-Sting Yourself

First, get inside or to a cool place. Then, remove the stinger by scraping a fingernail over the area, like you would to get a splinter out. Do not squeeze the stinger or use tweezers unless you absolutely can't get it out any other way because squeezing it may release more venom.

2. Put It on Ice

Wash the area with soap and water and apply a cool compress to reduce swelling. Continue icing the spot for 20 minutes every hour. Place a washcloth or towel between the ice and your skin.

3. Treat It Right

With a parent's permission, take an antihistamine and gently rub a hydrocortisone cream on the sting site.

4. Hands Off

Make sure you don't scratch the sting. You'll just increase the pain and swelling.

5. Recognise Danger

If you experience severe burning and itching, swelling of the throat and/or mouth, difficulty breathing, weakness or nausea, or if you already know you are allergic to bees, get to a hospital immediately.

193

GETTING THE SHOT

Capturing good photographs of wild animals can be tough. To get amazing pictures of them, nature photographers often tap into their wild side, thinking and even acting like the creatures they're snapping. Whether tracking deadly snakes or swimming with penguins, the artists must be daring — but they also need to know when to keep their distance. Three amazing photographers tell their behind-the-scenes stories of how they got these incredible shots.

Check out this book!

GUIDE TO PHOTOGRAPHY

FANG FOCUS

PHOTOGRAPHER: Mattias Klum
ANIMAL: Jameson's mamba
SHOOT SITE: Cameroon, Africa

"The Jameson's mamba is beautiful but dangerous. It produces highly toxic venom. My team searched for weeks for the reptile, asking locals about the best spots to see one. At last we came across a Jameson's mamba peeking out from tree leaves. Carefully, I inched closer. It's important to make this kind of snake think that you don't see it. Otherwise it might feel threatened and strike you. At about 1.4 metres (4.5 ft) away, I took the picture. Then I backed up and the snake slid off."

SECRETS FROM
AMAZING WILDLIFE PHOTOGRAPHERS

Usually solitary creatures, oceanic whitetip sharks have been observed swimming with pods of pilot whales.

SHARK TALE

PHOTOGRAPHER: Brian Skerry
ANIMAL: Oceanic whitetip shark
SHOOT SITE: The Bahamas

"I wanted to photograph an endangered oceanic whitetip shark. So I set sail with a group of scientists to an area where some had been sighted. Days later, the dorsal fin of a whitetip rose from the water near our boat. One scientist was lowered in a metal cage into the water to observe the fish. Then I dived in. Because I wasn't behind the protective bars, I had to be very careful. These 2.7-metre (9-ft) sharks can be aggressive, but this one was just curious. She swam around us for two hours and allowed me to take pictures of her. She was the perfect model."

LEAPS and BOUNDS

PHOTOGRAPHER: Nick Nichols
ANIMAL: Bengal tiger
SHOOT SITE: Bandhavgarh National Park, India

Fewer than 2,500 Bengal tigers are left in the wild.

"While following a tiger along a cliff, I saw him leap from the edge to his secret watering hole and take a drink. I wanted a close-up of the cat, but it wouldn't have been safe to approach him. Figuring he'd return to the spot, I set up a camera on the cliff that shoots off an infrared beam. Walking into the beam triggers the camera to click. The device was there for three months, but this was the only shot I got of the cat. Being near tigers makes the hair stand up on my arm. It was a gift to encounter such a magnificent creature."

QUIZ WHIZ

Discover just how much you know about exploration with this quiz!

Write your answers on a piece of paper. Then check them below.

1 Where on Earth are you most likely to spot a blue-footed boobie?
a. Germany
b. Ghana
c. Galápagos Islands
d. Greece

2 **True or false?** The deepest known blue hole is about 200 metres (660 ft) deep.

3 This risky but rewarding job evaluates eruptions and follows lava flow.
a. volcanologist
b. conservationist
c. psychologist
d. agriculturalist

4 Giraffes sometimes use their tongues to clean their _____.

5 Which kind of animals does veterinarian Jan Pol treat in his practice?
a. horses
b. hedgehogs
c. kittens
d. all of the above

Not **STUMPED** yet? Check out the *NATIONAL GEOGRAPHIC KIDS QUIZ WHIZ* collection for more crazy **EXPLORATION** questions!

ANSWERS: 1. c; 2. True 3. a; 4. ears; 5. d

HOMEWORK HELP

How to Write a Perfect Essay

Need to write an essay? Does the assignment feel as big as climbing Mount Everest? Fear not. You're up to the challenge! The following step-by-step tips will help you with this monumental task.

1 **BRAINSTORM.** Sometimes the subject matter of your essay is chosen for you, sometimes it's not. Either way, you have to decide what you want to say. Start by brainstorming some ideas, writing down any thoughts you have about the subject. Then read over everything you've come up with and consider which idea you think is the strongest. Ask yourself what you want to write about the most. Keep in mind the goal of your essay. Can you achieve the goal of the assignment with this topic? If so, you're good to go.

2 **WRITE A TOPIC SENTENCE.** This is the main idea of your essay, a statement of your thoughts on the subject. Again, consider the goal of your essay. Think of the topic sentence as an introduction that tells your readers what the rest of your essay will be about.

3 **OUTLINE YOUR IDEAS.** Once you have a good topic sentence, you then need to support that main idea with more detailed information, facts, thoughts and examples. These supporting points answer one question about your topic sentence — 'Why'? This is where research and perhaps more brainstorming come in. Then organise these points in the way you think makes the most sense, probably in order of importance. Now you have an outline for your essay.

4 **ON YOUR MARKS, GET SET, WRITE!** Follow your outline, using each of your supporting points as the topic sentence of its own paragraph. Use descriptive words to get your ideas across to readers. Go into detail, using specific information to tell your story or make your point. Stay on track, making sure that everything you include is somehow related to the main idea of your essay. Use transitions to make your writing flow.

5 **WRAP IT UP.** Finish your essay with a conclusion that summarises your entire essay and restates your main idea.

6 **PROOFREAD AND REVISE.** Check for errors in spelling, capitalisation, punctuation and grammar. Look for ways to make your writing clear, understandable and interesting. Use descriptive verbs, adjectives or adverbs when possible. It also helps to have someone else read your work to point out things you might have missed. Then make the necessary corrections and changes in a second draft. Repeat this revision process once more to make your final draft as good as you can.

197

WONDERS of NATURE

Tiny bioluminescent shrimp known as sea fireflies glitter on the rocks and sand in Okayama, Japan.

Biomes

A BIOME, OFTEN CALLED A MAJOR LIFE ZONE, is one of the natural world's major communities where plants and animals adapt to their specific surroundings. Biomes are classified depending on the predominant vegetation, climate and geography of a region. They can be divided into six major types: forest, freshwater, marine, desert, grassland and tundra. Each biome consists of many ecosystems.

Biomes are extremely important. Balanced ecological relationships among biomes help to maintain the environment and life on Earth as we know it. For example, an increase in one species of plant, such as an invasive one, can cause a ripple effect throughout a whole biome.

FOREST

Forests occupy about a third of Earth's land area. There are three major types of forests: tropical, temperate and boreal (taiga). Forests are home to a diversity of plants, some of which may hold medicinal qualities for humans, as well as thousands of animal species, some still undiscovered. Forests can also absorb carbon dioxide, a greenhouse gas, and give off oxygen.

The rabbit-sized royal antelope lives in West Africa's dense forests.

FRESHWATER

Most water on Earth is salty, but freshwater ecosystems — including lakes, ponds, wetlands, rivers and streams — usually contain water with less than one percent salt concentration. The countless animal and plant species that live in freshwater biomes vary from continent to continent, but they include algae, frogs, turtles, fish and the larvae of many insects.

The place where freshwater and salt water meet is called an estuary.

MARINE

The marine biome covers almost three-quarters of Earth's surface, making it the largest habitat on our planet. Oceans make up the majority of the saltwater marine biome. Coral reefs are considered to be the most biodiverse of any of the biome habitats. The marine biome is home to more than one million plant and animal species.

Estimated to be up to 100,000 years old, seagrass growing in the Mediterranean Sea may be the oldest living thing on Earth.

DESERT

Covering about a fifth of Earth's surface, deserts are places where precipitation is less than 25 centimetres (10 in) a year. Although most deserts are hot, there are other kinds as well. The four major kinds of deserts are hot, semiarid, coastal and cold. Far from being barren wastelands, deserts are biologically rich habitats.

Some sand dunes in the Sahara are tall enough to bury a 50-storey building.

GRASSLAND

Biomes called grasslands are characterised by having grasses instead of large shrubs or trees. Grasslands generally have precipitation for only about half to three-quarters of the year. If it were more, they would become forests. Grasslands can be divided into two types: tropical (savannahs) and temperate. Some of the world's largest land animals, such as elephants, live there.

Grasslands in North America are called prairies; in South America, they're called pampas.

TUNDRA

The coldest of all biomes, a tundra is characterised by an extremely cold climate, simple vegetation, little precipitation, poor nutrients and a short growing season. There are two types of tundra: Arctic and alpine. A tundra is home to few kinds of vegetation. Surprisingly, though, quite a few animal species can survive the tundra's extremes, such as wolves, caribou and even mosquitoes.

Formed 10,000 years ago, the Arctic tundra is the world's youngest biome.

10 WILD FACTS ABOUT THE AMAZON

The **AMAZON'S** **BLUE MORPHO BUTTERFLY** appears in **DIFFERENT COLOURS** when observed from **DIFFERENT ANGLES.**

The Amazon BIOME spans eight countries: **BRAZIL, BOLIVIA, PERU, ECUADOR, COLOMBIA, VENEZUELA, GUYANA** and **SURINAME,** plus the territory of **FRENCH GUIANA.**

The Amazon isn't just a **RAINFOREST.** Its other **ECOSYSTEMS INCLUDE FLOODPLAIN FORESTS, SAVANNAHS AND RIVERS.**

The **FLOODED FORESTS** of the **AMAZON** are among the only **PLACES ON EARTH** where **FISH FEED** on **FRUITS** and **SEEDS.**

Scientists think that some **PLANTS** in the Amazon can be **USED TO FIGHT CANCER.**

The Amazon is home to BOLDLY COLOURED MACAWS, which mate for life and can LIVE FOR UP TO 60 YEARS.

15 PERCENT of all the FRESHWATER ON EARTH can be FOUND in the AMAZON BASIN.

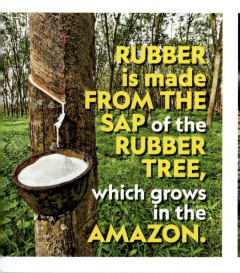

RUBBER is made FROM THE SAP of the RUBBER TREE, which grows in the AMAZON.

The AMAZON BIOME is HOME to 10 percent of the WORLD'S KNOWN SPECIES — including the endangered GIANT OTTER.

SPANNING MORE THAN 6 MILLION SQUARE KILOMETRES (2.3 million sq miles), the Amazon BIOME is about TWICE THE SIZE OF INDIA.

THE OC

PACIFIC OCEAN

STATS

Surface area
169,479,000 sq km (65,436,200 sq miles)

Portion of Earth's water area
47 percent

Greatest depth
Challenger Deep
(in the Mariana Trench)
-10,994 m (-36,070 ft)

Surface temperatures
Summer high: 32°C (90°F)
Winter low: -2°C (28°F)

Tides
Highest: 9 m (30 ft) near Korean Peninsula
Lowest: 0.3 m (1 ft) near Midway Islands

Cool creatures: giant Pacific octopus,
bottlenose whale, clownfish, great
white shark

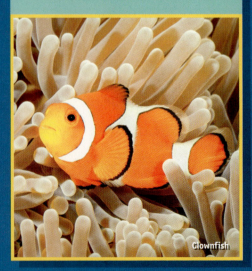

Clownfish

ATLANTIC OCEAN

STATS

Surface area
91,526,300 sq km (35,338,500 sq miles)

Portion of Earth's water area
25 percent

Greatest depth
Puerto Rico Trench
-8,605 m (-28,232 ft)

Surface temperatures
Summer high: 32°C (90°F)
Winter low: -2°C (28°F)

Tides
Highest: 16 m (52 ft)
Bay of Fundy, Canada
Lowest: 0.5 m (1.5 ft)
Gulf of Mexico and Mediterranean Sea

Cool creatures: blue whale, Atlantic spotted
dolphin, sea turtle, bottlenose dolphin

Bottlenose dolphin

EANS

INDIAN OCEAN

STATS

Surface area
74,694,800 sq km (28,839,800 sq miles)

Portion of Earth's water area
21 percent

Greatest depth
Java Trench
-7,125 m (-23,376 ft)

Surface temperatures
Summer high: 34°C (93°F)
Winter low: -2°C (28°F)

Tides
Highest: 11 m (36 ft)
Lowest: 0.6 m (2 ft)
Both along Australia's west coast

Cool creatures: humpback whale, Portuguese man-of-war, dugong (sea cow), leatherback turtle

ARCTIC OCEAN

STATS

Surface area
13,960,100 sq km (5,390,000 sq miles)

Portion of Earth's water area
4 percent

Greatest depth
Molloy Deep
-5,669 m (-18,599 ft)

Surface temperatures
Summer high: 5°C (41°F)
Winter low: -2°C (28°F)

Tides
Less than 0.3 m (1 ft) variation throughout the ocean

Cool creatures: beluga whale, orca, harp seal, narwhal

Leatherback turtle

Narwhal

To see the major oceans and bays in relation to landmasses, look at the map on pages 256 and 257.

Weather and Climate

Weather is the condition of the atmosphere — temperature, wind, humidity and precipitation — at a given place at a given time. Climate, however, is the average weather for a particular place over a long period of time. Different places on Earth have different climates, but climate is not a random occurrence. It is a pattern that is controlled by factors such as latitude, elevation, prevailing winds, the temperature of ocean currents and location on land relative to water. Climate is generally constant, but evidence indicates that human activity is causing a change in its patterns.

WEATHER EXTREMES

MOST SNOW RECORDED IN ONE SEASON: 29 metres (95 ft) in Mount Baker, Washington, U.S.A.

FASTEST TEMPERATURE RISE: 27.2 degrees in two minutes, in Rapid City, South Dakota, U.S.A.

HEAVIEST HAILSTONE: 1 kilogram (2.25 lb) in Gopalganj, Bangladesh

GLOBAL CLIMATE ZONES

Climatologists, people who study climate, have created different systems for classifying climates. One that is often used is called the Köppen system, which classifies climate zones according to precipitation, temperature and vegetation. It has five major categories — tropical, dry, temperate, cold and polar — with a sixth category for locations where high elevations override other factors.

Climate
Tropical Dry Temperate Cold Polar

Climate CHANGE

A POLAR BEAR ON A PIECE OF MELTING ICEBERG

Rising Temperatures, Explained

Fact: The world is getting warmer.
Earth's surface temperature has been increasing. In the past 50 years, our planet has warmed twice as fast as in the 50 years before that. This is the direct effect of climate change, which refers not only to the increase in Earth's average temperature (known as global warming), but also to its long-term effects on winds, rain and ocean currents. Global warming is the reason glaciers and polar ice sheets are melting — resulting in rising sea levels and shrinking habitats. This makes survival for some animals a big challenge. Warming also means more flooding along the coasts and drought for inland areas.

Why are temperatures climbing?
Some of the recent climate changes can be tied to natural causes — such as changes in the sun's intensity, the unusually warm ocean

SCIENTISTS ARE CONCERNED THAT GREENLAND'S ICE SHEET HAS BEGUN TO MELT IN SUMMER. BIRTHDAY CANYON, SHOWN HERE, WAS CARVED BY MELTWATER.

currents of El Niño and volcanic activity — but human activities are the greatest contributor.

Everyday activities that require burning fossil fuels, such as driving petrol-powered cars, contribute to global warming. These activities produce greenhouse gasses, which enter the atmosphere and trap heat. At the current rate, Earth's global average temperature is projected to rise some three degrees Celsius (5.4°F) by the year 2100, and it will get even warmer after that. And as the climate continues to warm, it will unfortunately continue to affect the environment and our society in many ways.

WATER CYCLE

Precipitation falls

Water storage in ice and snow

Water vapour condenses in clouds

Water filters into the ground

Meltwater and surface runoff

Freshwater storage

Evaporation

Groundwater discharge

Water storage in ocean

The amount of water on Earth is more or less constant —

only the form changes. As the sun warms Earth's surface, liquid water is changed into water vapour in a process called **evaporation.** Water on the surface of plants' leaves turns into water vapour in a process called **transpiration.** As water vapour rises into the air, it cools and changes form again. This time, it becomes clouds in a process called **condensation.** Water droplets fall from the clouds as **precipitation,** which then travels as groundwater or runoff back to the lakes, rivers and oceans, where the cycle (shown above) starts all over again.

To a meteorologist — a person who studies the weather — a 'light rain' is less than 0.5 millimetre (1/48 in). A 'heavy rain' is more than 4 millimetres (1/6 in).

You drink the same water as the dinosaurs! Earth has been recycling water for more than four billion years.

A MELTING WORLD

If all the ice on Earth melted, the world's oceans would rise 66 metres (216 ft). But how high is that exactly? Check out this chart to see what might end up underwater.

THE STATUE OF LIBERTY 93 metres (305 ft)

12 GIRAFFES 66 metres (216 ft)

5 SCHOOL BUSES 61 metres (200 ft)

6 ORCAS 59 metres (192 ft)

THE SKY IS FALLING

THE SKY CAN'T ACTUALLY FALL, BUT MOISTURE IN THE AIR CAN AND DOES.

'PRECIPITATION' IS A FANCY WORD
FOR THE WET STUFF THAT FALLS FROM THE SKY.

Precipitation is rain, freezing rain, sleet, snow or hail. It forms when water vapour in the air condenses into clouds, gets heavier and drops to the ground. Precipitation can ruin a picnic, but life on Earth couldn't exist without it.

Develops when ice crystals fall towards the ground, partly melt and then refreeze. This happens mainly in winter when air near the ground is below freezing temperatures.

SLEET

RAIN

Formed when ice crystals in high, cold clouds get heavy and fall. Even in summer, falling ice crystals could remain frozen, but warm air near the ground melts them into raindrops.

FREEZING RAIN

Falls during the winter when rain freezes immediately as it hits a surface. Freezing rain creates layers of ice on the roads and causes dangerous driving conditions.

Produced when ice crystals in clouds get heavy enough to fall. The air has to be cold enough all the way down for the crystals to stay frozen.

SNOW

HAIL

Formed inside thunderstorms when ice crystals covered in water pass through patches of freezing air in the tops of cumulonimbus clouds. The water on the ice crystals freezes. The crystals become heavy and fall to the ground.

Types of Clouds

If you want a clue about the weather, look up at the clouds. They'll tell a lot about the condition of the air and what weather might be on the way. Clouds are made of both air and water. On fair days, warm air currents rise up and push against the water in clouds, keeping it from falling. But as the raindrops in a cloud get bigger, it's time to set them free. The bigger raindrops become too heavy for the air currents to hold up, and they fall to the ground.

How Much Does a Cloud Weigh?

A light, fluffy cumulus cloud typically weighs about 98,000 kilograms (216,000 lb). That's about the weight of 18 elephants. A rain-soaked cumulonimbus cloud typically weighs 48 million kilograms (105.8 million lb), or about the same as 9,000 elephants.

1 STRATUS These clouds make the sky look like a bowl of thick grey porridge. They hang low in the sky, blanketing the day in dreary darkness. Stratus clouds form when cold, moist air close to the ground moves over a region.

2 CIRRUS These wispy tufts of clouds are thin and hang high up in the atmosphere where the air is extremely cold. Cirrus clouds are made of tiny ice crystals.

3 CUMULONIMBUS These are the monster clouds. Rising air currents force fluffy cumulus clouds to swell and shoot upward, as much as 21,000 metres (70,000 ft). When these clouds bump against the top of the troposphere, or the tropopause, they flatten out on top like tabletops.

4 CUMULUS These white, fluffy clouds make people sing, "Oh, what a beautiful morning!" They form low in the atmosphere and look like marshmallows. They often mix with large patches of blue sky. Formed when hot air rises, cumulus clouds usually disappear when the air cools at night.

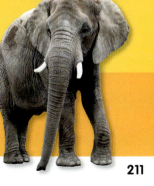

Lightning!

There are about 3,000 **LIGHTNING FLASHES** on Earth every minute.

LIGHTNING SAFETY TIPS

INSIDE

Stay inside for 30 minutes after the last lightning or thunder.

Don't take baths or showers or wash dishes.

Avoid using landline phones (mobile phones are okay), computers, TVs and other electrical equipment.

OUTSIDE

Get into an enclosed structure or vehicle and shut the windows.

Stay away from bodies of water.

Avoid tall objects such as trees.

If you're in the open, crouch down (but do not lie flat) in the lowest place you can find.

Clouds suddenly appeared on the horizon, the sky turned dark and it started to rain as Sabrina was hiking through the Grand Canyon with her parents.

As lightning flashed around them, Sabrina and her parents ran for cover. "When it stopped raining, we thought it was safe," says Sabrina. They started to hike back to their car along the trail. Then *zap!* A lightning bolt struck nearby. It happened so fast that the family didn't know what hit them. A jolt of electricity shot through their bodies. "It felt like a strong tingling over my whole body," says Sabrina. "It really hurt."

Sabrina and her family were lucky. The lightning didn't zap them directly, and they recovered within minutes. Some people aren't so lucky. Lightning kills thousands of people each year.

Lightning is a giant electric spark similar to the small spark you get when you walk across a carpet and touch a metal doorknob — but much stronger. One flash can contain a billion volts of electricity — enough to light a 100-watt incandescent bulb for three months. Lightning crackles through the air at a temperature five times hotter than the surface of the sun. The intense heat makes the surrounding air expand rapidly, creating a sound we know as thunder. Getting hit by lightning is rare, but everyone must be careful.

"For the first few years after I was struck, I was so scared every time there was a storm," says Sabrina. "Now I'm not scared. But I'm always cautious."

What Is a Tornado?

THE ENHANCED FUJITA SCALE

The Enhanced Fujita (EF) Scale, named after tornado expert T. Theodore Fujita, classifies tornadoes based on wind speed and the intensity of damage that they cause.

EF0
105–137 km/h winds
(65–85 mph)
Slight damage

EF1
138–177 km/h winds
(86–110 mph)
Moderate damage

EF2
178–217 km/h winds
(111–135 mph)
Substantial damage

EF3
218–266 km/h winds
(136–165 mph)
Severe damage

EF4
267–322 km/h winds
(166–200 mph)
Massive damage

EF5
More than 322 km/h winds
(200+ mph)
Catastrophic damage

TORNADOES, ALSO KNOWN AS TWISTERS, are funnels of rapidly rotating air that are created during a thunderstorm. With wind speeds of up to 483 kilometres an hour (300 mph), tornadoes have the power to pick up and destroy everything in their path.

THIS ROTATING FUNNEL OF AIR, formed in a cumulus or cumulonimbus cloud, became a tornado when it touched the ground.

TORNADOES HAVE OCCURRED ON EVERY CONTINENT EXCEPT ANTARCTICA.

HURRICANE
HAPPENINGS

A storm is coming! But is it a tropical cyclone, a hurricane or a typhoon? These weather events go by different names depending on where they form and how fast their winds get. Strong tropical cyclones are called hurricanes in the Atlantic and parts of the Pacific Ocean; in the western Pacific they are called typhoons. But any way you look at it, these storms pack a punch.

2,221
(1,380 miles)
KILOMETRES

Diameter of the most massive tropical cyclone ever recorded, 1979's Typhoon Tip

27.8°C
(82°F)

Water surface temperature necessary for a tropical cyclone to form

16.6

Average number of tropical storms each year in the Northeast and Central Pacific Basins

50
(164 feet)
METRES

Depth of warm ocean water needed to fuel the storm

31

Number of days Hurricane John lasted in 1994

12.1

Average number of tropical storms in the Atlantic Basin each year

408

(254 mph)

KILOMETRES AN HOUR

Strongest gust of storm wind ever recorded

20–40

(12–25 miles)

KILOMETRES

Diameter of a hurricane eye

HURRICANE NAMES FOR 2022

Hurricane names come from six official international lists. The names alternate between male and female. When a storm becomes a hurricane, a name from the list is used, in alphabetical order. Each list is reused every six years. A name is 'retired' if that hurricane caused a lot of damage or many deaths. Check out the names for Atlantic hurricanes in 2022:

Alex	Hermine	Owen
Bonnie	Ian	Paula
Colin	Julia	Richard
Danielle	Karl	Shary
Earl	Lisa	Tobias
Fiona	Martin	Virginie
Gaston	Nicole	Walter

SCALE OF HURRICANE INTENSITY

CATEGORY	ONE	TWO	THREE	FOUR	FIVE
DAMAGE	Minimal	Moderate	Extensive	Extreme	Catastrophic
WINDS	119–153 km/h (74–95 mph)	154–177 km/h (96–110 mph)	178–208 km/h (111–129 mph)	209–251 km/h (130–156 mph)	252 km/h or higher (157+ mph)

(DAMAGE refers to wind and water damage combined.)

Avalanche!

A million tonnes (984,207 tons) of snow rumble 13 kilometres (8 miles) downhill, kicking up a cloud of snow dust visible 161 kilometres (100 miles) away.

This is not a scene from a disaster movie — this describes reality one day in April 1981. The mountain was Mount Sanford in Alaska, U.S.A., and the event was one of history's biggest avalanches. Amazingly, no one was hurt, and luckily, avalanches this big are rare.

An avalanche is a moving mass of snow that may contain ice, soil, rocks and uprooted trees. The height of a mountain, the steepness of its slope and the type of snow lying on it all help determine the likelihood of an avalanche. Avalanches begin when an unstable mass of snow breaks away from a mountainside and moves downhill. The growing river of snow picks up speed as it rushes down the mountain. Avalanches have been known to reach speeds of 249 kilometres an hour (155 mph) — about the same as the record for downhill skiing.

To protect yourself and stay safe when you play in the mountains, follow our safety tips.

90 percent of AVALANCHE INCIDENTS are triggered by humans.

Safety TIPS

SAFETY FIRST
Before heading out, check for avalanche warnings.

EQUIPMENT
When hiking, carry safety equipment, including a long probe, a small shovel and an emergency avalanche rescue beacon that signals your location.

NEVER GO IT ALONE
Don't hike in the mountain wilderness without a companion.

IF CAUGHT
If caught in the path of an avalanche, try to get to the side of it. If you can't, grab a tree as an anchor.

Wildfires!

more people and animals, including an estimated 5,000 koalas.

Although the impact of the wildfires was devastating, Australia has worked

A deadly combination of drought and lightning sparked one of the worst ecological disasters in Australia. The recent wildfires, which burned for several months between late 2019 and early 2020, devastated parts of the country, charring a total of 17 million hectares (42 million acres) of land across the country — an area larger than England. A collective effort of firefighters targeting the blaze from the ground and the air — as well as welcome rain — finally contained the flames. But not before the fires destroyed thousands of homes and killed or injured even

its way towards recovery. Massive financial contributions from the Australian government, as well as private donations, have helped to rebuild homes and habitats for animals, especially koalas, which are a vulnerable species. One welcome sign of renewal and recovery? The birth of a healthy baby koala, born at the Australian Reptile Park outside of Sydney. The baby (above) was part of their breeding programme, aimed to replenish the animal's population. The joey, appropriately named 'Ash', served as a beacon of hope for the future of Australia's native wildlife.

Locusts!

T ypically, locusts, a type of grasshopper, are harmless. They don't sting, bite or cause much destruction on their own. But in large numbers, they can cause a lot of damage. Case in point: the swarms of locusts that descended upon Pakistan in 2020. Considered the worst infestation in decades, billions of locusts feasted on fields of crops. And because each locust can eat its own body weight in food daily, these massive swarms can consume as much food as 35,000 people in a 24-hour period. These effects were catastrophic for farmers, who lost entire harvests to the hungry insects, and have raised concerns about food shortages.

Why were the bugs so bad? Experts say dampness from heavy rains and cyclones sparked unusually active breeding among the locusts, causing their population to skyrocket in Pakistan as well as East Africa, India and parts of the Arabian Peninsula. Things got so grim that Pakistan declared a state of emergency to secure funding to help farmers. Authorities in Pakistan and India also agreed to work together to fight the locusts. By sharing data and resources, they were able to work to put this plague behind them.

QUIZ WHIZ

Quiz yourself to find out if you're a natural when it comes to nature knowledge!

Write your answers on a piece of paper. Then check them below.

1 **True or false?** The Pacific Ocean covers 15 percent of Earth's water area.

2 If all the ice on Earth melted, the world's oceans would rise as high as _____ .
a. five school buses
b. the Statue of Liberty
c. six orcas
d. all of the above

3 The birth of a baby _____ at the Australian Reptile Park was a sign of hope after the Australian wildfires of 2019 and 2020.
a. kangaroo
b. crocodile
c. koala
d. wombat

4 **True or false?** The Amazon biome is about twice the size of India.

5 Snow is produced when ice crystals in clouds get heavy enough to _____.
a. melt
b. fall
c. evaporate
d. freeze

Not **STUMPED** yet? Check out the *NATIONAL GEOGRAPHIC KIDS QUIZ WHIZ* collection for more crazy **NATURE** questions!

HOMEWORK HELP

Presentations Made Easy

TIP: Make sure you practise your presentation a few times. Stand in front of a mirror or ask a parent to record you so you can see if you need to work on anything, such as eye contact.

Does the thought of public speaking start your stomach churning like a tornado? Would you rather get caught in an avalanche than give a speech?

Giving a presentation does not have to be a natural disaster. The basic format is very similar to that of a written essay. There are two main elements that make up a good presentation — the writing and the presentation. As you write your presentation, remember that your audience will be hearing the information as opposed to reading it. Follow the guidelines below, and there will be clear skies ahead.

Writing Your Material

Follow the steps in the 'How to Write a Perfect Essay' section on page 197, but prepare your report to be spoken rather than written.

Try to keep your sentences short and simple. Long, complex sentences are harder to follow. Limit yourself to just a few key points. You don't want to overwhelm your audience with too much information. To be most effective, hit your key points in the introduction, elaborate on them in the body and then repeat them once again in your conclusion.

A PRESENTATION HAS THREE BASIC PARTS:

- **Introduction** — This is your chance to engage your audience and really capture their interest in the subject you are presenting. Use a funny personal experience or a dramatic story, or start with an intriguing question.

- **Body** — This is the longest part of your report. Here you elaborate on the facts and ideas you want to convey. Give information that supports your main idea, and expand on it with specific examples or details. In other words, structure your presentation in the same way you would a written essay, so that your thoughts are presented in a clear and organised manner.

- **Conclusion** — This is the time to summarise the information and emphasise your most important points to the audience one last time.

Preparing Your Delivery

1 Practice makes perfect. Practise! Practise! Practise! Confidence, enthusiasm and energy are key to delivering an effective presentation, and they can best be achieved through rehearsal. Ask family and friends to be your practice audience and give you feedback when you're done. Were they able to follow your ideas? Did you seem knowledgeable and confident? Did you speak too slowly or too fast, too softly or too loudly? The more times you practise giving your report, the more you'll master the material. Then you won't have to rely so heavily on your notes or papers, and you will be able to give your report in a relaxed and confident manner.

2 Present with everything you've got. Be as creative as you can. Incorporate videos, sound clips, slide presentations, charts, diagrams and photos. Visual aids help stimulate your audience's senses and keep them intrigued and engaged. They can also help to reinforce your key points. And remember that when you're giving a presentation, you're a performer. Take charge of the spotlight and be as animated and entertaining as you can. Have fun with it.

3 Keep your nerves under control. Everyone gets a little nervous when speaking in front of a group. That's normal. But the more preparation you've done — meaning plenty of researching, organising and rehearsing — the more confident you'll be. Preparation is the key. And if you make a mistake or stumble over your words, just regroup and keep going. Nobody's perfect, and nobody expects you to be.

HISTORY
HAPPENS

Massive 10-metre (32-ft)-tall sandstone pillar statues line the interior of the temple of Ramses II in Abu Simbel, Egypt.

Ancient World
ADVENTURE

KOURION

WHERE: Cyprus
BUILT: 13th century B.C.

COOL FACT: Kourion's 3,500-seat amphitheatre survived an earthquake in A.D. 364 that levelled the rest of the city. It's still used for performances today.

AYUTTHAYA

WHERE: Thailand
BUILT: About A.D. 1350

COOL FACT: Home to hundreds of thousands of people at the end of the 17th century, this former capital of the Siamese Kingdom was one of the world's largest cities.

FORBIDDEN CITY

WHERE: China
BUILT: Between A.D. 1406 and A.D. 1420

COOL FACT: The 73-hectare (180-acre) imperial compound in Beijing is rumoured to have more than 9,999 rooms and was home to 24 Chinese emperors over a nearly 500-year span.

Ever wonder what it was like on Earth hundreds of years ago? Check out these amazing ancient sites. Visiting them is like taking a time machine into the past!

PAMUKKALE

WHERE: Turkey
BUILT: About 200 B.C.

COOL FACT: People flocked to this ancient spa town to bathe in its hot springs, which are said to have healing powers. Today, tourists still visit, floating above submerged ruins of ancient columns.

PALENQUE

WHERE: Mexico
BUILT: About A.D. 500

COOL FACT: This ancient Maya city-state's buildings, including temples and tombs, were built without the use of metal tools, pack animals or even the wheel.

TIMBUKTU

WHERE: Mali
BUILT: About A.D. 1100

COOL FACT: Once known as the fabled 'City of Gold', Africa's Timbuktu was a centre of learning and culture in the 15th and 16th centuries and is home to a still standing university.

THE LOST CITY OF POMPEII

When will the volcano that buried this ancient civilisation blow again?

A deafening boom roars through Pompeii's crowded marketplace. The ground shakes violently, throwing the midday shoppers off balance and toppling stands of fish and meat. People start screaming and pointing towards Mount Vesuvius, a massive volcano that rises above the bustling city, located in what is now southern Italy.

Vesuvius has been silent for nearly 2,000 years, but it roars back to life, shooting ash and smoke into the air. Almost overnight, the city and most of its residents have vanished under a blanket of ash and lava.

Now, almost 2,000 years later, scientists agree that Vesuvius is overdue for another major eruption — but no one knows when it will happen. Three million people live in the volcano's shadow, in the modern-day city of Naples, Italy. Correctly predicting when the eruption might take place will mean the difference between life and death for many.

THE SKY IS FALLING

Thanks to excavations that started in 1748 and continue to this day, scientists have been able to re-create almost exactly what happened in Pompeii on that terrible day in A.D. 79.

"The thick ash turned everything black," says Pompeii expert Andrew Wallace-Hadrill.

"People couldn't see the sun. All the landmarks disappeared. They didn't have the foggiest idea which way they were going."

Some people ran for their lives, clutching their valuable coins and jewellery. Other people took shelter in their homes. But the debris kept falling. Piles grew as deep as 2.7 metres (9 ft) in some places, blocking doorways and caving in roofs.

Around midnight, the first of four searing-hot clouds, or surges, of ash, pumice, rock and toxic gas rushed down the mountainside. Travelling towards Pompeii at up to 290 kilometres an hour (180 mph), it scorched everything in its path. Around 7 a.m., 18 hours after the

TODAY, MILLIONS OF TOURISTS VISIT THE RUINS OF POMPEII, INCLUDING THE FORUM, BELOW.

THIS ARTIST'S CONCEPT RE-CREATES THE FORUM AT POMPEII AS IT LOOKED THE DAY OF THE ERUPTION IN A.D. 79. THE FORUM WAS THE CENTRE OF PUBLIC LIFE.

eruption, the last fiery surge buried the city.

LOST AND FOUND

Visiting the ruins of Pompeii today is like going back in time. The layers of ash actually helped preserve buildings, artwork and even the forms of bodies. "It gives you the feeling you can reach out and touch the ancient world," Wallace-Hadrill says.

There are kitchens with pots on the stove and bakeries with loaves of bread — now turned to charcoal — still in the ovens. Narrow corridors lead to magnificent mansions with elaborate gardens and fountains. Mosaics, or designs made out of tiles, decorate the walls and floors.

WARNING SIGNS

Pompeii's destruction may be ancient history, but there's little doubt that disaster will strike again. Luckily, people living near Vesuvius today will be likely to receive evacuation warnings before the volcano blows.

Scientists are closely monitoring Vesuvius for shifts in the ground, earthquakes and rising levels of certain gasses, which could be signs of an upcoming eruption. The Italian government is also working on a plan to help people flee the area in the event of a natural disaster.

CREEPY CASTS

Volcanic ash settled around many of the victims at the moment of death. When the bodies decayed, holes remained inside the solid ash. Scientists poured plaster into the holes to preserve the shapes of the victims.

10 ENDURING FACTS ABOUT THE GREAT WALL OF CHINA

In the 13th century, Mongolian Genghis Khan led the first — and only — army to breach the wall in its history.

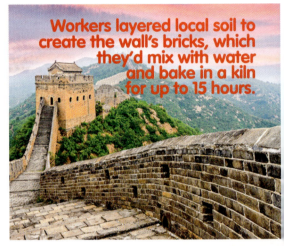

Workers layered local soil to create the wall's bricks, which they'd mix with water and bake in a kiln for up to 15 hours.

The wall — designed to keep invaders from the north out of China — **was built over a period of nearly 2,000 years.**

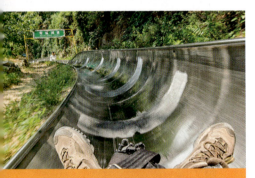

You can **ride a TOBOGGAN** from the top of the Great Wall to the ground below.

10 million people visit the Great Wall of China each year.

MORTAR CREATED WITH STICKY RICE FLOUR WAS USED TO HOLD THE WALL'S BRICKS TOGETHER AND MAKE IT STRONGER.

Smoke signals from the wall's watchtowers **alerted troops** if an enemy was spotted approaching.

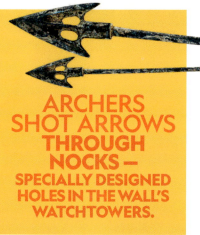

ARCHERS SHOT ARROWS **THROUGH NOCKS —** SPECIALLY DESIGNED HOLES IN THE WALL'S WATCHTOWERS.

You can camp out on certain portions of the Great Wall.

The **Great Wall of China** measures **21,196 KILOMETRES** (13,171 miles) — that's more than twice the length of the continent of Africa.

227

PiRATES!

MEET THREE OF HISTORY'S MOST FEARSOME HIGH-SEAS BADDIES.

Yo-ho, yo-ho — *uh-oh!* A mysterious ship on the horizon flying a skull-and-crossbones flag wasn't a welcome sight to sailors in the 18th and 19th centuries. That flag meant one thing: pirates. Faced with faster, cannon-crammed vessels typically crewed by pirates, a ship's captain was left with two choices: lower their sails and surrender — or turn and fight.

Life wasn't one big swashbuckling adventure for the pirates, however. Lousy food, cramped quarters, stinky crewmates and hurricanes were all part of the job. Still, a handful of pirates managed to enjoy success at sea ... and inspired fear in those who were unfortunate enough to meet them face-to-face. Check out some of history's most famous pirates.

RACHEL WALL

REIGN OF TERROR New England coast, U.S.A., late 1700s

Rachel Wall and her husband, George, worked together as pirates, targeting small islands off the coast of Maine in the Atlantic Ocean. After storms, they'd stop their ship and raise a distress flag. When passersby responded to Rachel's screams for help, they were robbed — or worse — for their trouble. After just two summers of piracy, Rachel and George killed at least 24 men and raked in about $6,000, plus an unknown amount of valuable goods. They later sold their loot, pretending they found it washed up on a beach.

CRIME DOESN'T PAY Eventually the law caught up with Rachel Wall. In 1789, she made history when she was the last woman to be hanged in the state of Massachusetts.

CHENG I SAO

REIGN OF TERROR South China Sea, 1801–1810

Cheng I Sao ruled a pirate fleet of nearly 2,000 ships. Sometimes called Madame Cheng, she turned to crime after she married a famous pirate. More than 80,000 buccaneers—men, women and even children—reported to Madame Cheng. They seized loot in all sorts of ways: selling 'protection' from pirate attacks, raiding ships and kidnapping for ransom. Madame Cheng was best known for paying her pirates cash for each head they brought back from their assaults. (Yikes!)

CRIME DOESN'T PAY — USUALLY Every government attempt to stop Madame Cheng was a failure. Rumour has it that after she retired from piracy, she started a second career as a smuggler. She died peacefully at the age of 69.

BLACKBEARD

REIGN OF TERROR North America's East Coast and the Caribbean, 1713–1718

Nobody knows Blackbeard's real name—historians think it might've been Edward Teach—but he's arguably history's most famous pirate. He began his career as a privateer, or a kind of legal pirate, who was hired by the British government to attack enemy fleets and steal their goods.

Blackbeard abandoned privateering in 1713 and went full-pirate when he sailed to the Caribbean on a French ship that was gifted to him by another pirate, adding cannons to the vessel and renaming it *Queen Anne's Revenge*. He terrified his enemies by strapping pistols and knives across his chest and sticking smoking cannon fuses in his beard. According to legend, Blackbeard hid a treasure somewhere ... but it's never been found.

CRIME DOESN'T PAY A few years into Blackbeard's time as a pirate, he was nabbed by the British Navy. They executed him and stuck his head on the front of a ship as a way to warn wannabe pirates to stay away from seafaring crime.

ROYAL

Check out what some of history's most

FIT FOR A QUEEN

Though militaries of the past were made up mostly of men, a few notable women—royal and otherwise—rode into battle, leading troops to victory. Not much is known about many of them. Check out what we *do* know about fierce females on the battlefield.

Armour for All

The few historical accounts of royal women in battle say that they most likely donned the same gear as men. They're usually described as wearing hauberks: garments made of metal that covered the arms, torso and upper legs.

Legendary Look

Many images of armour-clad women depict fictional figures like Minerva, the Roman goddess of women and warfare. According to legend, Minerva's father, Jupiter, swallowed her pregnant mother after a prophecy foretold that their unborn child would grow up to defeat him. When Minerva eventually escaped from inside Jupiter, she was wearing full battle armour and ready to fight her father.

MINERVA

Secret Suit

Though some historical paintings depict women in metal armour, no one knows for sure how accurate these illustrations are. That means the exact appearance of women's armour in the past is still a mystery, but historians think it looked similar to what men wore, like the suit above worn by English nobility during the 16th century.

Knight Me

In 1149, when invaders threatened to take over the town of Tortosa, Spain, local women threw on men's clothing and fought off the enemy. Spanish count Ramon Berenguer IV was so impressed that he created the Order of the Hatchet, granting the women rights similar to those of knights, such as not having to pay taxes.

CHECK OUT THE BOOK!

THE BOOK OF **Queens**

Custom Fit

Joan of Arc is one of history's most famous warriors. During the 15th century, France's King Charles VII presented the military leader with armour tailored to fit her perfectly.

RUMBLE

fearsome fighters wore on the battlefield.

So Much Metal

Being a knight sounds exciting, but wearing armour was not. Mail armour, invented around the third century B.C., was made of interlocking metal circles layered over quilted fabric to protect against arrows. Plate armour, invented around the late 1300s, was heavy and hard to see out of. But because it was made of bands of steel over leather, it defended against heavy blows while allowing for movement. The best protection? Probably a combination of both.

MAIL ARMOUR

PLATE ARMOUR

FIT FOR A KING

On the battlefield, sturdy armour meant the difference between life and death. Good armour protected its wearer against a variety of weapons while still allowing them to move easily. Discover what kings and their soldiers wore throughout history.

Works of Art

Today, Japanese samurai are famous for their long blades known as *katanas*, but their armour during the Heian period (A.D. 794–1185) was just as well known. Samurai armour, called *o-yoroi* (pronounced oh-YO-roy, above), was made of metal and leather, and designed to deflect blades and arrows. It consisted of multiple pieces laced together, including the *kabuto* (helmet), the *menpo* (face mask) and extra leg and arm guards. Some pieces were decorated so beautifully that today they're regarded as works of art.

Cat Fight

The Aztec Empire, which reigned over central Mexico from 1345 to 1521, was known for a group of warriors called the *ocelotl* (pronounced oh-seh-LO-tl), meaning 'jaguars'. In addition to wearing regular armour in battle, these jaguar fighters donned symbols of their namesake. One example was a helmet shaped like a jaguar head, with room for the soldier to peek out from below the teeth. And they sometimes wore capes made from real jaguar pelts. These outfits were thought to transfer the fierceness of the jaguar to the wearer.

SIXTH-CENTURY STATUE OF A JAGUAR WARRIOR

Animal Armour

Throughout history, some animals donned armour along with their soldiers, including battle horses and even elephants. War elephants, first used in what is now India during the 12th century, were sometimes dressed in fancy sets of metal armour weighing more than 159 kilograms (350 lb). A few were also adorned with 'tusk swords', which were metal weapons mounted on the elephants' tusks. Other elephants were saddled with carriages where archers could sit and fire on their enemies.

THE BOOK OF **KINGS**

CHECK OUT THE BOOK!

7 COOL THINGS ABOUT THE TOWER OF LONDON

As a palace, the Tower of London was a great place to live. As a prison, it wasn't so nice — especially because so many prisoners lost their lives. The place has been a lot of things in its nearly 1,000-year history. Today tourists can explore the Tower, in England, in the United Kingdom. Here are seven reasons why the Tower was — and still is — a cool place to be (as long as you weren't a prisoner, that is).

1
Ravens are like local superheroes. Well, sort of. Legend says if the ravens that live on the Tower grounds ever leave, the Tower will crumble and a disaster will befall England. No one knows when the ravens first showed up, but Charles II took the legend so seriously that in the 1670s he decreed that six ravens be kept there all the time. Today there are still always six — plus a couple of spares, just in case.

2
If you lived at the Tower today, your mum or dad might be in charge. The 35 Yeoman Warders and their families are among the few still allowed to live at the Tower. Established in 1509 as bodyguards for the king, today they give tours and manage the day-to-day details of the Tower. They're called 'beefeaters', possibly because their job once allowed them to eat beef from the king's table.

3
You need a secret password at night. Called the 'Word', the password changes every 24 hours and is a must-have to enter the Tower after hours. It's written on a piece of paper and delivered to the yeoman on duty for the night.

4
You might see a ghost. Queen Anne Boleyn, who was executed on orders from her husband, King Henry VIII, is said to wander the grounds without her head. One building is believed to be so haunted that dogs refuse to enter.

5

You'd have lots of bling. England's crown jewels are still guarded in the Tower's Jewel House, a dazzling display of crowns, robes, jewellery and sceptres that dates back hundreds of years. More than 23,500 diamonds, sapphires, rubies and other gems adorn the royal collection.

6

You'd never have to worry about a prison break. The Tower was so secure that only a few escape attempts succeeded. In 1716, one man sneaked out dressed in women's clothing. In 1100, a prisoner threw such a wild party for the guards that they didn't notice him climbing over the wall to meet a waiting boat!

7

You could find buried gold. In 1662, a goldsmith named John Barkstead supposedly hid £50,000 worth of stolen gold somewhere in the Tower grounds. Many have searched for the loot, but it has never been found.

MONARCHS
OF ENGLAND AND THE UNITED KINGDOM

England first became a united kingdom under the kings of Wessex, who drove out Viking invaders in the 10th century. The English kings conquered Wales in the 13th century, and the kingdoms of England and Scotland were joined together in 1603. After 1707, the country was known as the United Kingdom and now includes Northern Ireland. Many different houses have ruled the country; the current queen, Elizabeth II, is a member of the House of Windsor.

HOUSE OF WESSEX

Egbert (802–839)
Aethelwulf (839–855)
Aethelbald (855–860)
Aethelbert (860–866)
Aethelred (866–871)
Alfred the Great (871–899)
Edward the Elder (899–925)
Athelstan (925–939)
Edmund the Magnificent (939–946)
Eadred (946–955)
Eadwig (Edwy) All-Fair (955–959)
Edgar the Peaceable (959–975)
Edward the Martyr (975–978)
Aethelred the Unready (978–1013)

HOUSE OF DENMARK

Sweyn Forkbeard (1014)

HOUSE OF WESSEX
RESTORED, FIRST TIME

Aethelred the Unready (1014–1016)
Edmund Ironside (1016)

HOUSE OF DENMARK
RESTORED

Canute the Great (1016–1035)
Harold I Harefoot (1035–1040)
Harthacanute (1040–1042)

HOUSE OF WESSEX
RESTORED, SECOND TIME

Edward the Confessor (1042–1066)
Harold II (1066)

NORMANS

William I the Conqueror (1066–1087)
William II Rufus (1087–1100)
Henry I Beauclerc (1100–1135)
Stephen (1135–1154)
Matilda (1141)

PLANTAGENET
Angevin Line

Henry II Curtmantle (1154–1189)
Richard I the Lionheart (1189–1199)
John Lackland (1199–1216)
Henry III (1216–1272)
Edward I Longshanks (1272–1307)
Edward II (1307–1327)
Edward III (1327–1377)
Richard II (1377–1399)

Lancastrian Line

Henry IV Bolingbroke (1399–1413)
Henry V (1413–1422)
Henry VI (1422–1461, 1470–1471)

Yorkist Line

Edward IV (1461–1470, 1471–1483)
Edward V (1483)
Richard III Crookback (1483–1485)

HOUSE OF TUDOR

Henry VII Tudor (1485–1509)
Henry VIII (1509–1547)
Edward VI (1547–1553)
Lady Jane Grey (1553)
Mary I Tudor (1553–1558)
Elizabeth I (1558–1603)

HOUSE OF STUART

James I (1603–1625)
Charles I (1625–1649)

King Henry VII had more than 60 palaces and homes.

KING WILLIAM I THE CONQUEROR

KING JOHN LACKLAND

THE COMMONWEALTH
Oliver Cromwell* (1649–1658)
Richard Cromwell* (1658–1659)

HOUSE OF STUART
RESTORED
Charles II (1660–1685)
James II (1685–1688)

HOUSE OF ORANGE AND STUART
William III (1689–1702)
Mary II (1689–1694)

HOUSE OF STUART
Anne (1702–1714)

HOUSE OF HANOVER
George I (1714–1727)
George II (1727–1760)
George III (1760–1820)
George IV (1820–1830)
William IV (1830–1837)
Victoria (1837–1901)

HOUSE OF SAXE-COBURG-GOTHA
Edward VII (1901–1910)

HOUSE OF WINDSOR
George V (1910–1936)
Edward VIII (1936)
George VI (1936–1952)
Elizabeth II (1952–present)

*Held title of Lord Protector

Elizabeth I's court ate 8,200 sheep, 2,330 deer, 1,240 oxen, 1,870 pigs, 760 calves and 53 wild boar in one year.

Charles, Prince of Wales, wrote a children's book about an old man who lives in a cave.

Queen Elizabeth signs documents 'Elizabeth R.'—the R standing for Regina, which means 'queen' in Latin.

In 1976, Queen Elizabeth became the first British royal to send an email.

QUEEN ELIZABETH I

QUEEN VICTORIA

KING HENRY VIII

QUEEN ELIZABETH II

235

LEADERS OF THE WORLD

Each of the 195 independent countries in the world has its own leader or leaders. Whatever the leader is called, he or she takes charge of the direction of the country's growth — politically, economically and socially.

Some countries have more than one person who has an executive role in the government. That second person is often a prime minister or a chancellor. This varies depending on the type of government in the country.

Over the next several pages, the countries and their leaders are listed in alphabetical order according to the most commonly used version of each country's name. Disputed areas such as Northern Cyprus and Taiwan, and dependencies such as Bermuda, Greenland and Puerto Rico, which belong to independent nations, are not

included in this listing. The date given for leaders taking office is the date of their first term.

Note the colour key at the bottom of the pages, which assigns a colour to each country based on the continent on which it is located.

NOTE: These facts are current as of press time.

Colour Key by Continent

Afghanistan

President
Ashraf Ghani
Took office: 29 September 2014

Albania

President
Ilir Meta
Took office: 24 July 2017

Prime Minister
Edi Rama
Took office: 10 September 2013

Algeria

President
Abdelmadjid Tebboune
Took office: 12 December 2019

Prime Minister
Abdelaziz Djerad
Took office: 28 December 2019

> To learn more about world leaders, go online:
> **cia.gov/resources/ world-leaders/ foreign-governments/**

Andorra

Co-Prince
Emmanuel Macron
Took office: 14 May 2017

Co-Prince
Archbishop Joan-Enric Vives i Sicília
Took office: 12 May 2003

Executive Council President
Xavier Espot Zamora
Took office: 16 May 2019

Angola

President João Manuel Goncalves Lourenço
Took office: 26 September 2017

Antigua and Barbuda

Governor General
Rodney Williams
Took office: 14 August 2014

Prime Minister
Gaston Browne
Took office: 13 June 2014

Argentina

President
Alberto Ángel Fernández
Took office: 10 December 2019

> As a **LAW PROFESSOR, ALBERTO FERNÁNDEZ** was so **POPULAR** that students would line up to **TAKE SELFIES WITH HIM.**

Armenia

President Armen Sarkissian
Took office: 9 April 2018

Prime Minister
Nikol Pashinyan
Took office: 8 May 2018

Australia

Governor General
Sir David Hurley
Took office: 1 July 2019

Prime Minister
Scott Morrison
Took office: 24 August 2018

COLOUR KEY ● Africa ● Australia, New Zealand and Oceania

Austria

President
Alexander Van Der Bellen
Took office: 26 January 2017

Chancellor
Sebastian Kurz
Took office: 2 January 2020

Azerbaijan

President Ilham Aliyev
Took office: 31 October 2003

Prime Minister
Ali Asadov
Took office: 8 October 2019

Bahamas

Governor General
Cornelius A. Smith
Took office: 28 June 2019

Prime Minister
Hubert Minnis
Took office: 11 May 2017

Bahrain

King Hamad bin Isa
al-Khalifa
Began reign: 6 March 1999

Prime Minister
Salman bin Hamad al-Khalifa
Took office: 11 November 2020

Bangladesh

President Abdul Hamid
Took office: 24 April 2013

Prime Minister
Sheikh Hasina
Took office: 6 January 2009

Barbados

Governor General
Sandra Mason
Took office: 8 January 2018

Prime Minister
Mia Mottley
Took office: 25 May 2018

Belarus

President
Aleksandr Lukashenko
Took office: 20 July 1994

Prime Minister
Roman Golovchenko
Took office: 4 June 2020

Belgium

King Philippe
Began reign: 21 July 2013

Prime Minister
Alexander De Croo
Took office: 1 October 2020

Belize

Governor General
Sir Colville Norbert Young, Sr.
Took office: 17 November 1993

Prime Minister
Dean Oliver Barrow
Took office: 8 February 2008

Benin

President Patrice Talon
Took office: 6 April 2016

Bhutan

King Jigme Khesar
Namgyel Wangchuck
Began reign: 14 December 2006

Prime Minister
Lotay Tshering
Took office: 7 November 2018

THE KING OF BHUTAN is officially known as the DRAGON KING.

Bolivia

President
Luis Arce
Took office: 8 November 2020

Bosnia and Herzegovina

Presidency members:
Milorad Dodik
Sefik Dzaferovic
Zeljko Komsic
Took office: 20 November 2018

Chairman of the Council of Ministers Zoran Tegeltija
Took office: 5 December 2019

Botswana

President
Mokgweetse Eric Masisi
Took office: 1 April 2018

Brazil

President
Jair Bolsonaro
Took office: 1 January 2019

Brunei

Sultan Hassanal Bolkiah
Began reign: 5 October 1967

Bulgaria

President
Rumen Radev
Took office: 22 January 2017

Prime Minister
Boyko Borissov
Took office: 4 May 2017

Burkina Faso

President Roch Marc Christian Kabore
Took office: 29 December 2015

Prime Minister
Christophe Dabiré
Took office: 24 January 2019

Burundi

President
Evariste Ndayishimiye
Took office: 18 June 2020

Cabo Verde

President
Jorge Carlos Fonseca
Took office: 9 September 2011

Prime Minister
Ulisses Correia e Silva
Took office: 22 April 2016

Cambodia

King Norodom Sihamoni
Began reign: 29 October 2004

Prime Minister
Hun Sen
Took office: 14 January 1985

Cameroon

President
Paul Biya
Took office: 6 November 1982

Prime Minister
Joseph Dion Ngute
Took office: 4 January 2019

Canada

Governor General
Julie Payette
Took office: 2 October 2017

Prime Minister
Justin Trudeau
Took office: 4 November 2015

> **JUSTIN TRUDEAU and his YOUNGER BROTHER were both BORN ON CHRISTMAS DAY.**

Central African Republic

President
Faustin-Archange Touadera
Took office: 30 March 2016

Prime Minister
Firmin Ngrébada
Took office: 25 February 2019

Chad

President
Lt. Gen. Idriss Déby Itno
Took office: 4 December 1990

Chile

President
Sebastián Piñera Echenique
Took office: 11 March 2018

China

President
Xi Jinping
Took office: 14 March 2013

Premier
Li Keqiang
Took office: 16 March 2013

Hello From Costa Rica

Three-toed sloth

Colombia

President
Iván Duque Márquez
Took office: 7 August 2018

Comoros

President Azali Assoumani
Took office: 26 May 2016

Congo

President
Denis Sassou-Nguesso
Took office: 25 October 1997

Prime Minister
Clement Mouamba
Took office: 24 April 2016

Costa Rica

President
Carlos Alvarado Quesada
Took office: 8 May 2018

Elected at 38, CARLOS ALVARADO QUESADA is Costa Rica's YOUNGEST PRESIDENT in more than 100 years.

Côte d'Ivoire (Ivory Coast)

President
Alassane Dramane Ouattara
Took office: 4 December 2010

Prime Minister
Hamed Bakayoko
Took office: 30 July 2020

Croatia

President
Zoran Milanovic
Took office: 18 February 2020

Prime Minister
Andrej Plenkovic
Took office: 19 October 2016

Cuba

President Miguel
Díaz-Canel Bermúdez
Took office: 10 October 2019

Prime Minister
Manuel Marrero Cruz
Took office: 21 December 2019

Cyprus

President
Nikos Anastasiades
Took office: 28 February 2013

Czechia (Czech Republic)

President Milos Zeman
Took office: 8 March 2013

Prime Minister
Andrej Babis
Took office: 13 December 2017

Democratic Republic of the Congo

President
Felix Tshisekedi
Took office: 24 January 2019

Prime Minister
Sylvestre Ilunga Ilukamba
Took office: 20 May 2019

Denmark

Queen Margrethe II
Began reign: 14 January 1972

Prime Minister
Mette Frederiksen
Took office: 27 June 2019

Djibouti

President
Ismail Omar Guelleh
Took office: 8 May 1999

Prime Minister
Abdoulkader Kamil Mohamed
Took office: 1 April 2013

Dominica

President
Charles A. Savarin
Took office: 2 October 2013

Prime Minister
Roosevelt Skerrit
Took office: 8 January 2004

Dominican Republic

President
Luis Rodolfo Abinader
Took office: 16 August 2020

Ecuador

President
Lenín Moreno Garces
Took office: 24 May 2017

Egypt

President
Abdelfattah Elsisi
Took office: 8 June 2014

Prime Minister
Mostafa Madbouly
Took office: 7 June 2018

El Salvador

President Nayib Armando Bukele Ortez
Took office: 1 June 2019

Equatorial Guinea

President Teodoro Obiang Nguema Mbasogo
Took office: 3 August 1979

Prime Minister
Francisco Pascual Eyegue Obama Asue
Took office: 23 June 2016

Eritrea

President Isaias Afwerki
Took office: 8 June 1993

Estonia

President
Kersti Kaljulaid
Took office: 10 October 2016

Prime Minister
Juri Ratas
Took office: 23 November 2016

Aside from Estonian, KERSTI KALJULAID speaks ENGLISH, FINNISH, FRENCH and RUSSIAN.

Eswatini (Swaziland)

King Mswati III
Began reign: 25 April 1986

Prime Minister
Ambrose Mandvulo Dlamini
Took office: 27 October 2018

Ethiopia

President
Sahle-Work Zewde
Took office: 25 October 2018

Prime Minister Abiy Ahmed
Took office: 2 April 2018

SAHLE-WORK ZEWDE is ETHIOPIA'S FIRST FEMALE PRESIDENT.

Fiji

President
Jioji Konousi Konrote
Took office: 12 November 2015

Prime Minister
Voreqe 'Frank' Bainimarama
Took office: 22 September 2014

Finland

President Sauli Niinistö
Took office: 1 March 2012

Prime Minister Sanna Marin
Took office: 10 December 2019

SAULI NIINISTÖ is a FORMER CHAIRMAN of the FINNISH FOOTBALL ASSOCIATION.

France

President Emmanuel Macron
Took office: 14 May 2017

Prime Minister Jean Castex
Took office: 3 July 2020

Gabon

President
Ali Ben Bongo Ondimba
Took office: 16 October 2009

Prime Minister Rose Christiane Ossouka Raponda
Took office: 16 July 2020

Gambia

President Adama Barrow
Took office: 19 January 2017

Georgia

President
Salome Zourabichvili
Took office: 16 December 2018

Prime Minister
Giorgi Gakharia
Took office: 8 September 2019

Germany

President
Frank-Walter Steinmeier
Took office: 19 March 2017

Chancellor Angela Merkel
Took office: 22 November 2005

Ghana

President Nana Addo Dankwa Akufo-Addo
Took office: 7 January 2017

Greece

President
Ekaterini Sakellaropoulou
Took office: 13 March 2020

Prime Minister
Kyriakos Mitsotakis
Took office: 8 July 2019

Grenada

Governor General
Cecile La Grenade
Took office: 7 May 2013

Prime Minister
Keith Mitchell
Took office: 20 February 2013

Guatemala

President
Alejandro Giammattei
Took office: 14 January 2020

Guinea

President
Alpha Condé
Took office: 21 December 2010

Prime Minister
Ibrahima Fofana
Took office: 22 May 2018

Guinea-Bissau

President
Umaro Cissoko Embalo
Took office: 27 February 2020

Prime Minister
Nuno Nabiam
Took office: 27 February 2020

COLOUR KEY ● Africa ● Australia, New Zealand and Oceania

Guyana

President
Mohammed Irfaan Ali
Took office: 2 August 2020

Haiti

President
Jovenel Moise
Took office: 7 February 2017

Prime Minister
Joseph Jouthe
Took office: 4 March 2020

Honduras

President
Juan Orlando
Hernandez Alvarado
Took office: 27 January 2014

Hungary

President Janos Ader
Took office: 10 May 2012

Prime Minister
Viktor Orban
Took office: 29 May 2010

Iceland

President
Guðni Thorlacius
Jóhannesson
Took office: 1 August 2016

Prime Minister
Katrin Jakobsdóttir
Took office: 30 November 2017

Guðni Jóhannesson once said he'd BAN PINEAPPLE PIZZA if he could.

India

President
Ram Nath Kovind
Took office: 25 July 2017

Prime Minister
Narendra Modi
Took office: 26 May 2014

Indonesia

President Joko Widodo
Took office: 20 October 2014

JOKO WIDODO is a former FURNITURE MAKER.

Iran

Supreme Leader
Ayatollah Ali
Hoseini-Khamenei
Took office: 4 June 1989

President
Hasan Fereidun Rohani
Took office: 3 August 2013

Iraq

President
Barham Salih
Took office: 2 October 2018

Prime Minister
Mustafa al-Kadhimi
Took office: 7 May 2020

Greetings From Germany

Neuschwanstein Castle

● Asia ● Europe ● North America ● South America

Ireland (Éire)

President
Michael D. Higgins
Took office: 11 November 2011

Prime Minister
Micheál Martin
Took office: 27 June 2020

> **MICHAEL D. HIGGINS has published four collections of POETRY.**

Israel

President
Reuven Rivlin
Took office: 27 July 2014

Prime Minister
Binyamin Netanyahu
Took office: 31 March 2009

Italy

President Sergio Mattarella
Took office: 3 February 2015

Prime Minister
Giuseppe Conte
Took office: 1 June 2018

Jamaica

Governor General
Sir Patrick L. Allen
Took office: 26 February 2009

Prime Minister
Andrew Holness
Took office: 3 March 2016

Japan

Emperor Naruhito
Began reign: 1 May 2019

Prime Minister Yoshihide Suga
Took office: 16 September 2020

Jordan

King Abdullah II
Began reign: 7 February 1999

Prime Minister
Bisher Al-Khasawneh
Took office: 7 October 2020

> **King Abdullah II made a CAMEO APPEARANCE in an episode of *STAR TREK: VOYAGER*.**

Kazakhstan

President
Kassym-Jomart Tokayev
Took office: 20 March 2019

Prime Minister
Askar Mamin
Took office: 25 February 2019

Welcome to Madagascar

Avenue of the Baobabs

COLOUR KEY ● Africa ● Australia, New Zealand and Oceania

Kenya

President
Uhuru Kenyatta
Took office: 9 April 2013

> **UHURU KENYATTA'S first name means 'FREEDOM' in Swahili.**

Kiribati

President
Taneti Maamau
Took office: 11 March 2016

Kosovo

Acting President
Vjosa Osmani
Took office: 5 November 2020

Prime Minister
Avdullah Hoti
Took office: 3 June 2020

> **VJOSA OSMANI speaks Serbian, English and Turkish.**

Kuwait

Amir Nawaf al-Ahmad al-Jabir al-Sabah
Began reign: 30 September 2020

Prime Minister Sabah Al-Khalid al-Hamad al-Sabah
Took office: 19 November 2019

Kyrgyzstan

President
Sadyr Japarov
Took office: 28 January 2021

Prime Minister
Ulukbek Maripov
Took office: 3 February 2021

Laos

President
Bounnyang Vorachit
Took office: 20 April 2016

Prime Minister
Thongloun Sisoulit
Took office: 20 April 2016

Latvia

President Egils Levits
Took office: 8 July 2019

Prime Minister
Krisjanis Karins
Took office: 23 January 2019

Lebanon

President Michel Awn
Took office: 31 October 2016

Prime Minister
Saad Hariri
Took office: 22 October 2020

Lesotho

King Letsie III
Began reign: 7 February 1996

Prime Minister
Moeketsi Majoro
Took office: 20 May 2020

Liberia

President George Weah
Took office: 22 January 2018

Libya

Prime Minister
Fayiz al-Saraj
Took office: December 2015

Liechtenstein

Prince Hans Adam II
Began reign: 13 November 1989

Prime Minister
Adrian Hasler
Took office: 27 March 2013

Lithuania

President
Gitanas Nauseda
Took office: 12 July 2019

Prime Minister
Saulius Skvernelis
Took office: 13 December 2016

Luxembourg

Grand Duke Henri
Began reign: 7 October 2000

Prime Minister
Xavier Bettel
Took office: 4 December 2013

> **GRAND DUKE HENRI is a member of the INTERNATIONAL OLYMPIC COMMITTEE.**

Madagascar

President Andry Rajoelina
Took office: 21 January 2019

Prime Minister
Christian Ntsay
Took office: 6 June 2018

Malawi

President
Lazarus Chakwera
Took office: 28 June 2020

Malaysia

King Sultan Abdullah Sultan Ahmad Shah
Installed: 24 January 2019

Prime Minister
Tan Sri Muhyiddin Yassin
Took office: 1 March 2020

Maldives

President Ibrahim 'Ibu' Mohamed Solih
Took office: 17 November 2018

Mali

President of transitional government: Bah Ndaw
Took office: 25 September 2020

Prime Minister Moctar Ouane
Took office: 27 September 2020

Malta

President George Vella
Took office: 4 April 2019

Prime Minister Robert Abela
Took office: 13 January 2020

Marshall Islands

President David Kabua
Took office: 13 January 2020

Mauritania

President Mohamed Cheikh El Ghazouani
Took office: 1 August 2019

Prime Minister Mohamed Ould Bilal
Took office: 6 August 2020

Mauritius

President Pritivirajsing Roopun
Took office: 2 December 2019

Prime Minister Pravind Jugnauth
Took office: 23 January 2017

Mexico

President Andres Manuel Lopez Obrador
Took office: 1 December 2018

Micronesia

President David W. Panuelo
Took office: 11 May 2019

Moldova

President Igor Dodon
Took office: 23 December 2016

Prime Minister Ion Chicu
Took office: 14 November 2019

Monaco

Prince Albert II
Began reign: 6 April 2005

Minister of State Pierre Dartout
Took office: 1 September 2020

Mongolia

President Khaltmaa Battulga
Took office: 10 July 2017

Prime Minister Ukhnaa Khurelsukh
Took office: 4 October 2017

UKHNAA KHURELSUKH is a motorbike enthusiast.

Montenegro

President Milo Djukanovic
Took office: 20 May 2018

Prime Minister Zdravko Krivokapic
Took office: 4 December 2020

MILO DJUKANOVIC is a big BASKETBALL FAN.

Morocco

King Mohammed VI
Began reign: 30 July 1999

Prime Minister Saad-Eddine al-Othmani
Took office: 17 March 2017

Mozambique

President Filipe Jacinto Nyusi
Took office: 15 January 2015

Prime Minister Carlos Agostinho Do Rosario
Took office: 17 January 2015

Myanmar (Burma)

President Win Myint
Took office: 30 March 2018

Namibia

President Hage Geingob
Took office: 21 March 2005

HAGE GEINGOB has a rugby stadium named after him.

Nauru

President Lionel Aingimea
Took office: 27 August 2019

Nepal

President Bidhya Devi Bhandari
Took office: 29 October 2015

Prime Minister Khadga Prasad (KP) Sharma Oli
Took office: 15 February 2018

Netherlands

King Willem-Alexander
Began reign: 30 April 2013

Prime Minister Mark Rutte
Took office: 14 October 2010

COLOUR KEY ● Africa ● Australia, New Zealand and Oceania

New Zealand

Governor General
Dame Patricia Lee Reddy
Took office: 28 September 2016

Prime Minister
Jacinda Ardern
Took office: 26 October 2017

JACINDA ARDERN grew up on an APPLE FARM.

Nicaragua

President José Daniel Ortega Saavedra
Took office: 10 January 2007

Niger

President
Issoufou Mahamadou
Took office: 7 April 2011

Prime Minister
Brigi Rafini
Took office: 7 April 2011

Nigeria

President Maj. Gen. (ret.) Muhammadu Buhari
Took office: 29 May 2015

North Korea

Supreme Leader
Kim Jong-un
Took office: 17 December 2011

Assembly President
Choe Ryong Hae
Took office: 11 April 2019

North Macedonia

President Stevo Pendarovski
Took office: 12 May 2019

Prime Minister Zoran Zaev
Took office: 31 August 2020

Norway

King Harald V
Began reign: 17 January 1991

Prime Minister
Erna Solberg
Took office: 16 October 2013

ERNA SOLBERG plays games on her iPad TO DE-STRESS.

Oman

Sultan Haytham bin Tariq bin Taimur Al-Said
Began reign: 11 January 2020

Pakistan

President
Arif Alvi
Took office: 9 September 2018

Prime Minister
Imran Khan
Took office: 18 August 2018

Palau

President Tommy Esang Remengesau, Jr.
Took office: 17 January 2013

Tommy Remengesau, Jr., is the FIRST PALAUAN to be ELECTED PRESIDENT FOUR TIMES.

Panama

President
Laurentino 'Nito' Cortizo Cohen
Took office: 1 July 2019

Papua New Guinea

Governor General
Grand Chief Sir Bob Dadae
Took office: 28 February 2017

Prime Minister
James Marape
Took office: 30 May 2019

Paraguay

President
Mario Abdo Benitez
Took office: 15 August 2018

Peru

President
Francisco Sagasti
Took office: 17 November 2020

FRANCISCO SAGASTI has composed and written the lyrics to SIX SONGS.

Philippines

President
Rodrigo Duterte
Took office: 30 June 2016

Poland

President
Andrzej Duda
Took office: 6 August 2015

Prime Minister
Mateusz Morawiecki
Took office: 11 December 2017

Portugal

President
Marcelo Rebelo de Sousa
Took office: 9 March 2016

Prime Minister
António Costa
Took office: 26 November 2015

● Asia ● Europe ● North America ● South America

Qatar

**Amir Tamim bin Hamad
Al Thani**
Began reign: 25 June 2013

**Prime Minister
Sheikh Khalid bin Khalifa bin
Abdulaziz Al Thani**
Took office: 28 January 2020

Romania

**President
Klaus Werner Iohannis**
Took office: 21 December 2014

**Prime Minister
Ludovic Orban**
Took office: 4 November 2019

**KLAUS IOHANNIS
is a former high
school PHYSICS
TEACHER.**

Russia

**President Vladimir
Vladimirovich Putin**
Took office: 7 May 2012

**Premier
Mikhail Mishustin**
Took office: 16 January 2020
*Note: Russia is in both Europe and Asia, but
its capital is in Europe, so it is classified
here as a European country.*

**VLADIMIR PUTIN
SWIMS LAPS and
LIFTS WEIGHTS
every day.**

Rwanda

**President
Paul Kagame**
Took office: 22 April 2000

**Prime Minister
Edouard Ngirente**
Took office: 30 August 2017

Samoa

**Head of State Tuimaleali'ifano
Va'aletoa Sualauvi II**
Took office: 21 July 2017

**Prime Minister Tuila'epa
Lupesoliai Sailele Malielegaoi**
Took office: 23 November 1998

**Tuimaleali'ifano
Va'aletoa Sualauvi II
is a former
POLICE OFFICER.**

San Marino

**Co-Chiefs of State:
Captain Regent
Alessandro Cardelli
Captain Regent Mirko Dolcini**
Took office: 1 October 2020

**Secretary of State
for Foreign and Political
Affairs Luca Beccari**
Took office: 8 January 2020

Sao Tome and Principe

President Evaristo Carvalho
Took office: 3 September 2016

**Prime Minister
Jorge Bom Jesus**
Took office: 3 December 2018

Saudi Arabia

**King and Prime Minister
Salman bin Abd al-Aziz
Al Saud**
Began reign: 23 January 2015

Senegal

President Macky Sall
Took office: 2 April 2012

**MACKY SALL
worked as a
GEOLOGIST before
entering politics.**

Serbia

**President
Aleksandar Vucic**
Took office: 31 May 2017

Prime Minister Ana Brnabic
Took office: 29 June 2017

Seychelles

**President
Wavel Ramkalawan**
Took office: 26 October 2020

Sierra Leone

**President
Julius Maada Bio**
Took office: 4 April 2018

Singapore

President Halimah Yacob
Took office: 14 September 2017

**Prime Minister
Lee Hsien Loong**
Took office: 12 August 2004

Slovakia

President Zuzana Caputova
Took office: 15 June 2019

**Prime Minister
Igor Matovic**
Took office: 21 March 2020

Slovenia

President Borut Pahor
Took office: 22 December 2012

**Prime Minister
Janez Jansa**
Took office: 13 March 2020

Solomon Islands

**Governor General
David Vunagi**
Took office: 8 July 2019

**Prime Minister
Manessah Sogavare**
Took office: 24 April 2019

COLOUR KEY ● Africa ● Australia, New Zealand and Oceania

Somalia

President
Mohamed Abdullahi
Mohamed 'Farmaajo'
Took office: 8 February 2017

Prime Minister
Mohamed Hussein Roble
Took office: 27 September 2020

South Africa

President
Matamela Cyril Ramaphosa
Took office: 15 February 2018

Cyril Ramaphosa ENJOYS TROUT FISHING.

South Korea

President
Moon Jae-in
Took office: 10 May 2017

South Sudan

President
Salva Kiir Mayardit
Took office: 9 July 2011

Spain

King Felipe VI
Began reign: 19 June 2014

President of the Government
Pedro Sánchez Pérez-Castejón
Took office: 2 June 2018

Sri Lanka

President
Gotabaya Rajapaksa
Took office: 18 November 2019

St. Kitts and Nevis

Governor General
Samuel W. T. Seaton
Took office: 2 September 2015

Prime Minister
Timothy Harris
Took office: 18 February 2015

St. Lucia

Governor General
Neville Cenac
Took office: 12 January 2018

Prime Minister
Allen Chastanet
Took office: 7 June 2016

Postcard From Singapore

The view from the top of the Singapore Flyer, one of the tallest Ferris wheels in the world

St. Vincent and the Grenadines

**Governor General
Susan Dougan**
Took office: 1 August 2019

**Prime Minister
Ralph E. Gonsalves**
Took office: 29 March 2001

**SUSAN DOUGAN
is the
FIRST FEMALE
governor general of
St. Vincent and
the Grenadines.**

Sudan

President
Vacant

**Chairman of the
Sovereignty Council:
General Abd-al-Fatah
al-Burhan Abd-al-Rahman**
Took office: August 2019

Suriname

**President
Chandrikapersad Santokhi**
Took office: 16 July 2020

Sweden

King Carl XVI Gustaf
Began reign: 19 September 1973

**Prime Minister
Stefan Löfven**
Took office: 3 October 2014

**STEFAN LÖFVEN
spent 15 years
WORKING AS
A WELDER
in a factory.**

Switzerland

**President of the
Swiss Confederation
Simonetta Sommaruga**
Took office: 1 January 2020

**Federal Council members:
Viola Amherd, Guy Parmelin,
Ueli Maurer, Ignazio Cassis,
Alain Berset, Karin Keller-
Sutter**
Took office: Dates vary

Syria

**President
Bashar al-Asad**
Took office: 17 July 2000

**Prime Minister
Hussein Arnous**
Took office: 30 August 2020

Tajikistan

President Emomali Rahmon
Took office: 19 November 1992

**Prime Minister
Qohir Rasulzoda**
Took office: 23 November 2013

**EMOMALI
RAHMON has
nine children —
SEVEN daughters
and TWO sons.**

Tanzania

**President
John Magufuli**
Took office: 5 November 2015

**JOHN MAGUFULI
did press-ups
on the campaign
trail to prove his
FITNESS.**

Thailand

**King Wachiralongkon
Bodinthrathepphay-
awarangkun**
Began reign: 1 December 2016

**Prime Minister
General Prayut Chan-ocha**
Took office: 25 August 2014

**Prayut Chan-ocha
WRITES
POP SONGS.**

Timor-Leste (East Timor)

**President
Francisco Guterres**
Took office: 20 May 2017

**Prime Minister
Taur Matan Ruak**
Took office: 22 June 2018

Togo

President Faure Gnassingbé
Took office: 4 May 2005

**Prime Minister
Victoire Tomegah Dogbe**
Took office: 28 September 2020

Tonga

King Tupou VI
Began reign: 18 March 2012

**Prime Minister
Pohiva Tu'i'onetoa**
Took office: 27 September 2019

Trinidad and Tobago

**President
Paula-Mae Weekes**
Took office: 19 March 2018

**Prime Minister
Keith Rowley**
Took office: 9 September 2015

Tunisia

President
Kais Saied
Took office: 23 October 2019

Prime Minister
Hichem Mechichi
Took office: 2 September 2020

Turkey

President
Recep Tayyip Erdogan
Took office: 28 August 2014

Turkmenistan

President Gurbanguly Berdimuhamedow
Took office: 14 February 2007

Tuvalu

Governor General
Iakoba Taeia Italeli
Took office: 16 April 2010

Prime Minister
Kausea Natano
Took office: 19 September 2019

Uganda

President
Yoweri Kaguta Museveni
Took office: 26 January 1986

Ukraine

President
Volodymyr Zelenskyy
Took office: 20 May 2019

Prime Minister
Denys Shmyhal
Took office: 4 March 2020

A former actor, **VOLODYMYR ZELENSKYY** has appeared in **SEVERAL FILMS.**

United Arab Emirates

President Khalifa bin Zayid al-Nuhayyan
Took office: 3 November 2004

Prime Minister
Muhammad bin Rashid al-Maktum
Took office: 5 January 2006

United Kingdom

Queen Elizabeth II
Began reign: 6 February 1952

Prime Minister
Boris Johnson
Took office: 24 July 2019

United States

President
Joe Biden
Took office: 20 January 2021

Uruguay

President
Luis Alberto Lacalle Pou
Took office: 1 March 2020

Luis Alberto Lacalle Pou is an **AVID SURFER.**

Uzbekistan

President
Shavkat Mirziyoyev
Took office: 8 September 2016

Prime Minister
Abdulla Aripov
Took office: 14 December 2016

Vanuatu

President Tallis Obed Moses
Took office: 6 July 2017

Prime Minister
Bob Loughman
Took office: 20 April 2020

Vatican City

Supreme Pontiff
Pope Francis
Took office: 13 March 2013

Secretary of State
Cardinal Pietro Parolin
Took office: 15 October 2013

POPE FRANCIS is a fan of **TANGO DANCING.**

Venezuela

President
Nicolas Maduro Moros
Took office: 19 April 2013

Vietnam

President
Nguyen Phu Trong
Took office: 23 October 2018

Prime Minister
Nguyen Xuan Phuc
Took office: 7 April 2016

Yemen

President
Abd Rabuh Mansur Hadi
Took office: 21 February 2012

Prime Minister
Maeen Abd al-Malik Saeed
Took office: 15 October 2018

Zambia

President
Edgar Lungu
Took office: 25 January 2015

Zimbabwe

President
Emmerson Dambudzo Mnangagwa
Took office: 24 November 2017

● Asia ● Europe ● North America ● South America

QUIZ WHIZ

Go back in time to seek the answers to this history quiz!

Write your answers on a piece of paper. Then check them below.

1 **True or false?** Historians think Blackbeard's real name might have been Edward Teach, but they don't know for sure.

2 Mortar created with _____ was used to hold the Great Wall of China's bricks together.
- a. sticky rice
- b. glue
- c. bubble gum
- d. dumpling dough

3 Ayutthaya, an ancient capital of the Siamese Kingdom, was known as one of the world's _____ cities.
- a. richest
- b. smallest
- c. tallest
- d. largest

4 **True or false?** Legend has it that the Roman goddess Venus was born wearing full battle armour.

5 About how many gems make up the royal collection of crown jewels, housed in the Tower of London?
- a. 235
- b. 2,350
- c. 23,500
- d. 230,500

Not **STUMPED** yet? Check out the *NATIONAL GEOGRAPHIC KIDS QUIZ WHIZ* collection for more crazy **HISTORY** questions!

ANSWERS: 1. True; **2.** a; **3.** d; **4.** False. The legend is about the Roman goddess Minerva.; **5.** C

HOMEWORK HELP

Brilliant Biographies

Malala Yousafzai

A biography is the story of a person's life. It can be a brief summary or a long book. Biographers — those who write biographies — use many different sources to learn about their subjects. You can write your own biography of a famous person you find inspiring.

How to Get Started

Choose a subject you find interesting. If you think Cleopatra is cool, you have a good chance of getting your readers interested, too. If you're bored by ancient Egypt, your readers will be snoring after your first paragraph.

Your subject can be almost anyone: an author, an inventor, a celebrity, a politician or a member of your family. To find someone to write about, ask yourself these simple questions:

1. Who do I want to know more about?
2. What did this person do that was special?
3. How did this person change the world?

Do Your Research

- Find out as much about your subject as possible. Read books, news articles and encyclopedia entries. Watch video clips and movies and search the internet. Conduct interviews, if possible.
- Take notes, writing down important facts and interesting stories about your subject.

Write the Biography

- Come up with a title. Include the person's name.
- Write an introduction. Consider asking a probing question about your subject.
- Include information about the person's childhood. When was this person born? Where did he or she grow up? Who did he or she admire?
- Highlight the person's talents, accomplishments and personal attributes.
- Describe the specific events that helped to shape this person's life. Did this person ever have a problem and overcome it?
- Write a conclusion. Include your thoughts about why it is important to learn about this person.
- Once you have finished your first draft, revise and then proofread your work.

Here's a **SAMPLE BIOGRAPHY** of Malala Yousafzai, a human rights advocate and the youngest ever recipient of the Nobel Peace Prize. Of course, there is so much more for you to discover and write about on your own!

Malala Yousafzai

Malala Yousafzai was born in Pakistan on 12 July 1997. Malala's father, Ziauddin, a teacher, made it a priority for his daughter to receive a proper education. Malala loved school. She learned to speak three languages and even wrote a blog about her experiences as a student.

Around the time Malala turned 10, the Taliban — a group of strict Muslims who believe women should stay at home — took over the region where she lived. The Taliban did not approve of Malala's outspoken love of learning. One day, on her way home from school, Malala was shot in the head by a Taliban gunman. Very badly injured, she was sent to a hospital in England.

Not only did Malala survive the shooting — she thrived. She used her experience as a platform to fight for girls' education worldwide. She began speaking out about educational opportunities for all. Her efforts gained worldwide attention, and she was eventually awarded the Nobel Peace Prize in 2014 at the age of 17. She is the youngest person to earn the prestigious prize.

Each year on 12 July, World Malala Day honours her heroic efforts to bring attention to human rights issues.

Granite peaks rise above Lake Pehoé in Torres del Paine National Park in Chile's Patagonia region.

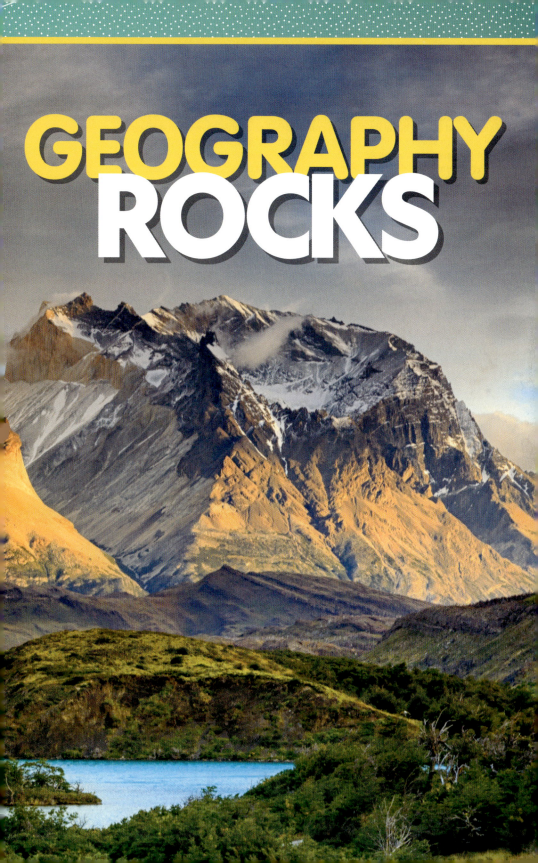

GEOGRAPHY
ROCKS

THE POLITICAL WORLD

Earth's land area is made up of seven continents, but people have divided much of the land into smaller political units called countries. Australia is a continent made up of a single country, and Antarctica is used for scientific research. But the other five continents include almost 200 independent countries. The political map shown here depicts boundaries — imaginary lines created by treaties — that separate countries. Some boundaries, such as the one between the United States and Canada, are very stable and have been recognised for many years.

See Europe map for more detail.

Winkel Tripel Projection

Other boundaries, such as the one between Sudan and South Sudan in northeast Africa, are relatively new and still disputed. Countries come in all shapes and sizes. Russia and Canada are giants; others, such as El Salvador and Qatar, are small. Some countries are long and skinny — look at Chile in South America! Still other countries — such as Indonesia and Japan in Asia — are made up of groups of islands. The political map is a clue to the diversity that makes Earth so fascinating.

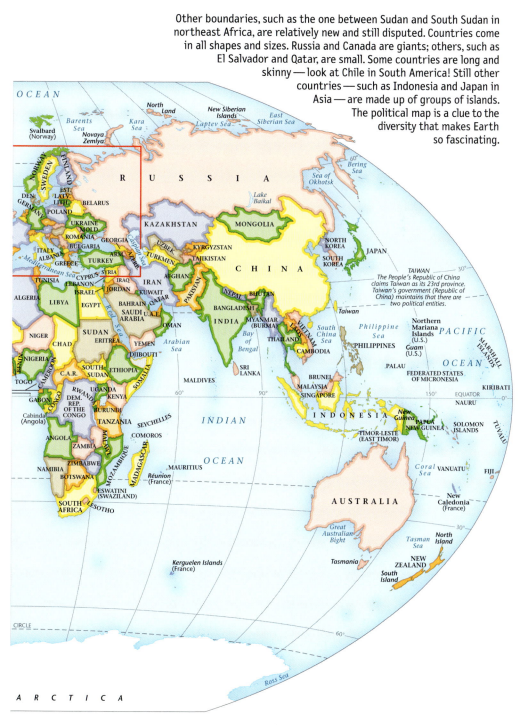

THE PHYSICAL WORLD

Earth is dominated by large landmasses called continents — seven in all — and by an interconnected global ocean that is divided into four parts by the continents. More than 70 percent of Earth's surface is covered by oceans, and the rest is made up of land areas.

Different landforms give variety to the surface of the continents. The Rocky Mountains divide North America, the Andes mark the western edge of South America and the Himalaya tower above South Asia. The Plateau of Tibet forms the rugged core of Asia,

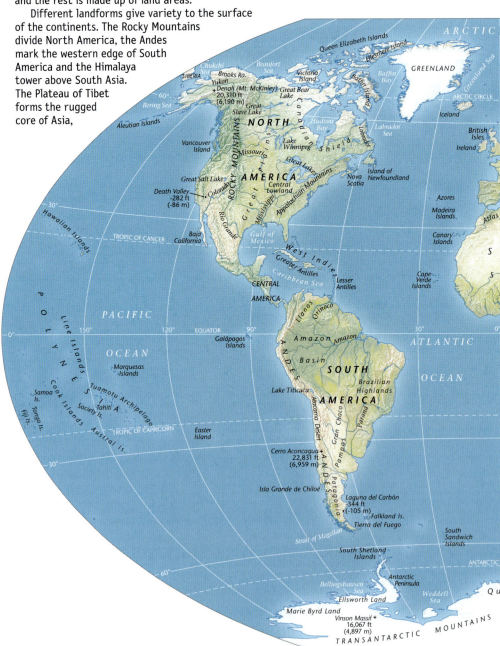

while the Northern European Plain extends from the North Sea to the Ural Mountains. Much of Africa is a plateau, and dry plains cover large areas of Australia. Mountains rise more than 4,877 metres (16,000 ft) above Antarctica's massive ice sheets. Mountains and trenches make the ocean floors as varied as any continent. A mountain chain called the Mid-Atlantic Ridge runs the length of the Atlantic Ocean. In the western Pacific, trenches drop deep into the ocean floor.

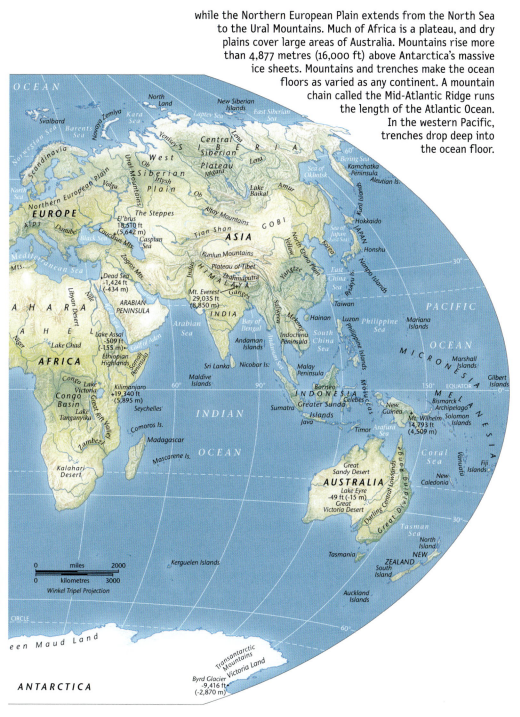

KINDS OF MAPS

Maps are special tools that geographers use to tell a story about Earth. Maps can be used to show just about anything related to places. Some maps show physical features, such as mountains or vegetation. Maps can also show climates or natural hazards and other things we cannot easily see. Other maps illustrate different features on Earth — political boundaries, urban centres and economic systems.

AN IMPERFECT TOOL

Maps are not perfect. A globe is a scale model of Earth with accurate relative sizes and locations. Because maps are flat, they involve distortions of size, shape and direction. Also, cartographers — people who create maps — make choices about what information to include. Because of this, it is important to study many different types of maps to learn the complete story of Earth. Three commonly found kinds of maps are shown on this page.

PHYSICAL MAPS. Earth's natural features — landforms, water bodies and vegetation — are shown on physical maps. The map above uses colour and shading to illustrate mountains, lakes, rivers and deserts of central South America. Country names and borders are added for reference, but they are not natural features.

POLITICAL MAPS. These maps represent characteristics of the landscape created by humans, such as boundaries, cities and place-names. Natural features are added only for reference. On the map above, capital cities are represented with a star inside a circle, while other cities are shown with black dots.

THEMATIC MAPS. Patterns related to a particular topic or theme, such as population distribution, appear on these maps. The map above displays the region's climate zones, which range from tropical wet (bright green) to tropical wet and dry (light green) to semiarid (dark yellow) to arid or desert (light yellow).

MAKING MAPS

Meet a Cartographer!

As a National Geographic cartographer, **Mike McNey** works with maps every day. Here, he shares more about his cool career.

National Geographic staff cartographers Mike McNey and Rosemary Wardley review a map of Africa for the *National Geographic Kids World Atlas*.

What exactly does a cartographer do?

I create maps specifically for books and atlases to help the text tell the story on the page. The maps need to fit into the size and the style of the book, with the final goal being that it's accurate and appealing for the reader.

What kinds of stories have you told with your maps?

Once, I created a map that showed the spread of the Burmese python population in Florida around the Everglades National Park. I've also made maps that show data like farmland, food production, cattle density and fish catch in a particular location, like the United States.

How do you rely on technology in your job?

All aspects of mapmaking are on the computer. This makes it much quicker to make a map. It also makes it easier to change anything on the map. If you want to change the colour of the rivers on the map, you just have to hit one button on the mouse.

How do you create your maps?

I work with geographic information systems (GIS), a computer software that allows us to represent any data on a specific location of the world, or even the entire world. Data can be anything from endangered species, animal ranges and population of a particular place. We also use remote systems, like satellites and aerial imagery, to analyse Earth's surface.

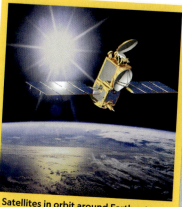

Satellites in orbit around Earth act as eyes in the sky, recording data about the planet's land and ocean areas. The data are converted to numbers transmitted back to computers specially programmed to interpret the data. They record it in a form that cartographers can use to create maps.

What will maps of the future look like?

In the future, you'll see more and more data on maps. I also think more online maps are going to be made in a way that you can switch from a world view to a local view to see data at any scale.

What's the best part of your job?

I love the combination of science and design involved in it. It's also fun to make maps interesting for kids.

UNDERSTANDING
MAPS

MAKING A PROJECTION

Globes present a model of Earth as it is — a sphere — but they are bulky and can be difficult to use and store. Flat maps are much more convenient but certain problems can result from transferring Earth's curved surface to a flat piece of paper, a process called projection. Imagine a globe that has been cut in half, like the one to the right. If a light is shined into it, the lines of latitude and longitude and the shapes of the continent will cast shadows that can be 'projected' onto a piece of paper, as shown here. Depending on how the paper is positioned, the shadows will be distorted in different ways.

KNOW THE CODE

Every map has a story to tell, but first you have to know how to read one. Maps represent information by using a language of symbols. When you know how to read these symbols, you can access a wide range of information. Look at the scale and compass rose or arrow to understand distance and direction (see box below).

To find out what each symbol on a map means, you must use the key. It's your secret decoder — identifying information by each symbol on the map.

There are three main types of map symbols: points, lines and areas. Points, which can be either dots or small icons, represent the location or the number of things, such as schools, cities or landmarks. Lines are used to show boundaries, roads or rivers and can vary in colour or thickness. Area symbols use pattern or colour to show regions, such as a sandy area or a neighbourhood.

SCALE AND DIRECTION

The scale on a map can be shown as a fraction, as words or as a line or bar. It relates distance on the map to distance in the real world. Sometimes the scale identifies the type of map projection. Maps may include an arrow to indicate north on the map or a compass rose to show all principal directions.

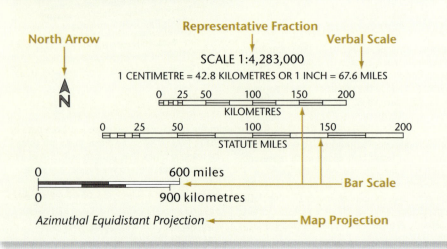

North Arrow

Representative Fraction

Verbal Scale

SCALE 1:4,283,000

1 CENTIMETRE = 42.8 KILOMETRES OR 1 INCH = 67.6 MILES

0 25 50 100 150 200
KILOMETRES

0 25 50 100 150 200
STATUTE MILES

0   600 miles
0   900 kilometres

Bar Scale

Azimuthal Equidistant Projection ← Map Projection

GEOGRAPHIC FEATURES

From roaring rivers to parched deserts, from underwater canyons to jagged mountains, Earth is covered with beautiful and diverse environments. Here are examples of the most common types of geographic features found around the world.

WATERFALL

Waterfalls form when a river reaches an abrupt change in elevation. At left, the Iguazú waterfall system — on the border of Brazil and Argentina — is made up of 275 falls.

VALLEY

Valleys, cut by running water or moving ice, may be broad and flat or narrow and steep, such as the Indus River Valley (above) in Ladakh, India.

RIVER

As a river moves through flatlands, it twists and turns. Above, the Rio Los Amigos winds through a rainforest in Peru.

MOUNTAIN

Mountains are Earth's tallest landforms, and Mount Everest (above) rises highest of all, at 8,850 metres (29,035 ft) above sea level.

GLACIER

Glaciers — 'rivers' of ice — such as Hubbard Glacier (above) in Alaska, U.S.A., move slowly from mountains to the sea. Global warming is shrinking them.

CANYON

Steep-sided valleys called canyons are created mainly by running water. Buckskin Gulch (above) in Utah, U.S.A., is the deepest 'slot' canyon in the American Southwest.

DESERT

Deserts are land features created by climate, specifically by a lack of water. Here, a camel caravan crosses the Sahara in North Africa.

AFRICA

In legends from Tanzania, Africa, witches ride on hyenas, not broomsticks.

Hippos sweat an oily red liquid that acts as sunscreen.

Hippopotamus

The massive continent of Africa, where humankind began millions of years ago, is second only to Asia in size. Stretching nearly as far from west to east as it does from north to south, Africa is home to both the longest river in the world (the Nile) and the largest hot desert on Earth (the Sahara).

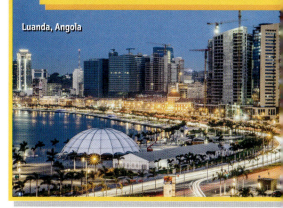
Luanda, Angola

DRAGON LIZARD SIGHTING

Scientists recently discovered a new species of dragon lizard in southern Africa. Known as the Swazi dragon lizard, the 33-centimetre (13-in) lizard has shield-like scales and hides in rock crevices.

ON LOCATION

Nigeria's film industry — also known as Nollywood — is the world's second largest film producer, ahead of Hollywood and behind India's Bollywood. Popular Nollywood films include the romantic comedy *The Wedding Party* and its sequel.

Great Pyramid, Great Numbers
How do the numbers for Earth's biggest pyramid stack up?

Due to erosion the pyramid is **9 metres (30 ft)** shorter than it was originally.

Weight of largest stone blocks: **14 tonnes (15 tons)**

Number of stone blocks: **2.3 million**

Number of builders: **20,000**

Angle at which the sides rise: **51°52"**

Height: **138 metres (451 ft)**

Angle at which the sides rise

Average length of each side: **230 metres (756 ft)**

MASSIVE DESERT

When it comes to deserts, the Sahara surely stands out! The massive stretch of sand is the largest hot desert in the world, reaching an area of 9.324 million square kilometres (3.6 million sq miles) — slightly smaller than the area of the United States.

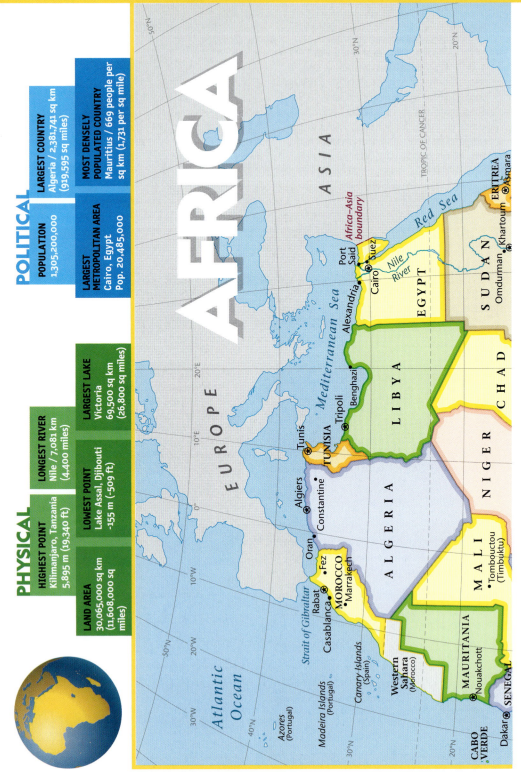

AFRICA

PHYSICAL

HIGHEST POINT
Kilimanjaro, Tanzania
5,895 m (19,340 ft)

LOWEST POINT
Lake Assal, Djibouti
-155 m (-509 ft)

LONGEST RIVER
Nile / 7,081 km
(4,400 miles)

LARGEST LAKE
Victoria
69,500 sq km
(26,800 sq miles)

LAND AREA
30,065,000 sq km
(11,608,000 sq miles)

POLITICAL

POPULATION
1,305,200,000

LARGEST METROPOLITAN AREA
Cairo, Egypt
Pop. 20,485,000

LARGEST COUNTRY
Algeria / 2,381,741 sq km
(919,595 sq miles)

MOST DENSELY POPULATED COUNTRY
Mauritius / 669 people per
sq km (1,731 per sq mile)

EUROPE

ASIA

Atlantic Ocean

Mediterranean Sea

Red Sea

Nile River

TROPIC OF CANCER

Africa-Asia boundary

Azores (Portugal)

Madeira Islands (Portugal)

Canary Islands (Spain)

Strait of Gibraltar

Rabat
Casablanca
MOROCCO
Marrakech
Fez
Oran
Algiers
Constantine

TUNISIA
Tunis

Tripoli
Benghazi

LIBYA

ALGERIA

Western Sahara (Morocco)

MAURITANIA
Nouakchott

SENEGAL
Dakar

CABO VERDE

MALI
Tombouctou (Timbuktu)

NIGER

CHAD

EGYPT
Alexandria
Cairo
Port Said
Suez

SUDAN
Omdurman
Khartoum

ERITREA
Asmara

Map Key
- ⊛ National capital
- • Other city
- ▲ Highest point (above sea level)
- ▼ Lowest point (below sea level)

Atlantic Ocean

Indian Ocean

Mozambique Channel

Gulf of Aden

SOMALIA
Mogadishu
SOMALILAND
DJIBOUTI Djibouti
Lake Assal (-155 m) -509 ft ▼
Addis Ababa
ETHIOPIA
SOUTH SUDAN
Juba
DARFUR
CENTRAL AFRICAN REPUBLIC
Bangui
N'Djamena
CAMEROON
Yaoundé
Douala
Malabo
EQUATORIAL GUINEA
São Tomé
SAO TOME & PRINCIPE
GABON
Libreville
Brazzaville
CONGO
Pointe-Noire
Cabinda (Angola)
Kinshasa
DEMOCRATIC REPUBLIC OF THE CONGO
Kisangani
Mbuji-Mayi
Kananga
Luanda
ANGOLA
NAMIBIA
Windhoek
BOTSWANA
Gaborone
NIGERIA
Kano
Abuja
Ogbomosho
Lagos
Porto-Novo
Cotonou
Lomé
BENIN
TOGO
GHANA
Accra
Ouagadougou
BURKINA FASO
Niamey
Bamako
THE GAMBIA
Banjul
GUINEA-BISSAU
Bissau
GUINEA
Conakry
SIERRA LEONE
Freetown
Monrovia
LIBERIA
Yamoussoukro
CÔTE D'IVOIRE (IVORY COAST)
Abidjan
UGANDA
Kampala
Lake Victoria
KENYA
Nairobi
Kilimanjaro 19,340 ft (5,895 m) ▲
Mombasa
Dar es Salaam
TANZANIA
Dodoma
RWANDA
Kigali
BURUNDI
Gitega
Bujumbura
MALAWI
Lilongwe
ZAMBIA
Lusaka
Lubumbashi
Kitwe
Kolwezi
Kanzani
ZIMBABWE
Harare
MOZAMBIQUE
Maputo
ESWATINI (SWAZILAND)
Lobamba
Mbabane
LESOTHO
Maseru
SOUTH AFRICA
Pretoria (Tshwane)
Johannesburg
Bloemfontein
Durban
Port Elizabeth
Cape Town
Victoria
SEYCHELLES
COMOROS
Moroni
MADAGASCAR
Antananarivo
MAURITIUS
Port Louis
Réunion (France)

SEYCHELLES
Victoria ⊛

St. Helena (U.K.)

Ascension (U.K.)

EQUATOR

TROPIC OF CAPRICORN

0
800 Miles
0
800 Kilometres
Azimuthal Equal-Area Projection

ANTARCTICA

Chinstrap penguin

Chinstrap penguins are named for the narrow black bands under their heads.

Antarctica experiences icequakes, which are like earthquakes that occur within an ice sheet.

This frozen continent may be a cool place to visit, but unless you're a penguin, you probably wouldn't want to hang out in Antarctica for long. The fact that it's the coldest, windiest and driest continent helps explain why humans never colonised this ice-covered land surrounding the South Pole.

Weddell seal

WARMER THAN EVER

With Antarctica experiencing record-breaking high temperatures, the continent as a whole is getting warmer. Temperatures hovering near 21°C (70°F) in February 2020 make the area one of the fastest-warming regions on Earth. Experts are racing to come up with ways to slow the effects of these dangerously high temps — and to save Antarctica from global warming's wrath.

GOING THE DISTANCE

Each year, a few dozen runners from around the world compete in the Antarctic Ice Marathon, where participants face an average temperature with windchill of -20°C (-4°F).

Annual Average Snowfall

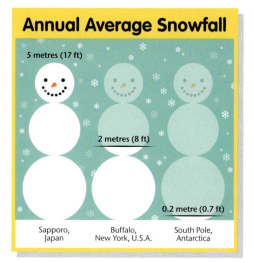

5 metres (17 ft)

2 metres (8 ft)

0.2 metre (0.7 ft)

| Sapporo, Japan | Buffalo, New York, U.S.A. | South Pole, Antarctica |

SEEING GREEN

Emerald icebergs? Only in Antarctica! Here you can spot these rare and beautiful bergs in a deep green hue. So how do these icebergs acquire their stunning shade? Experts say it could be a combo of the bluish tint of glacial ice and yellow-red glacial dust dredged up from deep below the surface.

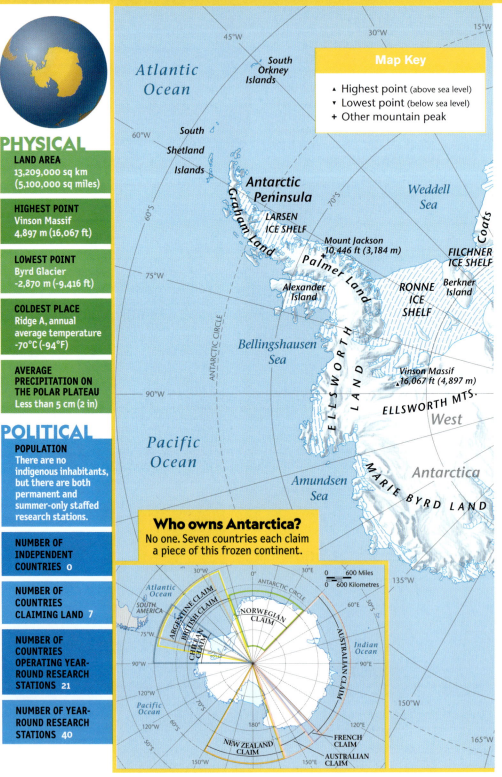

PHYSICAL

LAND AREA
13,209,000 sq km
(5,100,000 sq miles)

HIGHEST POINT
Vinson Massif
4,897 m (16,067 ft)

LOWEST POINT
Byrd Glacier
-2,870 m (-9,416 ft)

COLDEST PLACE
Ridge A, annual
average temperature
-70°C (-94°F)

**AVERAGE
PRECIPITATION ON
THE POLAR PLATEAU**
Less than 5 cm (2 in)

POLITICAL

POPULATION
There are no
indigenous inhabitants,
but there are both
permanent and
summer-only staffed
research stations.

**NUMBER OF
INDEPENDENT
COUNTRIES** 0

**NUMBER OF
COUNTRIES
CLAIMING LAND** 7

**NUMBER OF
COUNTRIES
OPERATING YEAR-
ROUND RESEARCH
STATIONS** 21

**NUMBER OF YEAR-
ROUND RESEARCH
STATIONS** 40

Map Key

▲ Highest point (above sea level)
▼ Lowest point (below sea level)
+ Other mountain peak

Atlantic
Ocean

South
Orkney
Islands

South
Shetland
Islands

Antarctic
Peninsula

Graham Land

LARSEN
ICE SHELF

Mount Jackson
10,446 ft (3,184 m)

Palmer Land

Alexander
Island

Weddell
Sea

Coats

FILCHNER
ICE SHELF

RONNE
ICE
SHELF

Berkner
Island

Bellingshausen
Sea

ANTARCTIC CIRCLE

Pacific
Ocean

E L L S W O R T H   L A N D

Vinson Massif
▲16,067 ft (4,897 m)

ELLSWORTH MTS.

West

Antarctica

Amundsen
Sea

M A R I E   B Y R D   L A N D

Who owns Antarctica?

No one. Seven countries each claim
a piece of this frozen continent.

Atlantic
Ocean

SOUTH
AMERICA

ARGENTINE CLAIM

BRITISH CLAIM

CHILEAN
CLAIM

NORWEGIAN
CLAIM

ANTARCTIC CIRCLE

AUSTRALIAN CLAIM

Indian
Ocean

Pacific
Ocean

NEW ZEALAND
CLAIM

FRENCH
CLAIM

AUSTRALIAN
CLAIM

0   600 Miles
0   600 Kilometres

ANTARCTICA

FIMBUL
ICE SHELF

RIISER-LARSEN
ICE SHELF

QUEEN MAUD LAND

ENDERBY
LAND

60°E

Indian
Ocean

Land

Valkyrie
Dome

Lambert
Glacier

MacKenzie Bay

AMERY ICE SHELF

75°E

AMERICAN

HIGHLAND

WEST
ICE SHELF

Ridge A

POLAR PLATEAU

East

90°E

South Pole

Antarctica

SHACKLETON
ICE SHELF

TRANSANTARCTIC MOUNTAINS

80°S

105°E

ROSS
ICE
SHELF

Byrd Glacier
-9,416 ft (-2,870 m)

WILKES LAND

Roosevelt
Island

Taylor
Glacier

Ross Island

Mount Erebus
12,448 ft
(3,794 m)

70°S

VICTORIA LAND

120°E

Ross
Sea

Talos
Dome

180°

60°S

Indian
Ocean

0   600 Miles

0   600 Kilometres

150°E   135°E

Azimuthal Equidistant Projection

269

ASIA

A whirling dervish performs in Istanbul, Turkey.

Chicken breast pudding is a popular dessert in Turkey.

China has only one time zone.

Made up of 46 countries, Asia is the world's largest continent. Just how big is it? From western Turkey to the eastern tip of Russia, Asia spans nearly half the globe! Home to more than four billion citizens — that's three out of five people on the planet — Asia's population is bigger than that of all the other continents combined.

Kuala Lumpur, Malaysia

FLYING HIGH

Native to Central Asia, the bar-headed goose can soar at altitudes higher than even helicopters can fly. Powerful lungs and strong wings allow these birds to cross over the Himalaya during their annual migration.

ON THE MOVE

About a third of the population of Mongolia moves seasonally. They live in portable huts called *ger* while travelling up to 112 kilometres (70 miles) on foot to find food sources for their livestock.

SAVING THE SNOW LEOPARDS

Countries with political tensions in Central and South Asia have found something to agree upon. 'Peace parks' — protected stretches of the snow leopard's native habitat — will soon appear in border areas shared by countries who have a history of disputes.

World's Deepest Lakes

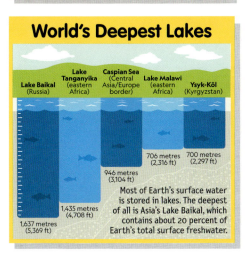

Lake Baikal (Russia)	Lake Tanganyika (eastern Africa)	Caspian Sea (Central Asia/Europe border)	Lake Malawi (eastern Africa)	Ysyk-Köl (Kyrgyzstan)
1,637 metres (5,369 ft)	1,435 metres (4,708 ft)	946 metres (3,104 ft)	706 metres (2,316 ft)	700 metres (2,297 ft)

Most of Earth's surface water is stored in lakes. The deepest of all is Asia's Lake Baikal, which contains about 20 percent of Earth's total surface freshwater.

PHYSICAL

LAND AREA
44,570,000 sq km
(17,208,000 sq miles)

HIGHEST POINT
Mount Everest,
China–Nepal
8,850 m (29,035 ft)

LOWEST POINT
Dead Sea,
Israel–Jordan
-427 m (-1,401 ft)

LONGEST RIVER
Yangtze, China
6,244 km (3,880 miles)

**LARGEST LAKE
ENTIRELY IN ASIA**
Lake Baikal, Russia
31,500 sq km
(12,200 sq miles)

POLITICAL

POPULATION
4,586,900,000

**LARGEST
METROPOLITAN AREA**
Tokyo, Japan
Pop. 37,435,000

**LARGEST COUNTRY
ENTIRELY IN ASIA**
China
9,596,960 sq km
(3,705,405 sq miles)

**MOST DENSELY
POPULATED COUNTRY**
Singapore
8,419 people
per sq km
(21,814 per sq mile)

A commonly accepted division between Asia and Europe — marked here by a maroon, dashed line — is formed by the Ural Mountains, Ural River, Caspian Sea, Caucasus Mountains and the Black Sea with its outlets, the Bosporus and Dardanelles.

EUROPE

Mediterranean Sea

Dardanelles
Bosporus
Izmir
TURKEY
Ankara
ARMENIA
GEORGIA
Tbilisi
Yerevan
Baku
LEBANON
Beirut
SYRIA
Damascus
Jerusalem
Amman
ISRAEL
Dead Sea
-1,424 ft
(-434 m)
JORDAN
AZERBAIJAN
Baghdad
IRAQ
Basra
Tehran
Mashhad
Medina
KUWAIT
Kuwait City
IRAN
Jeddah
SAUDI ARABIA
Manama
Mecca
Riyadh
BAHRAIN
Doha
QATAR
Dubai
Abu Dhabi
Muscat
Sanaa
UNITED ARAB EMIRATES
Aden
YEMEN
OMAN

Line of Russian control

Europe Asia

R   U
Nizhniy Tagil
Yekaterinburg
Tyumen'
Magnitogorsk
Chelyabinsk
Omsk
Nur-Sultan (Astana)
TURKMENISTAN
Qaraghandy
KAZAKHSTAN
UZBEKISTAN
Bishkek
Almaty
Ashgabat
Tashkent
Samarqand
KYRGYZSTAN
Dushanbe
TAJIKISTAN
AFGHANISTAN
Hotan
Kabul
Islamabad
Rawalpindi
Faisalabad
Lahore
PAKISTAN
Delhi
New Delhi
NEPAL
Jaipur
Kanpur
Karachi
Indore
Bhopal
Surat
INDIA
Mumbai
Pune
Hyderabad
Bengaluru
Chennai
SRI LANKA
Colombo
Sri Jayewardenepura Kotte
Male
MALDIVES

AFRICA

Arabian Sea

EQUATOR

Indian Ocean

0   800 Miles
0   800 Kilometres
Two-point Equidistant Projection

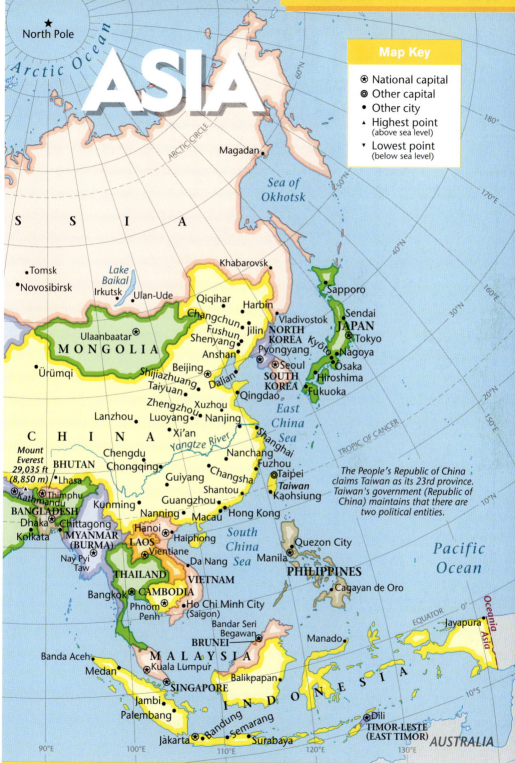

ASIA

Map Key

⊛ National capital
◎ Other capital
• Other city
▲ Highest point
  (above sea level)
▼ Lowest point
  (below sea level)

★ North Pole

Arctic Ocean

ARCTIC CIRCLE

R U S S I A

•Tomsk
•Novosibirsk
Lake Baikal
Irkutsk• •Ulan-Ude

Sea of Okhotsk

Magadan•

Khabarovsk•

Qiqihar• Harbin•
Changchun• •Vladivostok
Fushun• Jilin• **NORTH KOREA**
Shenyang• Pyongyang◎
MONGOLIA
Ulaanbaatar⊛ Anshan•
•Seoul⊛
SOUTH KOREA
Sapporo•
Sendai•
JAPAN
Kyoto •⊛Tokyo
Nagoya•
Osaka•
Hiroshima•
Fukuoka•

•Ürümqi
Beijing⊛
Shijiazhuang• Dalian•
Taiyuan•
Zhengzhou• Xuzhou•
Lanzhou• Luoyang• •Nanjing
Qingdao•

East China Sea

C H I N A
•Xi'an
Yangtze River
Mount Everest 29,035 ft (8,850 m)▲
BHUTAN
Chengdu•
Chongqing•
Nanchang•
Fuzhou•
Shanghai•
◎Taipei
Taiwan
Kaohsiung•

Lhasa•
⊛Kathmandu •Thimphu
BANGLADESH
Dhaka⊛
Guiyang• •Changsha
Shantou•
Kunming•
Guangzhou•
•Hong Kong
•Macau

Kolkata• Chittagong•
MYANMAR (BURMA)
Nanning•
Hanoi◎
Haiphong•

South China Sea

•Quezon City

Pacific Ocean

Nay Pyi Taw◎
LAOS
Vientiane◎
Da Nang•
Manila⊛

THAILAND
VIETNAM
PHILIPPINES
Cagayan de Oro•

Bangkok⊛ **CAMBODIA**
Phnom Penh◎
•Ho Chi Minh City (Saigon)

The People's Republic of China claims Taiwan as its 23rd province. Taiwan's government (Republic of China) maintains that there are two political entities.

TROPIC OF CANCER

Bandar Seri Begawan◎
BRUNEI
•Manado
Banda Aceh•
M A L A Y S I A
Medan•
Kuala Lumpur⊛
Balikpapan•
⊛**SINGAPORE**

EQUATOR Jayapura• *Oceania Asia*

Jambi•
Palembang•
I N D O N E S I A

•Dili
TIMOR-LESTE (EAST TIMOR)

Jakarta⊛ •Bandung •Semarang
Surabaya•

AUSTRALIA

90°E 100°E 110°E 120°E 130°E

273

AUSTRALIA,
NEW ZEALAND AND OCEANIA

Australia has no native hoofed animals.

At birth, a koala is about the size of a bee.

A koala munches on a eucalyptus leaf in Australia.

G'day, mate! This vast region, covering almost 8.5 million square kilometres (3.3 million sq miles), includes Australia — the world's smallest and flattest continent — and New Zealand, as well as a fleet of mostly tiny islands scattered across the Pacific Ocean. Also known as 'down under', most of the countries in this region are in the Southern Hemisphere, below the Equator.

Maori children of New Zealand in ceremonial clothing

COLOURFUL CRITTER

Almost half of known peacock spiders on the planet live in Western Australia. This eight-eyed spider, named for the bright blue markings on the males of the species, can jump a distance of more than 20 times its body length.

FLAT LAND

Australia has mountain ranges with low elevations compared to the other continents of the world. This makes it the flattest continent on Earth. Its highest point? Mount Kosciuszko, which is only about a quarter of the height of Mount Everest.

More Animals Than People

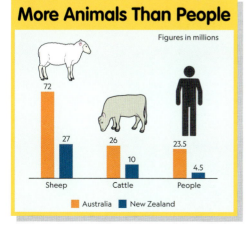

Figures in millions

72
27
26
10
23.5
4.5

Sheep   Cattle   People

■ Australia ■ New Zealand

BEACH IT

Beaches are bountiful in Australia! The continent boasts 10,000 beaches — more than any other country. Whether you're seeking sand, surf or natural beauty, you'll find a beach for that.

PHYSICAL

LAND AREA
8,490,000 sq km
(3,278,000 sq miles)

HIGHEST POINT*
Mount Wilhelm,
Papua New Guinea
4,509 m (14,793 ft)
*Includes Oceania

LOWEST POINT
Lake Eyre, Australia
-15 m (-49 ft)

LONGEST RIVER
Murray-Darling,
Australia
3,672 km (2,282 miles)

LARGEST LAKE
Lake Eyre, Australia
8,884 sq km
(3,430 sq miles)

POLITICAL

POPULATION
42,500,000

**LARGEST
METROPOLITAN AREA**
Melbourne, Australia
Pop. 4,870,000

LARGEST COUNTRY
Australia
7,741,220 sq km
(2,988,901 sq miles)

**MOST DENSELY
POPULATED COUNTRY**
Nauru
476 people per sq km
(1,250 per sq mile)

Map Key

⊛ National capital
• Other city
▲ Highest point
(above sea level)
▼ Lowest point
(below sea level)

Northern Mariana
Islands
(U.S.)
• Capital Hill

Guam
(U.S.)

M i c r o n e

PALAU
Melekeok ⊛

Yap
Islands

Truk Islands

Caroline Islands

Palikir ⊛

FEDERATED STATES
OF MICRONESIA

M e l a n

Oceania–Asia
boundary

PAPUA NEW GUINEA
▲ Mount Wilhelm
14,793 ft
(4,509 m)
Port Moresby

Honiara
Solomon Islands

C o r a l   S e a

Coral Sea
Islands
Territory
(Australia)

A U S T R A L I A

Brisbane

-49 ft
(-15 m)
Lake
Eyre

Perth

Darling River

Murray River

Adelaide
Sydney

Canberra,
A.C.T. ⊛

Lord Howe
Island
(Australia)

Melbourne

Indian
Ocean

Tasman
Sea

Tasmania
• Hobart

0   800 Miles
0   800 Kilometres

Mercator Projection

North Pacific
Ocean

Midway Is.
(U.S.)

TROPIC OF CANCER

Honolulu
Hawai'i
(U.S.)
Hilo

Wake Island
(U.S.)

Monday / Sunday

Johnston Atoll
(U.S.)

Bikini Atoll

MARSHALL
ISLANDS

Ralik Chain
Ratak Chain

Date Line

Kingman Reef
(U.S.)

Palmyra Atoll
(U.S.)

15°N

Majuro

Howland Island
(U.S.)

Kiritimati

Gilbert Islands

Tarawa

Baker Island
(U.S.)

EQUATOR

0°

Yaren
NAURU

Phoenix
Is.

Jarvis I.
(U.S.)

Line Islands

KIRIBATI

SOLOMON
ISLANDS

Santa Cruz
Islands

TUVALU

Funafuti

Tokelau
(N.Z.)

Marquesas
Islands

Wallis and
Futuna Is.
(France)

SAMOA

Apia

American
Samoa
(U.S.)

Pago
Pago

Tuamotu Archipelago

15°S

Port-
Vila
VANUATU

Suva

TONGA

Cook
Islands
(N.Z.)

Society Is.

Papeete

FIJI

Niue
(N.Z.)

Avarua

French Polynesia
(France)

Nouméa

Nuku'alofa

Austral Is.

TROPIC OF CAPRICORN

New
Caledonia
(France)

Norfolk Island
(Australia)

to Easter Island
(Chile)

Kermadec
Islands
(N.Z.)

South Pacific
Ocean

Pitcairn Island
(U.K.)

30°S

AUSTRALIA,
NEW ZEALAND AND OCEANIA

Auckland

NEW

ZEALAND

Wellington

Christchurch

Chatham Island
(N.Z.)

45°S

Date Line

165°E   180°   165°W   150°W   135°W

EUROPE

The Rubik's Cube was invented in Hungary, a country in Europe.

The national animal of Spain is the bull.

Acrobats build human castles at the La Mercè festival in Barcelona, Spain.

A cluster of peninsulas and islands jutting west from Asia, Europe is bordered by the Atlantic and Arctic Oceans and more than a dozen seas. Here you'll find a variety of scenery, from mountains to countryside to coastlines. Europe is also known for its rich culture and fascinating history, which make it one of the most visited continents on Earth.

Traditional dance performed in Greece

MORE TREES

Every time a baby is born or adopted in Wales, U.K., a tree is planted to create new woodlands across the country. Since 2008, more than 300,000 trees have been planted, enough to create some 140 hectares (346 acres) of new woods.

COOL COMEBACK

Bring back the bison! The European bison's numbers are increasing across the continent, thanks to recent conservation efforts. At one point, the animals' population was about 50, but now it is up to around 7,000 in the wild and captivity.

RECYCLING RIGHT

A leader in recycling, Lithuania boasts a rate of 74 percent for recycling plastic packaging — the highest of any European country. Its residents also recycle more than 90 percent of their bottles and cans.

Europe's Longest Rivers

Volga — 3,685 km (2,290 miles)
Danube — 2,848 km (1,770 miles)
Dnieper — 2,285 km (1,420 miles)
Rhine — 1,230 km (765 miles)
Elbe — 1,165 km (724 miles)

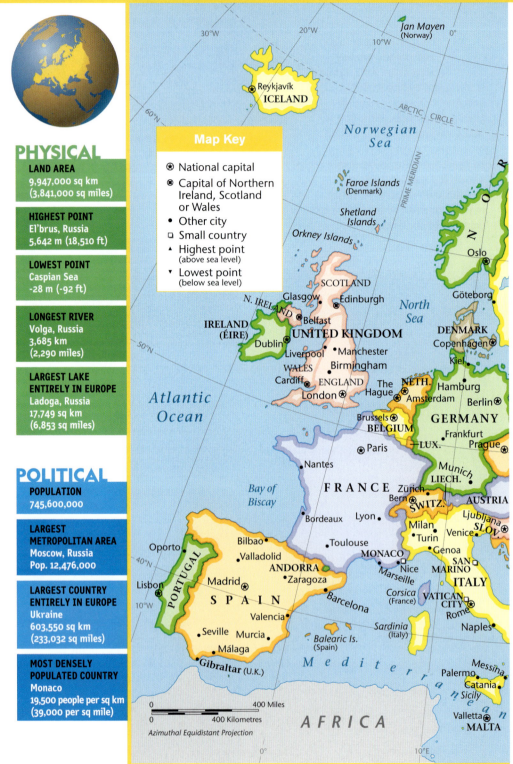

PHYSICAL

LAND AREA
9,947,000 sq km
(3,841,000 sq miles)

HIGHEST POINT
El'brus, Russia
5,642 m (18,510 ft)

LOWEST POINT
Caspian Sea
-28 m (-92 ft)

LONGEST RIVER
Volga, Russia
3,685 km
(2,290 miles)

**LARGEST LAKE
ENTIRELY IN EUROPE**
Ladoga, Russia
17,749 sq km
(6,853 sq miles)

POLITICAL

POPULATION
745,600,000

**LARGEST
METROPOLITAN AREA**
Moscow, Russia
Pop. 12,476,000

**LARGEST COUNTRY
ENTIRELY IN EUROPE**
Ukraine
603,550 sq km
(233,032 sq miles)

**MOST DENSELY
POPULATED COUNTRY**
Monaco
19,500 people per sq km
(39,000 per sq mile)

Map Key

⊛ National capital
⊗ Capital of Northern
   Ireland, Scotland
   or Wales
• Other city
▫ Small country
▲ Highest point
   (above sea level)
▼ Lowest point
   (below sea level)

Jan Mayen
(Norway)

30°W   20°W   10°W   0°

Reykjavík
ICELAND

ARCTIC CIRCLE

60°N

*Norwegian
Sea*

Faroe Islands
(Denmark)

Shetland
Islands

Orkney Islands

SCOTLAND

Glasgow   Edinburgh   *North
Sea*   Göteborg

N. IRELAND   Belfast   DENMARK
IRELAND   UNITED KINGDOM   Copenhagen
(ÉIRE)   Dublin
Liverpool •Manchester   Kiel
WALES   Birmingham   Hamburg
Cardiff   ENGLAND   The   NETH.
London   Hague   Amsterdam   Berlin

*Atlantic
Ocean*   Brussels   GERMANY
BELGIUM   Frankfurt
LUX.   Prague

Paris

Nantes   Munich
LIECH.

*Bay of
Biscay*   F R A N C E   Zürich   AUSTRIA
Bern   SWITZ.   Ljubljana
Bordeaux   Lyon   Milan   SLOV.
Oporto   Turin   Venice
Bilbao•   Toulouse   Genoa
Valladolid   MONACO   Nice   SAN
ANDORRA   Marseille   MARINO
Lisbon   Madrid   Zaragoza   ITALY
S P A I N   Barcelona   Corsica   VATICAN
(France)   CITY
Valencia   Rome
Sardinia   Naples•
Seville Murcia   (Italy)
Málaga   *Balearic Is.*
(Spain)
Gibraltar (U.K.)   M e d i t e r   Palermo   Messina
Catania
Sicily

0   400 Miles
0   400 Kilometres   Valletta
Azimuthal Equidistant Projection   A F R I C A   MALTA

0°   10°E

PRIME MERIDIAN

40°N

10°W

50°N

280

EUROPE

A commonly accepted division between Asia and Europe — marked here by a maroon, dashed line — is formed by the Ural Mountains, Ural River, Caspian Sea, Caucasus Mountains and the Black Sea with its outlets, the Bosporus and Dardanelles.

CRIMEA
Russia invaded Crimea in 2014 and, after secession from Ukraine was approved in a disputed and boycotted referendum held in Crimea, the Russian parliament voted to annex Crimea into the Russian Federation. The United Nations General Assembly subsequently adopted a nonbinding resolution declaring the annexation invalid and affirming Ukraine's territorial jurisdiction. As of 2019, Russia administers and controls all aspects of the peninsula, while Ukraine continues to maintain that Crimea is its sovereign territory.

Barents Sea

Murmansk

Asia
Europe

RUSSIA

Archangel

NORWAY
SWEDEN
FINLAND

Lake Ladoga

Helsinki

St. Petersburg

Stockholm
Tallinn
ESTONIA

Baltic Sea

Riga
LATVIA

Kaliningrad (Russia)

Gdańsk
LITHUANIA
Kaunas
Vilnius

Vitsyebsk
Minsk

BELARUS
Homyel'

POLAND
Warsaw
Bydgoszcz
Łódź
Wrocław
Kraków
CZECHIA
(CZECH REP.)
Vienna
SLOVAKIA
Bratislava
Budapest
HUNGARY
Zagreb
CROATIA
BOSNIA &
HERZEGOVINA
Belgrade
Sarajevo
SERBIA
MONTENEGRO
Podgorica
KOSOVO
Prishtinë
Tirana
N. MACED.
ALBANIA
Skopje
BULGARIA
Sofia

GREECE
Thessaloniki
Athens

Crete

Lake Ladoga

Yaroslavl'
Tver'
Moscow
Ryazan'
Smolensk
Bryansk
Kursk

Volga River
Kazan'
Nizhniy Novgorod
Penza
Saratov

Ufa

Samara Orenburg

KAZAKHSTAN

Volgograd
Astrakhan'

Kyiv
Poltava
Kharkiv
UKRAINE
Donets'k
L'viv
Vinnytsya
Dnipropetrovs'k
Rostov

MOLDOVA
Chișinău
Line of Russian control

Boundary claimed by Ukraine

-92 ft
(-28 m)

Caspian Sea

Odesa
CRIMEA
Simferopol'
Sevastopol'

El'brus
(5,642 m) 18,510 ft
Sochi

Grozny

Baku

ROMANIA
Bucharest

Varna

Black Sea

GEORGIA
AZERBAIJAN

Bosporus

Istanbul

Dardanelles

TURKEY

Sea

NORTHERN CYPRUS
Nicosia
CYPRUS

281

NORTH AMERICA

Guatemala's national bird is the quetzal, and its money is called the quetzal.

Wolf eyes glow in the dark.

A grey wolf walking along a forest trail during autumn in Minnesota, U.S.A.

From the Great Plains of the United States and Canada to the rainforests of Panama, North America stretches 8,850 kilometres (5,500 miles) from north to south. The third largest continent, North America can be divided into five regions: the mountainous west (including parts of Mexico and Central America's western coast), the Great Plains, the Canadian Shield, the varied eastern region (including Central America's lowlands and coastal plains) and the Caribbean.

Onlookers celebrate the opening of the Panama Canal expansion in 2016.

BIG BONES

Canada was once a hotbed of activity for dinosaurs. In fact, the skeleton of the largest *Tyrannosaurus rex* to date was recently uncovered by researchers at a site in Saskatchewan, Canada. Estimated to weigh more than an elephant, the giant dino — nicknamed 'Scotty' — stomped around some 68 million years ago.

BERRY GOOD

The United States is the world's largest producer of strawberries, with some 90 percent of the crops grown in the coastal climates of California. That's about 907 million kilograms (2 billion lb) of strawberries plucked from the state each year! Other top strawberry-producing states? Florida, Oregon, North Carolina and Washington.

BLOW ON

For the first time in history, wind recently surpassed hydroelectricity as the top source of renewable energy in the United States. Currently, the 60,000 wind turbines in the country can power 32 million homes across 41 states.

World's Longest Coastlines

Canada	243,048 km (151,023 miles)
Indonesia	54,716 km (33,998 miles)
Russia	37,653 km (23,397 miles)
Philippines	36,289 km (22,549 miles)
Japan	29,751 km (18,486 miles)

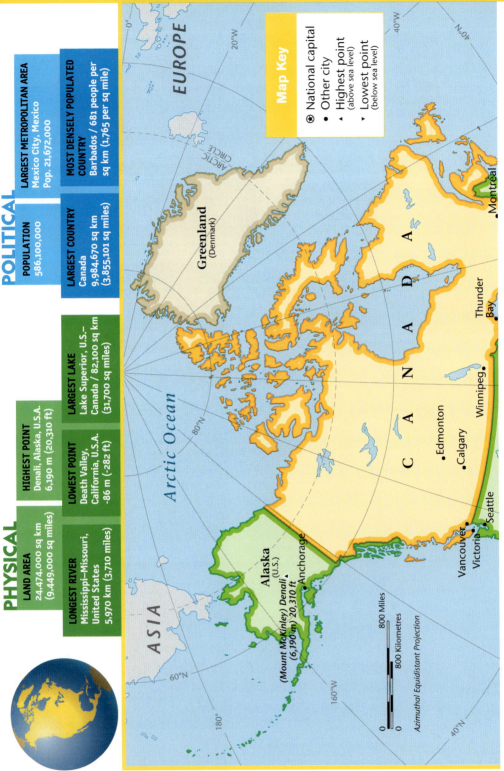

PHYSICAL

LAND AREA
24,474,000 sq km
(9,449,000 sq miles)

LONGEST RIVER
Mississippi–Missouri,
United States
5,970 km (3,710 miles)

HIGHEST POINT
Denali, Alaska, U.S.A.
6,190 m (20,310 ft)

LOWEST POINT
Death Valley,
California, U.S.A.
-86 m (-282 ft)

LARGEST LAKE
Lake Superior, U.S.—
Canada / 82,100 sq km
(31,700 sq miles)

POLITICAL

POPULATION
586,100,000

LARGEST COUNTRY
Canada
9,984,670 sq km
(3,855,101 sq miles)

LARGEST METROPOLITAN AREA
Mexico City, Mexico
Pop. 21,672,000

**MOST DENSELY POPULATED
COUNTRY**
Barbados / 681 people per
sq km (1,765 per sq mile)

Map Key

⊛ National capital
• Other city
▲ Highest point
(above sea level)
▼ Lowest point
(below sea level)

EUROPE

ASIA

Arctic Ocean

ARCTIC CIRCLE

Greenland
(Denmark)

C A N A D A

Montréal

Thunder
Bay

Winnipeg

Edmonton
Calgary

Seattle
Vancouver
Victoria

Alaska
(U.S.)
Denali ▲
(Mount McKinley) Denali
(6,190 m) 20,310 ft
Anchorage

800 Miles
0

800 Kilometres
0

Azimuthal Equidistant Projection

20°W
40°W
40°W
80°N
60°N
180°
160°W
40°N

284

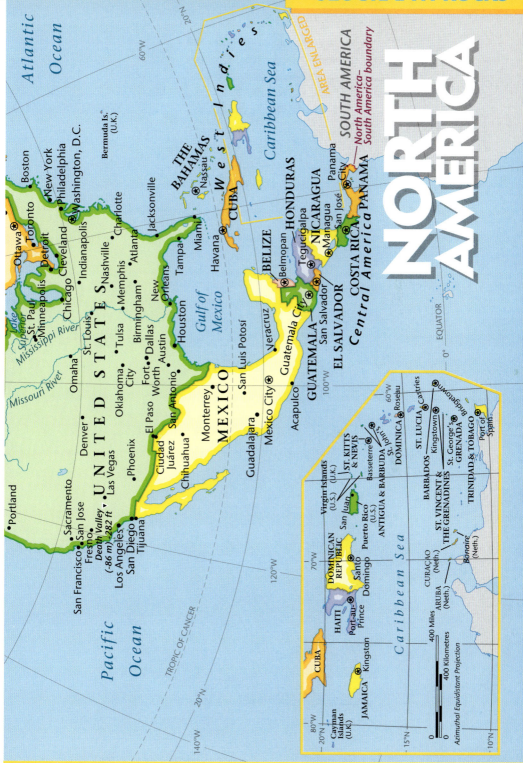

NORTH AMERICA

Atlantic Ocean

Pacific Ocean

UNITED STATES

MEXICO

Gulf of Mexico

Caribbean Sea

West Indies

AREA ENLARGED

SOUTH AMERICA

North America–South America boundary

Central America

Canada/US cities: Portland, Seattle area, San Francisco, Sacramento, San Jose, Fresno, Los Angeles, San Diego, Tijuana, Death Valley (-86 m) -282 ft, Las Vegas, Phoenix, Denver, Omaha, Oklahoma City, Tulsa, Dallas, Fort Worth, Austin, San Antonio, El Paso, Ciudad Juárez, Chihuahua, Monterrey

St. Paul, Minneapolis, Chicago, St. Louis, Memphis, Nashville, Birmingham, New Orleans, Houston, Indianapolis, Cleveland, Detroit, Toronto, Ottawa, Atlanta, Charlotte, Jacksonville, Tampa, Miami

Lake Superior, Mississippi River, Missouri River

Boston, New York, Philadelphia, Washington, D.C.

Bermuda Is. (U.K.)

THE BAHAMAS, Nassau

CUBA, Havana

BELIZE, Belmopan

GUATEMALA, Guatemala City

EL SALVADOR, San Salvador

HONDURAS, Tegucigalpa

NICARAGUA, Managua

COSTA RICA, San José

PANAMA, Panama City

Veracruz, San Luis Potosí, Mexico City, Guadalajara, Acapulco, Monterrey

TROPIC OF CANCER

EQUATOR

0°

20°N

60°W

100°W

120°W

140°W

70°W

80°W

15°N

10°N

20°N

Enlarged Caribbean inset:

Caribbean Sea

CUBA, Kingston

Cayman Islands (U.K.)

JAMAICA, Kingston

HAITI, Port-au-Prince

DOMINICAN REPUBLIC, Santo Domingo

Puerto Rico (U.S.), San Juan

Virgin Islands (U.S.) (U.K.)

ST. KITTS & NEVIS, Basseterre

ANTIGUA & BARBUDA, St. John's

DOMINICA, Roseau

ST. LUCIA, Castries

ST. VINCENT & THE GRENADINES, Kingstown

BARBADOS, Bridgetown

GRENADA, St. George's

TRINIDAD & TOBAGO, Port of Spain

Bonaire (Neth.)

CURAÇAO (Neth.)

ARUBA (Neth.)

400 Miles

400 Kilometres

Azimuthal Equidistant Projection

SOUTH AMERICA

Peru has more than 3,000 kinds of potatoes.

Turtles the size of compact cars once roamed South America.

A woman sells fruit in Chivay, Peru.

South America is bordered by three major bodies of water — the Caribbean Sea, Atlantic Ocean and Pacific Ocean. The world's fourth largest continent extends over a range of climates, from tropical in the north to subarctic in the south. South America produces a rich diversity of natural resources, including nuts, fruits, sugar, grains, coffee and chocolate.

Santiago Cathedral in Santiago, Chile

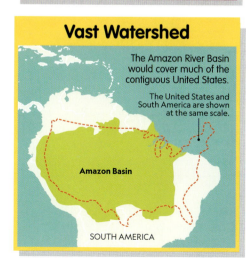

A HOME FOR ELEPHANTS

When elephants are rescued from circuses, where do they go? In South America, they may head to Elephant Sanctuary Brazil, the only rescue centre of its kind on the continent. The centre's 1,130 hectares (2,800 acres) of lush land offers a peaceful place for the pachyderms to roam.

OCEANS ALL AROUND

South America is surrounded by both the Pacific and Atlantic Oceans. Experts think that the two oceans used to be one massive body of water until North and South America joined together at the Isthmus of Panama some three million years ago. That move, scientists think, divided the original ocean into two. Today, Colombia and Chile are the only two countries in South America with a coastline on each ocean.

Vast Watershed

The Amazon River Basin would cover much of the contiguous United States.

The United States and South America are shown at the same scale.

Amazon Basin

SOUTH AMERICA

ANCIENT BRIDGE

Deep in the Peruvian Andes, a suspension bridge made of handwoven grass stretches more than 30 metres (100 ft) over a rushing river. Once used to connect two villages on either side of the river, the bridge, which dates back more than 500 years, is now more of a symbolic nod to the past. Each June, the suspension bridge is rebuilt and replaced by the local indigenous community.

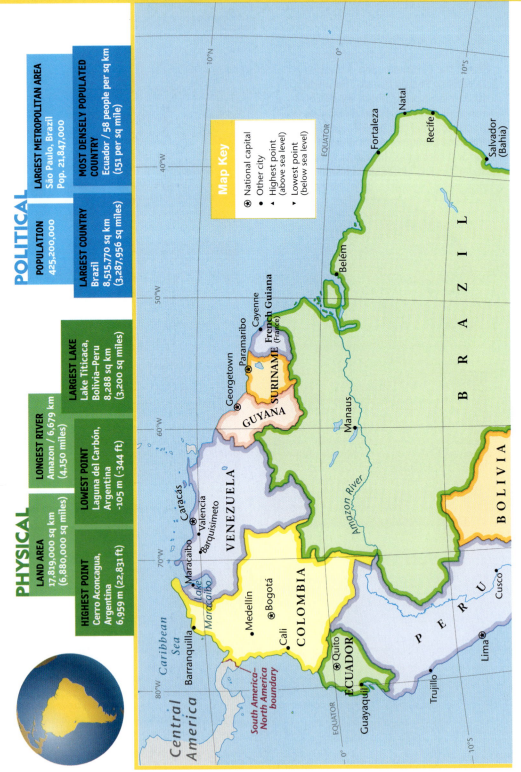

POLITICAL

POPULATION
425,200,000

LARGEST METROPOLITAN AREA
São Paulo, Brazil
Pop. 21,847,000

MOST DENSELY POPULATED COUNTRY
Ecuador / 58 people per sq km
(151 per sq mile)

LARGEST COUNTRY
Brazil
8,515,770 sq km
(3,287,956 sq miles)

PHYSICAL

LAND AREA
17,819,000 sq km
(6,880,000 sq miles)

HIGHEST POINT
Cerro Aconcagua, Argentina
6,959 m (22,831 ft)

LOWEST POINT
Laguna del Carbón, Argentina
-105 m (-344 ft)

LONGEST RIVER
Amazon / 6,679 km
(4,150 miles)

LARGEST LAKE
Lake Titicaca, Bolivia–Peru
8,288 sq km
(3,200 sq miles)

Map Key
⊛ National capital
• Other city
▲ Highest point (above sea level)
▼ Lowest point (below sea level)

Central America

Caribbean Sea

Barranquilla
Maracaibo
Lake Maracaibo
Medellín
Bogotá
Cali

COLOMBIA

Caracás
Valencia
Barquisimeto

VENEZUELA

Georgetown
Paramaribo
Cayenne
French Guiana (France)

GUYANA
SURINAME

Manaus

Amazon River

B R A Z I L

Belém

Fortaleza
Natal
Recife
Salvador (Bahia)

Quito
ECUADOR
Guayaquil

P E R U

Lima
Trujillo
Cusco

B O L I V I A

South America–North America boundary

EQUATOR

288

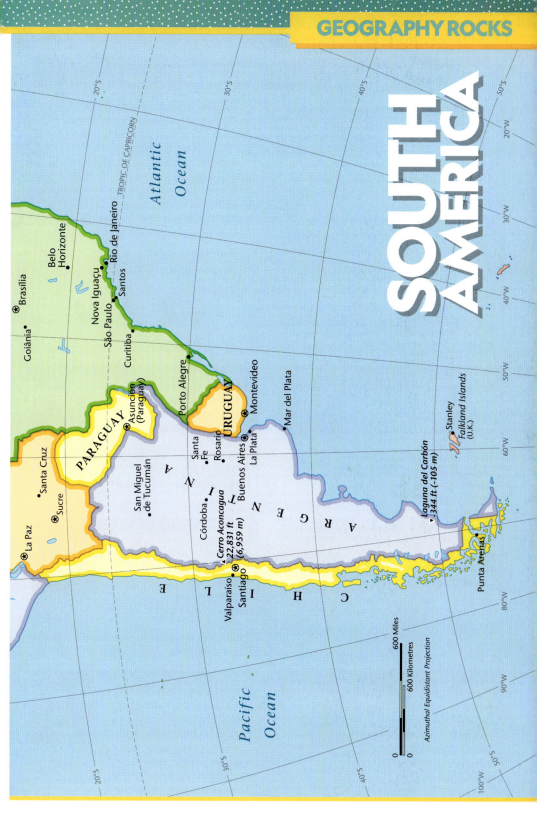

SOUTH AMERICA

Atlantic Ocean

Pacific Ocean

TROPIC OF CAPRICORN

20°S
30°S
40°S
50°S

20°W
30°W
40°W
50°W
60°W
70°W
80°W
90°W
100°W

Brasília
Goiânia
Belo Horizonte
Nova Iguaçu
Rio de Janeiro
Santos
São Paulo
Curitiba
Porto Alegre

Santa Cruz
Sucre
La Paz

PARAGUAY
Asunción (Paraguay)

URUGUAY
Montevideo
Mar del Plata

Santa Fe
Rosario
Buenos Aires
La Plata

San Miguel de Tucumán
Córdoba

ARGENTINA

▲ Cerro Aconcagua
22,831 ft
(6,959 m)

Valparaíso
Santiago

CHILE

Laguna del Carbón
344 ft (-105 m) ▼

Stanley
Falkland Islands (U.K.)

Punta Arenas

600 Miles
600 Kilometres
Azimuthal Equidistant Projection
0
0

COUNTRIES OF THE WORLD

The following pages present a general overview of all 195 independent countries recognised by the National Geographic Society, including the newest nation, South Sudan, which gained independence in 2011.

The flags of each independent country symbolise diverse cultures and histories. The statistical data cover highlights of geography and demography and provide a brief overview of each country. They present general characteristics and are not intended to be comprehensive. For example, not every language spoken in a specific country can be listed. Thus, languages shown are the most representative of that area. This is also true of the religions mentioned.

A country is defined as a political body with its own independent government, geographical space and, in most cases, laws, military and taxes.

Disputed areas such as Northern Cyprus and Taiwan, and dependencies of independent nations, such as Bermuda and Puerto Rico, are not included in this listing.

Note the colour key at the bottom of the pages and the locator map below, which assign a colour to each country based on the continent on which it is located. Some capital city populations include that city's metro area. All information is accurate as of press time.

Colour Key by Continent

Afghanistan

Area: 652,230 sq km (251,827 sq miles)
Population: 34,941,000
Capital: Kabul, pop. 4,114,000
Currency: afghani
Religions: Sunni Muslim, Shia Muslim
Languages: Afghan Persian (Dari), Pashto, Uzbek, Turkmen

Albania

Area: 28,748 sq km (11,100 sq miles)
Population: 3,057,000
Capital: Tirana, pop. 485,000
Currency: lek
Religions: Muslim, Roman Catholic, Orthodox
Languages: Albanian, Greek

Algeria

Area: 2,381,741 sq km (919,595 sq miles)
Population: 41,657,000
Capital: Algiers, pop. 2,729,000
Currency: Algerian dinar
Religion: Sunni Muslim
Languages: Arabic, French, Berber dialects

Andorra

Area: 468 sq km (181 sq miles)
Population: 86,000
Capital: Andorra la Vella, pop. 23,000
Currency: euro
Religion: Roman Catholic
Languages: Catalan, French, Castilian, Portuguese

Angola

Area: 1,246,700 sq km (481,353 sq miles)
Population: 30,356,000
Capital: Luanda, pop. 8,045,000
Currency: kwanza
Religions: Roman Catholic, Protestant, indigenous beliefs
Languages: Portuguese, Umbundu, other African languages

Antigua and Barbuda

Area: 443 sq km (171 sq miles)
Population: 86,000
Capital: St. John's, pop. 21,000
Currency: East Caribbean dollar
Religions: Anglican, Methodist, other Protestant, Roman Catholic
Languages: English, Antiguan Creole

Argentina

Area: 2,780,400 sq km
(1,073,518 sq miles)
Population: 44,694,000
Capital: Buenos Aires,
pop. 15,057,000
Currency: Argentine peso
Religion: Roman Catholic
Languages: Spanish, Italian, English, German, French

Armenia

Area: 29,743 sq km
(11,484 sq miles)
Population: 3,038,000
Capital: Yerevan,
pop. 1,083,000
Currency: Armenian dram
Religions: Armenian Apostolic, other Christian
Languages: Armenian, Russian

Australia

Area: 7,741,220 sq km
(2,988,901 sq miles)
Population: 23,470,000
Capital: Canberra, A.C.T.,
pop. 452,000
Currency: Australian dollar
Religions: Anglican, Roman Catholic, other Christian
Language: English

Austria

Area: 83,871 sq km (32,383 sq miles)
Population: 8,793,000
Capital: Vienna, pop. 1,915,000
Currency: euro
Religions: Roman Catholic, Protestant, Muslim
Languages: German, Turkish, Serbian, Croatian, Slovene, Hungarian

Azerbaijan

Area: 86,600 sq km
(33,436 sq miles)
Population: 10,047,000
Capital: Baku, pop. 2,313,000
Currency: Azerbaijani manat
Religions: Muslim, Russian Orthodox
Languages: Azerbaijani (Azeri), Russian, Armenian

Bahamas, The

Area: 13,880 sq km
(5,359 sq miles)
Population: 333,000
Capital: Nassau, pop. 280,000
Currency: Bahamian dollar
Religions: Baptist, Anglican, Roman Catholic, Pentecostal
Languages: English, Creole

3 cool things about THE BAHAMAS

1. Stretching for 200 kilometres (124 miles), the Bahamas' Andros Barrier Reef is the sixth largest coral reef on the planet.

2. There are 700 islands and islets that make up the Bahamas — and only 30 of them are inhabited.

3. The pink sand on Harbour Island's beach gets its colour from microscopic creatures known as foraminifera, which have bright pink or red shells.

Bahrain

Area: 760 sq km (293 sq miles)
Population: 1,443,000
Capital: Manama, pop. 600,000
Currency: Bahraini dinar
Religions: Muslim (Shia and Sunni), Christian
Languages: Arabic, English, Farsi, Urdu

Bangladesh

Area: 148,460 sq km
(57,321 sq miles)
Population: 159,453,000
Capital: Dhaka, pop. 20,284,000
Currency: taka
Religions: Muslim, Hindu
Language: Bangla (Bengali)

Barbados

Area: 430 sq km (166 sq miles)
Population: 293,000
Capital: Bridgetown, pop. 89,000
Currency: Barbadian dollar
Religions: Protestant, Roman Catholic
Languages: English, Bajan

Bhutan

Area: 38,394 sq km (14,824 sq miles)
Population: 766,000
Capital: Thimphu, pop. 203,000
Currencies: ngultrum, Indian rupee
Religions: Lamaistic Buddhist,
Indian- and Nepalese-influenced Hindu
Languages: Sharchhopka, Dzongkha, Lhotshamkha

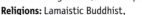

Belarus

Area: 207,600 sq km
(80,155 sq miles)
Population: 9,528,000
Capital: Minsk, pop. 2,017,000
Currency: Belarusian ruble
Religions: Eastern Orthodox, Roman Catholic
Languages: Russian, Belarusian

Bolivia

Area: 1,098,581 sq km
(424,164 sq miles)
Population: 11,306,000
Capitals: La Paz, pop. 1,835,000;
Sucre, pop. 278,000
Currency: boliviano
Religions: Roman Catholic, Protestant
Languages: Spanish, Quechua, Aymara, Guarani

Belgium

Area: 30,528 sq km (11,787 sq miles)
Population: 11,571,000
Capital: Brussels, pop. 2,065,000
Currency: euro
Religions: Roman Catholic, Muslim,
Protestant
Languages: Dutch, French, German

Bosnia and Herzegovina

Area: 51,197 sq km
(19,767 sq miles)
Population: 3,850,000
Capital: Sarajevo, pop. 343,000
Currency: convertible mark
Religions: Muslim, Orthodox, Roman Catholic
Languages: Bosnian, Serbian, Croatian

Belize

Area: 22,966 sq km (8,867 sq miles)
Population: 386,000
Capital: Belmopan, pop. 23,000
Currency: Belize dollar
Religions: Roman Catholic, Protestant
(includes Pentecostal, Seventh-Day Adventist,
Mennonite, Methodist)
Languages: English, Spanish, Creole, Maya

Botswana

Area: 581,730 sq km
(224,607 sq miles)
Population: 2,249,000
Capital: Gaborone, pop. 269,000
Currency: pula
Religions: Christian, Badimo
Languages: Setswana, Sekalanga, Sekgalagadi, English

Benin

Area: 112,622 sq km (43,484 sq miles)
Population: 11,341,000
Capitals: Porto-Novo, pop. 285,000;
Cotonou, pop. 688,000
Currency: Communauté Financière Africaine franc
Religions: Muslim, Roman Catholic, Protestant, Vodoun
Languages: French, Fon, Yoruba, tribal languages

Brazil

Area: 8,514,877 sq km
(3,287,611 sq miles)
Population: 208,847,000
Capital: Brasília, pop. 4,559,000
Currency: Brazilian real
Religions: Roman Catholic, Protestant
Language: Portuguese

Brunei

Area: 5,765 sq km
(2,226 sq miles)
Population: 451,000
Capital: Bandar Seri Begawan,
pop. 241,000
Currency: Brunei dollar
Religions: Muslim, Christian, Buddhist, indigenous beliefs
Languages: Malay, English, Chinese

Burkina Faso

Area: 274,200 sq km
(105,869 sq miles)
Population: 19,743,000
Capital: Ouagadougou,
pop. 2,653,000
Currency: Communauté Financière Africaine franc
Religions: Muslim, Catholic, animist
Languages: French, African languages

Bulgaria

Area: 110,879 sq km
(42,811 sq miles)
Population: 7,058,000
Capital: Sofia, pop. 1,277,000
Currency: Bulgarian lev
Religions: Eastern Orthodox, Muslim
Languages: Bulgarian, Turkish, Romany

Burundi

Area: 27,830 sq km (10,745 sq miles)
Population: 11,845,000
Capital: Bujumbura, pop. 954,000;
Gitega, pop. 120,000
Currency: Burundi franc
Religions: Roman Catholic, Protestant, Muslim
Languages: Kirundi, French, Swahili

SNAPSHOT Bhutan

A sacred site, Paro Taktsang — or Tiger's Nest Monastery — sits at the edge of a cliff some 915 metres (3,000 ft) above Paro, Bhutan.

● Asia ● Europe ● North America ● South America

Cabo Verde

Area: 4,033 sq km (1,557 sq miles)
Population: 568,000
Capital: Praia, pop. 168,000
Currency: Cape Verdean escudo
Religions: Roman Catholic, Protestant
Languages: Portuguese, Crioulo

Cameroon

Area: 475,440 sq km (183,568 sq miles)
Population: 25,641,000
Capital: Yaoundé, pop. 3,822,000
Currency: Communauté Financière Africaine franc
Religions: Roman Catholic, Protestant, Muslim, animist
Languages: African languages, English, French

Cambodia

Area: 181,035 sq km (69,898 sq miles)
Population: 16,450,000
Capital: Phnom Penh, pop. 2,014,000
Currency: riel
Religion: Buddhist
Language: Khmer

Canada

Area: 9,984,670 sq km (3,855,101 sq miles)
Population: 35,882,000
Capital: Ottawa, pop. 1,378,000
Currency: Canadian dollar
Religions: Roman Catholic, Protestant
Languages: English, French

SNAPSHOT Chile

A visitor gazes at the massive 'Mano del Desierto' ('Hand of the Desert') sculpture in Antofagasta, Chile.

COLOUR KEY ● Africa ● Australia, New Zealand and Oceania

Central African Republic

Area: 622,984 sq km (240,535 sq miles)
Population: 5,745,000
Capital: Bangui, pop. 870,000
Currency: Communauté Financière Africaine franc
Religions: Indigenous beliefs, Protestant, Roman Catholic, Muslim
Languages: French, Sangho, tribal languages

Comoros

Area: 2,235 sq km (863 sq miles)
Population: 821,000
Capital: Moroni, pop. 62,000
Currency: Comoran franc
Religion: Sunni Muslim
Languages: Arabic, French, Shikomoro

Chad

Area: 1,284,000 sq km (495,755 sq miles)
Population: 15,833,000
Capital: N'Djamena, pop. 1,372,000
Currency: Communauté Financière Africaine franc
Religions: Muslim, Protestant, Roman Catholic, animist
Languages: French, Arabic, Sara, indigenous languages

Congo

Area: 342,000 sq km (132,047 sq miles)
Population: 5,062,000
Capital: Brazzaville, pop. 2,308,000
Currency: Communauté Financière Africaine franc
Religions: Christian, animist, Muslim
Languages: French, Lingala, Monokutuba, Kikongo, local languages

Chile

Area: 756,102 sq km (291,932 sq miles)
Population: 17,925,000
Capital: Santiago, pop. 6,724,000
Currency: Chilean peso
Religions: Roman Catholic, Protestant
Languages: Spanish, English, indigenous languages

Costa Rica

Area: 51,100 sq km (19,730 sq miles)
Population: 4,987,000
Capital: San José, pop. 1,379,000
Currency: Costa Rican colón
Religions: Roman Catholic, Evangelical
Languages: Spanish, English

China

Area: 9,596,960 sq km (3,705,405 sq miles)
Population: 1,384,689,000
Capital: Beijing, pop. 20,035,000
Currency: yuan
Religions: folk religion, Buddhist, Christian
Languages: Standard Chinese or Mandarin, Yue or Cantonese, Wu, Minbei, Minnan, Xiang, Gan, regional

Côte d'Ivoire (Ivory Coast)

Area: 322,463 sq km (124,504 sq miles)
Population: 26,261,000
Capitals: Abidjan, pop. 5,059,000; Yamoussoukro, pop. 231,000
Currency: Communauté Financière Africaine franc
Religions: Muslim, Christian, indigenous beliefs
Languages: French, Dioula, native dialects

Colombia

Area: 1,138,910 sq km (439,735 sq miles)
Population: 48,169,000
Capital: Bogotá, pop. 10,779,000
Currency: Colombian peso
Religions: Roman Catholic, Protestant
Language: Spanish

Croatia

Area: 56,594 sq km (21,851 sq miles)
Population: 4,270,000
Capital: Zagreb, pop. 685,000
Currency: kuna
Religions: Roman Catholic, Orthodox
Languages: Croatian, Serbian

● Asia ● Europe ● North America ● South America

Cuba

Area: 110,860 sq km
(42,803 sq miles)
Population: 11,116,000
Capital: Havana, pop. 2,138,000
Currencies: Cuban peso, peso convertible
Religion: Roman Catholic
Language: Spanish

Cyprus

Area: 9,251 sq km (3,572 sq miles)
Population: 1,237,000
Capital: Nicosia, pop. 269,000
Currency: euro
Religions: Greek Orthodox, Muslim
Languages: Greek, Turkish, English

Czechia (Czech Republic)

Area: 78,867 sq km (30,451 sq miles)
Population: 10,686,000
Capital: Prague, pop. 1,299,000
Currency: Czech koruny
Religions: Roman Catholic, Protestant
Languages: Czech, Slovak

Democratic Republic of the Congo

Area: 2,344,858 sq km
(905,354 sq miles)
Population: 85,281,000
Capital: Kinshasa, pop. 13,743,000
Currency: Congolese franc
Religions: Roman Catholic, Protestant, Kimbanguist, Muslim
Languages: French, Lingala, Kingwana, Kikongo, Tshiluba

Denmark

Area: 43,094 sq km
(16,639 sq miles)
Population: 5,810,000
Capital: Copenhagen, pop. 1,334,000
Currency: Danish krone
Religions: Evangelical Lutheran, Muslim
Languages: Danish, Faroese, Greenlandic

Djibouti

Area: 23,200 sq km
(8,958 sq miles)
Population: 884,000
Capital: Djibouti, pop. 569,000
Currency: Djiboutian franc
Religions: Muslim, Christian
Languages: French, Arabic, Somali, Afar

Dominica

Area: 751 sq km (290 sq miles)
Population: 74,000
Capital: Roseau, pop. 15,000
Currency: East Caribbean dollar
Religions: Roman Catholic, Protestant
Languages: English, French patois

Dominican Republic

Area: 48,670 sq km
(18,792 sq miles)
Population: 10,299,000
Capital: Santo Domingo, pop. 2,245,000
Currency: Dominican peso
Religion: Roman Catholic
Language: Spanish

Ecuador

Area: 283,561 sq km
(109,483 sq miles)
Population: 16,499,000
Capital: Quito, pop. 1,848,000
Currency: U.S. dollar
Religions: Roman Catholic, Evangelical
Languages: Spanish, Quechua, other Amerindian languages

Egypt

Area: 1,001,450 sq km
(386,662 sq miles)
Population: 99,413,000
Capital: Cairo, pop. 20,485,000
Currencies: Egyptian pound
Religions: Muslim (mostly Sunni), Coptic Christian
Languages: Arabic, English, French

El Salvador

Area: 21,041 sq km
(8,124 sq miles)
Population: 6,187,000
Capital: San Salvador,
pop. 1,106,000
Currencies: U.S. dollar, El Salvador colón
Religions: Roman Catholic, Protestant
Languages: Spanish, Nahua

Equatorial Guinea

Area: 28,051 sq km
(10,831 sq miles)
Population: 797,000
Capital: Malabo, pop. 297,000
Currency: Communauté
Financière Africaine franc
Religions: Roman Catholic, pagan practises
Languages: Spanish, French, Fang, Bubi

Eritrea

Area: 117,600 sq km
(45,406 sq miles)
Population: 5,971,000
Capital: Asmara, pop. 929,000
Currency: nakfa
Religions: Muslim, Coptic Christian, Roman Catholic
Languages: Tigrigna (Tigrinya), Arabic, English, Tigre,
Kunama, Afar, other Cushitic languages

Estonia

Area: 45,228 sq km
(17,463 sq miles)
Population: 1,244,000
Capital: Tallinn, pop. 441,000
Currency: euro
Religions: Lutheran, Orthodox
Languages: Estonian, Russian

Eswatini (Swaziland)

Area: 17,364 sq km (6,704 sq miles)
Population: 1,087,000
Capitals: Mbabane, pop. 68,000;
Lobamba, pop. 5,800
Currency: lilangeni
Religions: Christian, Muslim
Languages: English, siSwati

Ethiopia

Area: 1,104,300 sq km
(426,372 sq miles)
Population: 108,386,000
Capital: Addis Ababa,
pop. 4,592,000
Currency: Ethiopian birr
Religions: Ethiopian Orthodox, Muslim, Protestant
Languages: Oromo, Amharic, Somali

3 cool things about ETHIOPIA

1. In an effort to improve deforestation rates, residents across Ethiopia planted more than 350 million trees in 12 hours in 2019, setting a world record.

2. Upon her appointment in 2018, Sahle-Work Zewde became Ethiopia's first female president—and its first woman leader in nearly 100 years.

3. A 'hidden' population of at least 100 lions was recently discovered in and around Ethiopia's Alatash National Park, an area thought to have lost its lions due to hunting and habitat destruction.

Fiji

Area: 18,274 sq km
(7,056 sq miles)
Population: 927,000
Capital: Suva, pop. 178,000
Currency: Fiji dollar
Religions: Protestant, Hindu,
Roman Catholic, Muslim
Languages: English, Fijian, Hindustani

Finland

Area: 338,145 sq km
(130,558 sq miles)
Population: 5,537,000
Capital: Helsinki, pop. 1,292,000
Currency: euro
Religion: Lutheran
Languages: Finnish, Swedish

● Asia ● Europe ● North America ● South America

France

Area: 643,801 sq km
(248,573 sq miles)
Population: 67,364,000
Capital: Paris, pop. 10,958,000
Currency: euro
Religions: Roman Catholic, Protestant, Muslim, Jewish
Language: French

Gambia, The

Area: 11,295 sq km (4,361 sq miles)
Population: 2,093,000
Capital: Banjul, pop. 443,000
Currency: dalasi
Religions: Muslim, Christian
Languages: English, Mandinka, Wolof, Fula

Gabon

Area: 267,667 sq km (103,347 sq miles)
Population: 2,119,000
Capital: Libreville, pop. 824,000
Currency: Communauté Financière Africaine franc
Religions: Christian, Muslim
Languages: French, Fang, Myene, Nzebi, Bapounou/Eschira, Bandjabi

Georgia

Area: 69,700 sq km (26,911 sq miles)
Population: 4,003,000
Capital: Tbilisi, pop. 1,077,000
Currency: lari
Religions: Orthodox Christian, Muslim, Armenian Apostolic
Languages: Georgian, Azeri, Armenian

SNAPSHOT
Ghana

A fisherman repairs a net in Accra, Ghana.

COLOUR KEY ● Africa ● Australia, New Zealand and Oceania

GEOGRAPHY ROCKS

Germany

Area: 357,022 sq km
(137,847 sq miles)
Population: 80,458,000
Capital: Berlin, pop. 3,557,000
Currency: euro
Religions: Roman Catholic, Protestant, Muslim
Language: German

Ghana

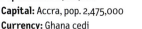

Area: 238,533 sq km (92,098 sq miles)
Population: 28,102,000
Capital: Accra, pop. 2,475,000
Currency: Ghana cedi
Religions: Christian, Muslim, traditional beliefs
Languages: Asante, Ewe, Fante, Boron (Brong),
Dagomba, Dangme, Dagarte (Dagaba),
Kokomba, English

Greece

Area: 131,957 sq km
(50,949 sq miles)
Population: 10,762,000
Capital: Athens, pop. 3,154,000
Currency: euro
Religions: Greek Orthodox, Muslim
Language: Greek

Grenada

Area: 344 sq km (133 sq miles)
Population: 112,000
Capital: St. George's, pop. 39,000
Currency: East Caribbean dollar
Religions: Roman Catholic, Pentecostal,
other Protestant
Languages: English, French patois

Guatemala

Area: 108,889 sq km (42,042 sq miles)
Population: 16,581,000
Capital: Guatemala City,
pop. 2,891,000
Currency: quetzal
Religions: Roman Catholic, Protestant, indigenous
Maya beliefs
Languages: Spanish, Amerindian languages

Guinea

Area: 245,857 sq km
(94,926 sq miles)
Population: 11,855,000
Capital: Conakry, pop. 1,889,000
Currency: Guinean franc
Religions: Muslim, Christian, indigenous beliefs
Languages: French, African languages

Guinea-Bissau

Area: 36,125 sq km
(13,948 sq miles)
Population: 1,833,000
Capital: Bissau, pop. 579,000
Currency: Communauté Financière Africaine franc
Religions: Muslim, Christian, indigenous beliefs
Languages: Crioulo, Portuguese, Pular, Mandingo

Guyana

Area: 214,969 sq km
(83,000 sq miles)
Population: 741,000
Capital: Georgetown, pop. 110,000
Currency: Guyanese dollar
Religions: Protestant, Hindu, Roman Catholic, Muslim
Languages: English, Guyanese Creole, Amerindian
languages, Caribbean Hindustani

Haiti

Area: 27,750 sq km
(10,714 sq miles)
Population: 10,788,000
Capital: Port-au-Prince,
pop. 2,704,000
Currencies: gourde, U.S. dollar
Religions: Roman Catholic, Protestant, voodoo
Languages: French, Creole

Honduras

Area: 112,090 sq km
(43,278 sq miles)
Population: 9,183,000
Capital: Tegucigalpa,
pop. 1,403,000
Currency: lempira
Religions: Roman Catholic, Protestant
Languages: Spanish, Amerindian dialects

● Asia ● Europe ● North America ● South America

Hungary

Area: 93,028 sq km (35,918 sq miles)
Population: 9,826,000
Capital: Budapest, pop. 1,764,000
Currency: forint
Religions: Roman Catholic, Calvinist, Lutheran
Language: Hungarian, English, German

Iraq

Area: 438,317 sq km (169,235 sq miles)
Population: 40,194,000
Capital: Baghdad, pop. 6,974,000
Currency: Iraqi dinar
Religions: Shia Muslim, Sunni Muslim
Languages: Arabic, Kurdish, Turkmen, Syriac, Armenian

Iceland

Area: 103,000 sq km (39,769 sq miles)
Population: 344,000
Capital: Reykjavík, pop. 216,000
Currency: Icelandic krona
Religions: Lutheran, Roman Catholic
Languages: Icelandic, English, Nordic languages

Ireland (Éire)

Area: 70,273 sq km (27,133 sq miles)
Population: 5,068,000
Capital: Dublin (Baile Átha Cliath), pop. 1,215,000
Currency: euro
Religions: Roman Catholic, Church of Ireland
Languages: English, Irish (Gaelic)

India

Area: 3,287,263 sq km (1,269,219 sq miles)
Population: 1,296,834,000
Capital: New Delhi, pop. 29,399,000
Currency: Indian rupee
Religions: Hindu, Muslim, Christian, Sikh
Languages: Hindi, Bengali, Telugu, Marathi, Tamil, Urdu, Gujarati, Kannada, Malayalam, Oriya, Panjabi, Assamese, English

Israel

Area: 20,770 sq km (8,019 sq miles)
Population: 8,425,000
Capital: Jerusalem, pop. 919,000
Currency: new Israeli sheqel
Religions: Jewish, Muslim
Languages: Hebrew, Arabic, English

Indonesia

Area: 1,904,569 sq km (735,358 sq miles)
Population: 262,787,000
Capital: Jakarta, pop. 10,639,000
Currency: Indonesian rupiah
Religions: Muslim, Protestant, Roman Catholic, Hindu
Languages: Bahasa Indonesia, English, Dutch, Javanese, local dialects

Italy

Area: 301,340 sq km (116,348 sq miles)
Population: 62,247,000
Capital: Rome, pop. 4,234,000
Currency: euro
Religion: Roman Catholic
Languages: Italian, German, French, Slovene

Iran

Area: 1,648,195 sq km (636,371 sq miles)
Population: 83,025,000
Capital: Tehran, pop. 9,014,000
Currency: Iranian rial
Religions: Shia Muslim, Sunni Muslim
Languages: Persian (Farsi), Aziri, Turkic dialects, Kurdish

Jamaica

Area: 10,991 sq km (4,244 sq miles)
Population: 2,812,000
Capital: Kingston, pop. 590,000
Currency: Jamaican dollar
Religions: Protestant, Roman Catholic
Languages: English, English patois

COLOUR KEY ● Africa ● Australia, New Zealand and Oceania

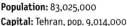

Japan

Area: 377,915 sq km (145,914 sq miles)
Population: 126,168,000
Capital: Tokyo, pop. 37,435,000
Currency: yen
Religions: Shinto, Buddhist
Language: Japanese

Kazakhstan

Area: 2,724,900 sq km (1,052,089 sq miles)
Population: 18,949,000
Capital: Nur-Sultan (Astana), pop. 1,118,000
Currency: tenge
Religions: Muslim, Russian Orthodox
Languages: Kazakh (Qazaq), Russian

Jordan

Area: 89,342 sq km (34,495 sq miles)
Population: 10,458,000
Capital: Amman, pop. 2,109,000
Currency: Jordanian dinar
Religions: Sunni Muslim, Christian
Languages: Arabic, English

Kenya

Area: 580,367 sq km (224,081 sq miles)
Population: 48,398,000
Capital: Nairobi, pop. 4,556,000
Currency: Kenyan shilling
Religions: Protestant, Roman Catholic, Muslim, indigenous beliefs
Languages: English, Kiswahili, indigenous languages

SNAPSHOT
India

Doused in colourful powder and water, friends celebrate Holi, an annual festival in India commemorating spring.

● Asia ● Europe ● North America ● South America

Kiribati

Area: 811 sq km (313 sq miles)
Population: 109,000
Capital: Tarawa, pop. 64,000
Currency: Australian dollar
Religions: Roman Catholic, Protestant
Languages: I-Kiribati, English

Kuwait

Area: 17,818 sq km (6,880 sq miles)
Population: 4,438,000
Capital: Kuwait City, pop. 3,052,000
Currency: Kuwaiti dinar
Religions: Sunni Muslim, Shia Muslim, Christian
Languages: Arabic, English

Kosovo

Area: 10,887 sq km (4,203 sq miles)
Population: 1,908,000
Capital: Prishtinë, pop. 207,000
Currencies: euro, Serbian dinar
Religions: Muslim, Roman Catholic, Serbian Orthodox
Languages: Albanian, Serbian, Bosnian

Kyrgyzstan

Area: 199,951 sq km (77,201 sq miles)
Population: 5,849,000
Capital: Bishkek, pop. 1,017,000
Currency: som
Religions: Muslim, Russian Orthodox
Languages: Kyrgyz, Uzbek, Russian

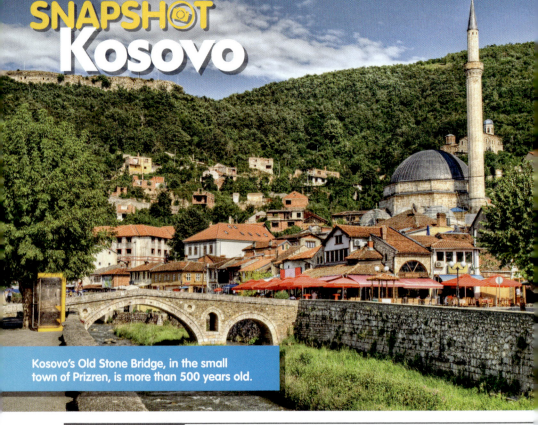

SNAPSHOT Kosovo

Kosovo's Old Stone Bridge, in the small town of Prizren, is more than 500 years old.

COLOUR KEY ● Africa ● Australia, New Zealand and Oceania

Laos

Area: 236,800 sq km
(91,429 sq miles)
Population: 7,234,000
Capital: Vientiane, pop. 673,000
Currency: Lao kip
Religions: Buddhist, Christian
Languages: Lao, French, English, ethnic languages

Libya

Area: 1,759,540 sq km
(679,362 sq miles)
Population: 6,755,000
Capital: Tripoli, pop. 1,161,000
Currency: Libyan dinar
Religions: Sunni Muslim, Christian
Languages: Arabic, Italian, English, Berber

Latvia

Area: 64,589 sq km
(24,938 sq miles)
Population: 1,924,000
Capital: Riga, pop. 634,000
Currency: euro
Religions: Lutheran, Orthodox
Languages: Latvian, Russian

Liechtenstein

Area: 160 sq km (62 sq miles)
Population: 39,000
Capital: Vaduz, pop. 5,000
Currency: Swiss franc
Religions: Roman Catholic, Protestant
Languages: German, Italian

Lebanon

Area: 10,400 sq km (4,015 sq miles)
Population: 6,100,000
Capital: Beirut, pop. 2,407,000
Currency: Lebanese pound
Religions: Muslim, Christian
Languages: Arabic, French, English, Armenian

Lithuania

Area: 65,300 sq km
(25,212 sq miles)
Population: 2,793,000
Capital: Vilnius, pop. 538,000
Currency: euro
Religions: Roman Catholic, Russian Orthodox
Languages: Lithuanian, Russian, Polish

Lesotho

Area: 30,355 sq km (11,720 sq miles)
Population: 1,962,000
Capital: Maseru, pop. 202,000
Currencies: loti, rand
Religions: Protestant, Roman Catholic
Languages: Sesotho, English, Zulu, Xhosa

Luxembourg

Area: 2,586 sq km (998 sq miles)
Population: 606,000
Capital: Luxembourg,
pop. 120,000
Currency: euro
Religion: Roman Catholic
Languages: Luxembourgish, German,
French, Portuguese

Liberia

Area: 111,369 sq km
(43,000 sq miles)
Population: 4,810,000
Capital: Monrovia,
pop. 1,467,000
Currency: Liberian dollar
Religions: Christian, Muslim, indigenous beliefs
Languages: English, indigenous languages

Madagascar

Area: 587,041 sq km
(226,658 sq miles)
Population: 25,684,000
Capital: Antananarivo,
pop. 3,210,000
Currency: Malagasy ariary
Religions: Christian, indigenous beliefs, Muslim
Languages: French, Malagasy, English

● Asia ● Europe ● North America ● South America

Malawi

Area: 118,484 sq km
(45,747 sq miles)
Population: 19,843,000
Capital: Lilongwe, pop. 1,075,000
Currency: Malawian kwacha
Religions: Christian, Muslim
Languages: Chichewa, Chinyanja,
other Bantu languages, English

Malaysia

Area: 329,847 sq km
(127,355 sq miles)
Population: 31,810,000
Capital: Kuala Lumpur,
pop. 7,780,000
Currency: Malaysian ringgit
Religions: Muslim, Buddhist, Christian, Hindu
Languages: Bahasa Malaysia (Malay), English,
Chinese, Tamil, Telugu, Malayalam

Maldives

Area: 298 sq km (115 sq miles)
Population: 392,000
Capital: Male, pop. 177,000
Currency: rufiyaa
Religion: Sunni Muslim
Languages: Dhivehi, English

Mali

Area: 1,240,192 sq km
(478,841 sq miles)
Population: 18,430,000
Capital: Bamako, pop. 2,529,000
Currency: Communauté
Financière Africaine franc
Religions: Muslim, Christian, animist
Languages: French, Bambara, African languages

Malta

Area: 316 sq km (122 sq miles)
Population: 449,000
Capital: Valletta, pop. 213,000
Currency: euro
Religion: Roman Catholic
Languages: Maltese, English

Marshall Islands

Area: 181 sq km (70 sq miles)
Population: 76,000
Capital: Majuro, pop. 31,000
Currency: U.S. dollar
Religions: Protestant, Roman Catholic,
Mormon
Languages: Marshallese, English

3 cool things about the MARSHALL ISLANDS

1. At just 36 years old, the Marshall Islands is one of the world's youngest nations. The chain of 1,200 islands and atolls gained its independence from the United States in 1986.

2. There are some 47 sunken ships and 270 aeroplanes dating back to World War II at the bottom of the Pacific Ocean off the coast of the Marshall Islands. This is a popular spot for scuba divers who flock to the tropical waters to explore the submerged ships and planes lying 30 metres (100 ft) below.

3. First debuted in 1946, the bikini is named after the Marshall Islands' Bikini Atoll. The designer of the two-piece bathing suit gave it the unique name as a nod to the ring-shaped reef, which was in the news at the time during World War II.

Mauritania

Area: 1,030,700 sq km
(397,955 sq miles)
Population: 3,840,000
Capital: Nouakchott, pop. 1,259,000
Currency: ouguiya
Religion: Muslim
Languages: Arabic, Pulaar, Soninke, Wolof,
French, Hassaniya

Mauritius

Area: 2,040 sq km (788 sq miles)
Population: 1,364,000
Capital: Port Louis, pop. 149,000
Currency: Mauritius rupee
Religions: Hindu, Roman Catholic,
Muslim, other Christian
Languages: Creole, Bhojpuri, French, English

COLOUR KEY ● Africa ● Australia, New Zealand and Oceania

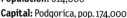

Mexico

Area: 1,964,375 sq km
(758,449 sq miles)
Population: 125,959,000
Capital: Mexico City,
pop. 21,672,000
Currency: Mexican peso
Religions: Roman Catholic, Protestant
Languages: Spanish, indigenous languages

Micronesia

Area: 702 sq km (271 sq miles)
Population: 104,000
Capital: Palikir, pop. 7,000
Currency: U.S. dollar
Religions: Roman Catholic, Protestant
Languages: English, Chuukese, Kosrean, Pohnpeian,
Yapese, other indigenous languages

Moldova

Area: 33,851 sq km
(13,070 sq miles)
Population: 3,438,000
Capital: Chisinau,
pop. 504,000
Currency: Moldovan leu
Religion: Eastern Orthodox
Languages: Moldovan, Russian, Gagauz

Monaco

Area: 2 sq km (1 sq mile)
Population: 39,000
Capital: Monaco, pop. 39,000
Currency: euro
Religion: Roman Catholic
Languages: French, English, Italian, Monegasque

Mongolia

Area: 1,564,116 sq km
(603,908 sq miles)
Population: 3,103,000
Capital: Ulaanbaatar,
pop. 1,553,000
Currency: tugrik
Religions: Buddhist, Muslim, Shamanist, Christian
Languages: Mongolian, Turkic, Russian

Montenegro

Area: 13,812 sq km
(5,333 sq miles)
Population: 614,000
Capital: Podgorica, pop. 174,000
Currency: euro
Religions: Orthodox, Muslim, Roman Catholic
Languages: Serbian, Montenegrin,
Bosnian, Albanian

Morocco

Area: 446,550 sq km
(172,414 sq miles)
Population: 34,314,000
Capital: Rabat, pop. 1,865,000
Currency: Moroccan dirham
Religion: Muslim
Languages: Arabic, Berber languages,
Tamazight, French

MOROCCO is home to the WORLD'S OLDEST UNIVERSITY, dating back to the NINTH CENTURY.

Mozambique

Area: 799,380 sq km
(308,642 sq miles)
Population: 27,234,000
Capital: Maputo, pop. 1,104,000
Currency: Mozambique metical
Religions: Christian, Muslim
Languages: Emakhuwa, Portuguese, Xichangana,
Cisena, Elomwe, Echuwabo, other local languages

Myanmar (Burma)

Area: 676,578 sq km
(261,228 sq miles)
Population: 55,623,000
Capital: Nay Pyi Taw,
pop. 1,176,000
Currency: kyat
Religions: Buddhist, Christian, Muslim
Languages: Burmese, ethnic languages

● Asia   ● Europe   ● North America   ● South America

Namibia

Area: 824,292 sq km
(318,261 sq miles)
Population: 2,533,000
Capital: Windhoek, pop. 417,000
Currencies: Namibian dollar,
South African rand
Religion: Christian
Languages: Indigenous languages, Afrikaans, English

Nepal

Area: 147,181 sq km
(56,827 sq miles)
Population: 29,718,000
Capital: Kathmandu, pop. 1,376,000
Currency: Nepalese rupee
Religions: Hindu, Buddhist, Muslim, Kirant
Languages: Nepali, Maithali, Bhojpuri, Tharu,
Tamang, Newar, Magar, Bajjika, Awadhi

Nauru

Area: 21 sq km (8 sq miles)
Population: 10,000
Capital: Yaren, pop. 1,000
Currency: Australian dollar
Religions: Protestant, Roman Catholic
Languages: Nauruan, English

Netherlands

Area: 41,543 sq km
(16,040 sq miles)
Population: 17,151,000
Capitals: Amsterdam, pop. 1,140,000;
The Hague, pop. 685,000
Currency: euro
Religions: Roman Catholic, Protestant, Muslim
Languages: Dutch, Frisian

SNAPSHOT
Norway

The brightly painted buildings along the Nidelva River in Trondheim, Norway, date back to the 18th century.

COLOUR KEY ● **Africa** ● **Australia, New Zealand and Oceania**

New Zealand

Area: 268,838 sq km
(103,799 sq miles)
Population: 4,546,000
Capital: Wellington, pop. 413,000
Currency: New Zealand dollar
Religions: Protestant, Roman Catholic,
Hindu, Buddhist, Maori Christian
Languages: English, Maori

North Macedonia

Area: 25,713 sq km
(9,928 sq miles)
Population: 2,119,000
Capital: Skopje, pop. 590,000
Currency: denar
Religions: Macedonian Orthodox, Muslim
Languages: Macedonian, Albanian, Turkish, Romany,
Aromanian, Serbian

Nicaragua

Area: 130,370 sq km
(50,336 sq miles)
Population: 6,085,000
Capital: Managua, pop. 1,055,000
Currency: córdoba oro
Religions: Roman Catholic, Protestant
Languages: Spanish, Miskito

Norway

Area: 323,802 sq km
(125,021 sq miles)
Population: 5,372,000
Capital: Oslo, pop. 1,027,000
Currency: Norwegian krone
Religion: Lutheran
Languages: Bokmal Norwegian, Nynorsk
Norwegian, Sami, Finnish

Niger

Area: 1,267,000 sq km
(489,191 sq miles)
Population: 19,866,000
Capital: Niamey, pop. 1,252,000
Currency: Communauté
Financière Africaine franc
Religion: Muslim
Languages: French, Hausa, Djerma

Oman

Area: 309,500 sq km
(119,499 sq miles)
Population: 4,613,000
Capital: Muscat, pop. 1,502,000
Currency: Omani rial
Religions: Muslim, Christian, Hindu
Languages: Arabic, English, Baluchi,
Urdu, Indian dialects

Nigeria

Area: 923,768 sq km
(356,669 sq miles)
Population: 203,453,000
Capital: Abuja, pop. 3,095,000
Currency: naira
Religions: Muslim, Christian, indigenous beliefs
Languages: English, Hausa, Yoruba,
Igbo (Ibo), Fulani

Pakistan

Area: 796,095 sq km
(307,374 sq miles)
Population: 207,863,000
Capital: Islamabad, pop. 1,095,000
Currency: Pakistani rupee
Religions: Sunni Muslim, Shia Muslim
Languages: Punjabi, Sindhi, Saraiki, Pashto, Urdu,
Baluchi, Hindko, Brahui, English, Burushaski

North Korea

Area: 120,538 sq km
(46,540 sq miles)
Population: 25,381,000
Capital: Pyongyang,
pop. 3,061,000
Currency: North Korean won
Religions: Buddhist, Confucianist, some Christian
Language: Korean

Palau

Area: 459 sq km (177 sq miles)
Population: 22,000
Capital: Ngerulmud
(on Babeldaob), pop. 277
Currency: U.S. dollar
Religions: Roman Catholic, Protestant, Modekngei
Languages: Palauan, Filipino, English

Panama

Area: 75,420 sq km (29,120 sq miles)
Population: 3,801,000
Capital: Panama City, pop. 1,822,000
Currency: U.S. dollar
Religions: Roman Catholic, Protestant
Languages: Spanish, English

Papua New Guinea

Area: 462,840 sq km (178,703 sq miles)
Population: 7,027,000
Capital: Port Moresby, pop. 375,000
Currency: kina
Religions: Protestant, Roman Catholic
Languages: Tok Pisin, English, Hiri Motu, other indigenous languages

Paraguay

Area: 406,752 sq km (157,048 sq miles)
Population: 7,026,000
Capital: Asunción (Paraguay), pop. 3,279,000
Currency: guaraní
Religions: Roman Catholic, Protestant
Languages: Spanish, Guarani

Peru

Area: 1,285,216 sq km (496,224 sq miles)
Population: 31,331,000
Capital: Lima, pop. 10,555,000
Currency: sol
Religions: Roman Catholic, Evangelical
Languages: Spanish, Quechua, Aymara

Philippines

Area: 300,000 sq km (115,831 sq miles)
Population: 105,893,000
Capital: Manila, pop. 13,699,000
Currency: Philippine peso
Religions: Roman Catholic, Protestant, Muslim
Languages: Filipino (Tagalog), English

Poland

Area: 312,685 sq km (120,728 sq miles)
Population: 38,421,000
Capital: Warsaw, pop. 1,776,000
Currency: zloty
Religion: Roman Catholic
Language: Polish

Portugal

Area: 92,090 sq km (35,556 sq miles)
Population: 10,355,000
Capital: Lisbon, pop. 2,942,000
Currency: euro
Religion: Roman Catholic
Languages: Portuguese, Mirandese

Qatar

Area: 11,586 sq km (4,473 sq miles)
Population: 2,364,000
Capital: Doha, pop. 637,000
Currency: Qatari rial
Religions: Muslim, Christian
Languages: Arabic, English

Romania

Area: 238,391 sq km (92,043 sq miles)
Population: 21,457,000
Capital: Bucharest, pop. 1,812,000
Currency: Romanian leu
Religions: Eastern Orthodox, Protestant, Roman Catholic
Languages: Romanian, Hungarian

Russia

Area: 17,098,242 sq km (6,601,665 sq miles)
Population: 144,478,000
Capital: Moscow, pop. 12,476,000
Currency: Russian ruble
Religions: Russian Orthodox, Muslim
Languages: Russian, Tatar, other local languages
Note: Russia is in both Europe and Asia, but its capital is in Europe, so it is classified here as a European country.

COLOUR KEY ● **Africa** ● **Australia, New Zealand and Oceania**

Rwanda

Area: 26,338 sq km (10,169 sq miles)
Population: 12,187,000
Capital: Kigali, pop. 1,095,000
Currency: Rwandan franc
Religions: Protestant, Roman Catholic, Muslim
Languages: Kinyarwanda, French, English, Kiswahili (Swahili)

San Marino

Area: 61 sq km (24 sq miles)
Population: 34,000
Capital: San Marino, pop. 4,000
Currency: euro
Religion: Roman Catholic
Language: Italian

Samoa

Area: 2,831 sq km (1,093 sq miles)
Population: 201,000
Capital: Apia, pop. 36,000
Currency: tala
Religions: Protestant, Roman Catholic, Mormon
Languages: Samoan (Polynesian), English

Sao Tome and Principe

Area: 964 sq km (372 sq miles)
Population: 204,000
Capital: São Tomé, pop. 80,000
Currency: dobra
Religions: Roman Catholic, Protestant
Languages: Portuguese, Forro

SNAPSHOT
Samoa

A wooden ladder leads down to the To Sua Ocean Trench swimming hole in Upolo, Samoa.

● Asia   ● Europe   ● North America   ● South America

Saudi Arabia

Area: 2,149,690 sq km
(830,000 sq miles)
Population: 33,091,000
Capital: Riyadh, pop. 7,071,000
Currency: Saudi riyal
Religion: Muslim
Language: Arabic

Singapore

Area: 697 sq km (269 sq miles)
Population: 5,996,000
Capital: Singapore,
pop. 5,868,000
Currency: Singapore dollar
Religions: Buddhist, Christian, Muslim, Taoist, Hindu
Languages: English, Mandarin, Malay, Tamil

Senegal

Area: 196,722 sq km
(75,955 sq miles)
Population: 15,021,000
Capital: Dakar, pop. 3,057,000
Currency: Communauté Financière Africaine franc
Religions: Muslim, Roman Catholic
Languages: French, Wolof, Pulaar, Jola, Mandinka

3 cool things about SINGAPORE

1. Singapore's mascot is the merlion, a half-fish, half-lion mythical creature said to represent Singapore's name in Malay, Singapura, which means 'Lion City'.

2. The country's Changi Airport features a butterfly garden, an indoor waterfall, a cinema and Singapore's tallest slide at four stories high.

3. Singapore's 'Night Safari', the world's first nighttime zoo, welcomes guests to check out animals in the dark.

Serbia

Area: 77,474 sq km (29,913 sq miles)
Population: 7,078,000
Capital: Belgrade, pop. 1,394,000
Currency: Serbian dinar
Religions: Serbian Orthodox, Roman Catholic, Protestant
Languages: Serbian, Hungarian, Bosniak, Romany

Seychelles

Area: 455 sq km (176 sq miles)
Population: 95,000
Capital: Victoria, pop. 28,000
Currency: Seychelles rupee
Religions: Roman Catholic, Protestant, Hindu, Muslim
Languages: Seychellois Creole, English, French

Slovakia

Area: 49,035 sq km
(18,933 sq miles)
Population: 5,445,000
Capital: Bratislava, pop. 433,000
Currency: euro
Religions: Roman Catholic, Protestant, Greek Catholic
Languages: Slovak, Hungarian, Romany

Sierra Leone

Area: 71,740 sq km
(27,699 sq miles)
Population: 6,312,000
Capital: Freetown, pop. 1,168,000
Currency: leone
Religions: Muslim, Christian
Languages: English, Mende, Temne, Krio

Slovenia

Area: 20,273 sq km
(7,827 sq miles)
Population: 2,102,000
Capital: Ljubljana,
pop. 286,000
Currency: euro
Religions: Roman Catholic, Muslim, Orthodox
Languages: Slovene, Serbian, Croatian, Italian, Hungarian

COLOUR KEY ● Africa ● Australia, New Zealand and Oceania

Solomon Islands

Area: 28,896 sq km
(11,157 sq miles)
Population: 660,000
Capital: Honiara, pop. 82,000
Currency: Solomon Islands dollar
Religions: Protestant, Roman Catholic
Languages: Melanesian pidgin, English,
indigenous languages

Somalia

Area: 637,657 sq km
(246,201 sq miles)
Population: 11,259,000
Capital: Mogadishu, pop. 2,180,000
Currency: Somali shilling
Religion: Sunni Muslim
Languages: Somali, Arabic, Italian, English

South Africa

Area: 1,219,090 sq km (470,693 sq miles)
Population: 55,380,000
Capitals: Pretoria (Tshwane),
pop. 2,473,000; Cape Town, pop.
4,524,000; Bloemfontein, pop. 465,000
Currency: rand
Religions: Christian, indigenous religions
Languages: isiZulu, isiXhosa, Afrikaans, Sepedi, Setswana,
English, Sesotho, Xitsonga, siSwati, Tshivenda, isiNdebele

South Korea

Area: 99,720 sq km
(38,502 sq miles)
Population: 51,418,000
Capital: Seoul, pop. 9,962,000
Currency: won
Religions: Christian, Buddhist
Languages: Korean, English

South Sudan

Area: 644,329 sq km
(248,777 sq miles)
Population: 10,205,000
Capital: Juba, pop. 386,000
Currency: South Sudanese pound
Religions: animist, Christian
Languages: English, Arabic, Dinke, Nuer,
Bari, Zande, Shilluk

Spain

Area: 505,370 sq km
(195,124 sq miles)
Population: 49,331,000
Capital: Madrid, pop. 6,559,000
Currency: euro
Religion: Roman Catholic
Languages: Castilian Spanish, Catalan,
Galician, Basque

Sri Lanka

Area: 65,610 sq km
(25,332 sq miles)
Population: 22,577,000
Capitals: Colombo, pop. 609,000;
Sri Jayewardenepura Kotte, pop. 103,000
Currency: Sri Lankan rupee
Religions: Buddhist, Muslim, Hindu, Christian
Languages: Sinhala, Tamil

St. Kitts and Nevis

Area: 261 sq km (101 sq miles)
Population: 53,000
Capital: Basseterre, pop. 14,000
Currency: East Caribbean dollar
Religions: Protestant, Roman Catholic
Language: English

St. Lucia

Area: 616 sq km (238 sq miles)
Population: 166,000
Capital: Castries,
pop. 22,000
Currency: East Caribbean dollar
Religions: Roman Catholic, Protestant
Languages: English, French patois

St. Vincent and the Grenadines

Area: 389 sq km (150 sq miles)
Population: 102,000
Capital: Kingstown, pop. 27,000
Currency: East Caribbean dollar
Religions: Protestant, Roman Catholic
Languages: English, Vincentian Creole English,
French patois

Sudan

Area: 1,861,484 sq km
(718,723 sq miles)
Population: 43,121,000
Capital: Khartoum,
pop. 5,678,000
Currency: Sudanese pound
Religions: Sunni Muslim, Christian
Languages: Arabic, English, Nubian, Ta Bedawie, Fur

Syria

Area: 185,180 sq km (71,498 sq miles)
Population: 19,454,000
Capital: Damascus, pop. 2,354,000
Currency: Syrian pound
Religions: Sunni Muslim, other Muslim
(includes Alawite), Christian, Druze
Languages: Arabic, Kurdish, Armenian, Aramaic,
Circassian, French

Suriname

Area: 163,820 sq km (63,251 sq miles)
Population: 598,000
Capital: Paramaribo, pop. 239,000
Currency: Suriname dollar
Religions: Protestant, Hindu, Roman Catholic,
Muslim
Languages: Dutch, English, Sranan Tongo,
Caribbean Hindustani, Javanese

Tajikistan

Area: 144,100 sq km
(55,637 sq miles)
Population: 8,605,000
Capital: Dushanbe,
pop. 894,000
Currency: somoni
Religions: Sunni Muslim, Shia Muslim
Languages: Tajik, Uzbek

Sweden

Area: 450,295 sq km
(173,860 sq miles)
Population: 10,041,000
Capital: Stockholm,
pop. 1,608,000
Currency: Swedish krona
Religion: Lutheran
Languages: Swedish, Sami, Finnish

Tanzania

Area: 947,300 sq km (365,754 sq miles)
Population: 55,451,000
Capitals: Dar es Salaam, pop.
6,368,000; Dodoma, pop. 262,000
Currency: Tanzanian shilling
Religions: Christian, Muslim, indigenous beliefs
Languages: Kiswahili (Swahili), Kiunguja (Swahili in
Zanzibar), English, Arabic, local languages

200 DIFFERENT LANGUAGES are SPOKEN in SWEDEN.

Thailand

Area: 513,120 sq km
(198,117 sq miles)
Population: 68,616,000
Capital: Bangkok, pop. 10,350,000
Currency: baht
Religions: Buddhist, Muslim, Christian
Languages: Thai, English

Switzerland

Area: 41,277 sq km
(15,937 sq miles)
Population: 8,293,000
Capital: Bern, pop. 426,000
Currency: Swiss franc
Religions: Roman Catholic, Protestant, Muslim
Languages: German, French, Italian, English, Romansh

Timor-Leste (East Timor)

Area: 14,874 sq km
(5,743 sq miles)
Population: 1,322,000
Capital: Dili, pop. 281,000
Currency: U.S. dollar
Religions: Roman Catholic, Protestant
Languages: Tetum, Portuguese, Indonesian, English

COLOUR KEY ● Africa ● Australia, New Zealand and Oceania

Togo

Area: 56,785 sq km
(21,925 sq miles)
Population: 8,176,000
Capital: Lomé, pop. 1,785,000
Currency: Communauté
Financière Africaine franc
Religions: Indigenous beliefs, Christian, Muslim
Languages: French, Ewe, Mina, Kabye, Dagomba

Turkey

Area: 783,562 sq km
(302,535 sq miles)
Population: 81,257,000
Capital: Ankara, pop. 5,018,000
Currency: Turkish lira
Religion: Muslim
Languages: Turkish, Kurdish,
other minority languages

Tonga

Area: 747 sq km (288 sq miles)
Population: 107,000
Capital: Nuku´alofa
(on Tongatapu), pop. 27,000
Currency: pa´anga
Religions: Protestant, Church of Latter-day Saints, Roman Catholic
Languages: Tongan, English

Turkmenistan

Area: 488,100 sq km
(188,456 sq miles)
Population: 5,411,000
Capital: Ashgabat, pop. 828,000
Currency: Turkmenistan new manat
Religions: Muslim, Eastern Orthodox
Languages: Turkmen, Russian, Uzbek

There are NO TRAFFIC LIGHTS in TONGA.

The GARAGUM DESERT COVERS 70 PERCENT of TURKMENISTAN.

Trinidad and Tobago

Area: 5,128 sq km (1,980 sq miles)
Population: 1,216,000
Capital: Port of Spain
(on Trinidad), pop. 544,000
Currency: Trinidad and Tobago dollar
Religions: Protestant, Roman Catholic, Hindu, Muslim
Languages: English, Creole, Caribbean Hindustani

Tuvalu

Area: 26 sq km (10 sq miles)
Population: 11,000
Capital: Funafuti
(on Funafuti Atoll), pop. 7,000
Currency: Australian dollar
Religions: Protestant, Baha'i
Languages: Tuvaluan, English, Samoan, Kiribati

Tunisia

Area: 163,610 sq km
(63,170 sq miles)
Population: 11,516,000
Capital: Tunis, pop. 2,328,000
Currency: Tunisian dinar
Religion: Muslim
Languages: Arabic, French, Berber (Tamazight)

Uganda

Area: 241,038 sq km
(93,065 sq miles)
Population: 40,854,000
Capital: Kampala, pop. 3,318,000
Currency: Ugandan shilling
Religions: Protestant, Roman Catholic, Muslim
Languages: English, Ganda (Luganda),
local languages, Swahili, Arabic

Ukraine

Area: 603,550 sq km
(233,032 sq miles)
Population: 41,597,000
Capital: Kyiv, pop. 2,973,000
Currency: hryvnia
Religions: Ukrainian Orthodox, Ukrainian Greek Catholic, Roman Catholic, Protestant, Jewish
Languages: Ukrainian, Russian

United Kingdom

Area: 243,610 sq km
(94,058 sq miles)
Population: 65,105,000
Capital: London, pop. 9,177,000
Currency: pound sterling
Religions: Anglican, Roman Catholic, Presbyterian, Methodist, Muslim, Hindu
Languages: English, Scots, Scottish Gaelic, Welsh, Irish

United Arab Emirates

Area: 83,600 sq km
(32,278 sq miles)
Population: 9,701,000
Capital: Abu Dhabi,
pop. 1,452,000
Currency: United Arab Emirates dirham
Religions: Muslim, Christian, Hindu
Languages: Arabic, Persian, English, Hindi, Urdu

United States

Area: 9,833,517 sq km
(3,796,741 sq miles)
Population: 321,004,000
Capital: Washington, D.C.,
pop. 672,000
Currency: U.S. dollar
Religions: Protestant, Roman Catholic, Jewish
Languages: English, Spanish, Native American

SNAPSHOT
Vietnam

Outdoor market in the streets of Hoi An, Vietnam

COLOUR KEY ● Africa ● Australia, New Zealand and Oceania

Uruguay

Area: 176,215 sq km
(68,037 sq miles)
Population: 3,369,000
Capital: Montevideo, pop. 1,745,000
Currency: Uruguayan peso
Religions: Roman Catholic, Protestant
Language: Spanish

**CAPYBARAS —
the world's largest
RODENT — are native
to URUGUAY.**

Uzbekistan

Area: 447,400 sq km
(172,742 sq miles)
Population: 30,024,000
Capital: Tashkent,
pop. 2,049,000
Currency: Uzbekistan sum
Religions: Muslim (mostly Sunni), Eastern Orthodox
Languages: Uzbek, Russian, Tajik

Vanuatu

Area: 12,189 sq km (4,706 sq miles)
Population: 288,000
Capital: Port Vila, pop. 53,000
Currency: vatu
Religions: Protestant, Roman Catholic, indigenous beliefs
Languages: Bislama, English, French, local languages

Vatican City

Area: .44 sq km (.17 sq mile)
Population: 1,000
Capital: Vatican City, pop. 1,000
Currency: euro
Religion: Roman Catholic
Languages: Italian, Latin, French

Venezuela

Area: 912,050 sq km
(352,144 sq miles)
Population: 31,689,000
Capital: Caracas, pop. 2,936,000
Currency: bolívar soberano
Religion: Roman Catholic
Languages: Spanish, numerous indigenous dialects

Vietnam

Area: 331,210 sq km
(127,881 sq miles)
Population: 97,040,000
Capital: Hanoi, pop. 4,480,000
Currency: dong
Religions: Buddhist, Roman Catholic, Hoa Hao, Cao Dai, Protestant, Muslim
Languages: Vietnamese, English, French, Chinese, Khmer

Yemen

Area: 527,968 sq km
(203,850 sq miles)
Population: 28,667,000
Capital: Sanaa, pop. 2,874,000
Currency: Yemeni rial
Religion: Muslim
Language: Arabic

Zambia

Area: 752,618 sq km
(290,587 sq miles)
Population: 16,445,000
Capital: Lusaka, pop. 2,647,000
Currency: Zambian kwacha
Religions: Protestant, Roman Catholic
Languages: Bemba, Nyanja, Tonga, Lozi, Chewa, Nsenga, Tumbuka, English

Zimbabwe

Area: 390,757 sq km
(150,872 sq miles)
Population: 14,030,000
Capital: Harare, pop. 1,521,000
Currency: Zimbabwe dollar
Religions: Protestant, Roman Catholic, indigenous beliefs
Languages: Shona, Ndebele, English

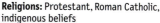
● Asia ● Europe ● North America ● South America

315

EUROPE
A VIEW FROM SPACE

POLITICAL EUROPE

Map Key

⊛ National capital

⊗ Capital of Northern Ireland, Scotland or Wales

• Other city

□ Small country

⬛ Country in the European Union

Reykjavík
ICELAND
ARCTIC CIRCLE

Norwegian Sea

Faroe Islands (Denmark)

PRIME MERIDIAN

Shetland Islands

Orkney Islands

SCOTLAND
Glasgow Edinburgh

N. IRELAND
Belfast

IRELAND (ÉIRE)
Dublin

UNITED KINGDOM
Liverpool Manchester
WALES Birmingham
Cardiff ENGLAND
London

North Sea

Oslo
Stockholm
Göteborg

Copenhagen
DENMARK
Kiel

Baltic Sea

Kaliningrad (Russia)

Gdańsk

Hamburg
Berlin
POLAND
Warsaw
Bydgoszcz
Łódź
Wrocław

The Hague
NETH.
Amsterdam

Brussels
BELGIUM

GERMANY
Frankfurt
LUX.

Paris

Nantes

FRANCE

Atlantic Ocean

Bay of Biscay

Bordeaux
Lyon

Munich
LIECH.
Zürich
Bern
SWITZ.

Prague
CZECHIA (CZECH REP.)
Kraków

Vienna
AUSTRIA
SLOV.
Ljubljana

SLOVAKIA
Bratislava
Budapest
HUNGARY

Oporto
Bilbao
Valladolid
ANDORRA
Zaragoza
Madrid
SPAIN
Valencia
Seville Murcia
Málaga
Gibraltar (U.K.)

Lisbon
PORTUGAL

Toulouse

MONACO
Nice
Marseille

Corsica (France)

Sardinia (Italy)

Balearic Is. (Spain)

Barcelona

Milan
Turin Venice
Genoa

SAN MARINO

VATICAN CITY
ITALY
Rome

Naples

Zagreb
CROATIA
BOSNIA & HERZEGOVINA
Sarajevo

Belgrade

MONTENEGRO
Podgorica

KOSOVO
Tirana
ALBANIA

Mediterranean Sea

Palermo
Sicily
Messina
Catania

Valletta
MALTA

AFRICA

0   400 Miles
0   400 Kilometres

60°N
20°W
50°N
40°N
10°W
0°
10°E
20°E

Barents Sea

Murmansk

FINLAND

Helsinki

Tallinn ⊛
ESTONIA

Rīga
LATVIA
LITHUANIA
Kaunas
Vilnius ⊛
Minsk

BELARUS
Homyel'

L'viv

U K R A I N E
Vinnytsya

MOLDOVA
Chişinău ⊛

ROMANIA

Bucharest ⊛

SERBIA
Prishtinë ⊛
BULGARIA
Sofia ⊛
Skopje ⊛
N. MACED.
Thessaloniki

GREECE
Athens ⊛

Crete

Archangel

R U S S I A

A commonly accepted division between Asia and Europe — marked here by a maroon, dashed line — is formed by the Ural Mountains, Ural River, Caspian Sea, Caucasus Mountains and the Black Sea with its outlets, the Bosporus and Dardanelles.

Asia
Europe

A S I A

St. Petersburg

Yaroslavl'

Tver'

Moscow ⊛

Ryazan'

Vitsyebsk
Smolensk

Bryansk

Kursk

Kyiv ⊛
Poltava
Kharkiv
Donets'k
Dnipropetrovs'k
Rostov

Line of
Russian
control

Boundary claimed
by Ukraine

Odesa
CRIMEA
Simferopol'
Sevastopol'

Varna
Bosporus

Istanbul

Dardanelles

T U R K E Y

NORTHERN CYPRUS
Nicosia ⊛
CYPRUS

Black Sea

Ufa

Kazan'

Nizhniy Novgorod

Samara
Orenburg

Penza

Saratov

Volgograd

Astrakhan'

KAZAKHSTAN

Groznyy

GEORGIA
AZERBAIJAN
Baku ⊛

Caspian Sea

CRIMEA
Russia invaded Crimea in 2014 and, after secession from Ukraine was approved in a disputed and boycotted referendum held in Crimea, the Russian parliament voted to annex Crimea into the Russian Federation. The United Nations General Assembly subsequently adopted a nonbinding resolution declaring the annexation invalid and affirming Ukraine's territorial jurisdiction. As of 2019, Russia administers and controls all aspects of the peninsula, while Ukraine continues to maintain that Crimea is its sovereign territory.

30°E   40°E   50°E   60°E   70°E   60°N

50°N

40°N

PHYSICAL EUROPE

Iceland

Norwegian
Sea

ARCTIC CIRCLE

Faroe Islands

S C A N D I N A V I A

Gulf of

PRIME MERIDIAN

Shetland
Islands

Outer Hebrides

Orkney
Islands

Highlands

Baltic

North
Sea

Jutland

Zealand

Ireland

Irish Sea

Great
Britain

British Isles

Celtic

Thames

N O R T H E R

Sea

Atlantic
Ocean

English Channel

Ruhr Valley

Elbe

Oder

Vistula

Rhine

C

Brittany

Seine

Loire

Danube

Bay of
Biscay

Massif
Central

A L P S

Mt. Blanc
15,781 ft
(4,810 m)

Po

Rhône

Cantabrian Mts.

Douro

Pyrenees

Riviera

Ligurian
Sea

A
p
e
n
n
i
n
e
s

Adriatic Sea

Iberian

Tagus

Ebro

Corsica

Balearic Sea

Peninsula

Sardinia

Baetic Mts.

Balearic Is.

Tyrrhenian
Sea

Strait of
Gibraltar

M e d i t e r r a n e a n

Sicily

Ionian
Sea

Etna
10,899 ft
(3,322 m)

S e a

A F R I C A

| | 400 Miles |
| 0 | 400 Kilometres |

30°W 60°N 20°W 50°N 40°N 10°W 0° 10°E 20°E

North Cape

Barents Sea

30°E   40°E   50°E   70°E   60°N

Kola Peninsula

ASIA

P L A N D

V I A N D

Pechora

U R A L   M O U N T A I N S

White Sea

Bothnia

Northern Dvina

Lake Region

Lake Onega

Kama

Lake Ladoga

Gulf of Finland

Western Dvina

Kama

E U R O P E A N   P L A I N

N

Central

Russian

Upland

Volga

60°E

50°N

Europe
Asia

Sea

Dnieper

Don

arpathian Mts.

Dniester

Volga

Don

Ural

-92 ft (-28 m)
Lowest point
in Europe
(at water level)

Sea of Azov

El'brus
18,510 ft (5,642 m)
Highest point in Europe

Caspian Sea

Crimea

CAUCASUS   MOUNTAINS

Danube

Black Sea

Balkan

Balkan Mts.

40°N

Peninsula

Bosporus

A commonly accepted division
between Asia and Europe — marked
here by a maroon, dashed line —
is formed by the Ural Mountains,
Ural River, Caspian Sea, Caucasus
Mountains and the Black Sea
with its outlets, the Bosporus
and Dardanelles.

Sea of Marmara

Dardanelles

Aegean Sea

Map Key

✛ Mountain peak

Peloponnesus

Crete

Cyprus

30°E   40°E

321

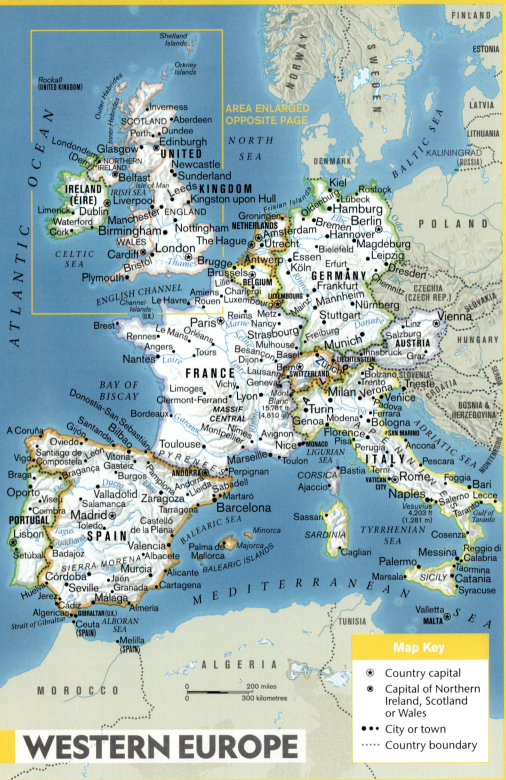

WESTERN EUROPE

Map Key

⊛ Country capital

⊛ Capital of Northern Ireland, Scotland or Wales

••• City or town

••••• Country boundary

AREA ENLARGED OPPOSITE PAGE

SPOTLIGHT ON THE UNITED KINGDOM AND IRELAND

The **UNITED KINGDOM** is made up of four countries: England, Northern Ireland, Scotland and Wales. The flag of the United Kingdom, known as the Union Flag, or Union Jack, combines the three crosses of the patron saints of England (St. George), Scotland (St. Andrew) and Ireland (St. Patrick).

First used in 1848, **IRELAND's** tricolour flag was officially adopted when Ireland became independent in 1922. Today, Ireland has a population of almost 5.1 million.

England's flag features the red cross of St. George on a white background. The English have been using it since the 12th century. England, by far the largest country in the United Kingdom, has around 55.3 million people.

Northern Ireland flies the Union Flag. It has a population of 1.8 million people.

Scotland's flag shows a diagonal white cross on a blue field, known as the Saltire, or St. Andrew's Cross. The English and Scottish flags were combined in 1606 as the flag for the union of England and Scotland. Scotland has a population of about 5.4 million people.

Wales was conquered by England in the 13th century. Considered a principality, not a kingdom, its red dragon flag is not part of the United Kingdom flag. Wales is mountainous, and most of its 3.1 million people live along the coast.

57 percent of residents in southeast SCOTLAND have BLUE EYES.

A 9,000-year-old polished STONE AXE was recently discovered BURIED in LIMERICK, IRELAND.

In WALES, SHEEP OUTNUMBER PEOPLE about three to one.

EASTERN EUROPE

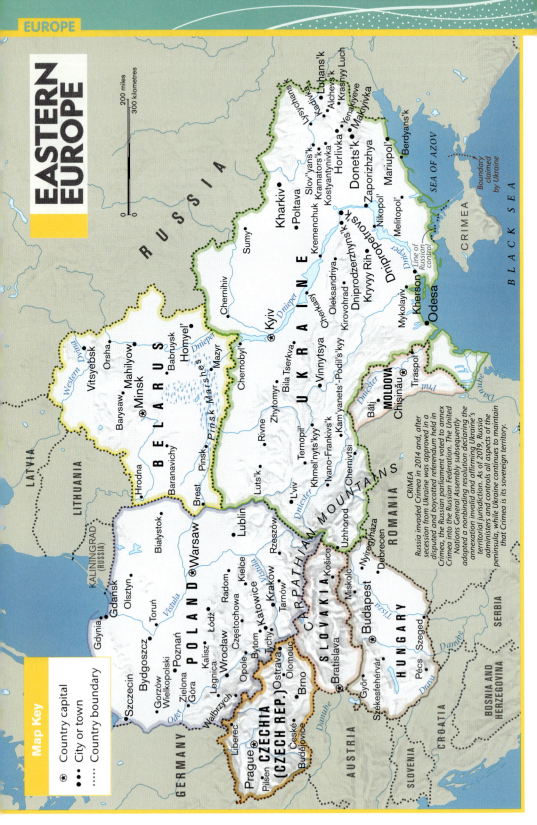

200 miles
300 kilometres

Map Key

⊛ Country capital
• • • City or town
• • • • • Country boundary

RUSSIA

LATVIA

LITHUANIA

KALININGRAD (RUSSIA)

BELARUS

Vitsyebsk
Orsha
Barysaw • Mahilyow
Minsk
Baranavichy
Hrodna
Brest

Western Dvina
Babruysk
Homyel'
Mazyr
Pinsk Marshes
Pinsk

UKRAINE

Sumy
Kharkiv
Poltava
Chernihiv
Kyiv ⊛
Chernobyl'
Zhytomyr
Rivne
Luts'k
L'viv
Ternopil'
Khmel'nyts'kyy
Ivano-Frankivs'k
Chernivtsi
Uzhhorod

Bila Tserkva
Vinnytsya
Kam"yanets'-Podil's'kyy

Kremenchuk
Cherkasy
Oleksandriya
Kirovohrad
Kryvyy Rih
Mykolayiv

Slov"yans'k
Kramators'k
Kostyantynivka
Horlivka
Donets'k
Nikopol'
Melitopol'
Zaporizhzhya
Dnipro
Dniprodzerzhyns'k

Lysychans'k
Sievierodonets'k
Luhans'k
Alchevs'k
Krasnyy Luch
Yenakiyeve
Makiyivka
Berdyans'k
Mariupol'

Kherson
Odesa

SEA OF AZOV

CRIMEA

BLACK SEA

Boundary claimed by Ukraine

Line of Russian control

Dnieper
Dniester

MOLDOVA
Chişinău ⊛
Tiraspol'
Bălţi

ROMANIA

CARPATHIAN MOUNTAINS

Prut
Danube

POLAND

Gdynia
Gdańsk
Olsztyn
Toruń
Bydgoszcz
Szczecin
Gorzów Wielkopolski
Poznań
Zielona Góra
Legnica
Wrocław
Opole
Wałbrzych
Białystok
Warsaw ⊛
Łódź
Radom
Lublin
Kielce
Częstochowa
Katowice
Bytom
Tychy
Kraków
Tarnów
Rzeszów

Vistula
Oder

GERMANY

CZECHIA (CZECH REP.)
Liberec
Prague ⊛
Pilsen
České Budějovice
Olomouc
Brno
Ostrava

SLOVAKIA
Košice
Bratislava ⊛

AUSTRIA

HUNGARY
Miskolc
Nyíregyháza
Debrecen
Budapest ⊛
Győr
Székesfehérvár
Szeged
Pécs

Tisza
Danube
Drava

SLOVENIA

CROATIA

BOSNIA AND HERZEGOVINA

SERBIA

CRIMEA
Russia invaded Crimea in 2014 and, after secession from Ukraine was approved in a disputed and boycotted referendum held in Crimea, the Russian parliament voted to annex Crimea into the Russian Federation. The United Nations General Assembly subsequently adopted a nonbinding resolution declaring the annexation invalid and affirming Ukraine's territorial jurisdiction. As of 2019, Russia administers and controls all aspects of the peninsula, while Ukraine continues to maintain that Crimea is its sovereign territory.

SVALBARD (NORWAY)

North East Land
Spitsbergen
Edgeøya
•Longyearbyen

0 — 200 miles
0 — 300 kilometres

ARCTIC CIRCLE

•Ísafjörður   •Akureyri
Neskaupstaður
ICELAND
Reykjavík   Vatnajökull   •Höfn
•Kópavogur
Keflavík

ARCTIC CIRCLE

0 — 200 miles
0 — 300 kilometres

Map Key

⊛ Country capital
••• City or town
••••• Country boundary

NORWEGIAN SEA

North Cape
BARENTS SEA
Søroya   •Hammerfest
•Tromsø

L A P L A N D

•Ivalo

LOFOTEN   *VESTERÅLEN*
Vestfjorden

•Kiruna
Kebnekaise
6,926 ft
(2,111 m)
•Bodø

•Rovaniemi

•Kemi

N O R W A Y

Ångermanälven   *Umeälven*   •Luleå

•Skellefteå   •Raahe

R U S S I A

F I N L A N D

•Oulu

Tornealven

ATLANTIC OCEAN

•Trondheim   *Trondheimsfjorden*

Norrland   Umeå

Gulf of Bothnia

•Kokkola
Jakobstad

•Kajaani
Nurmes

•Ålesund   •Örnsköldsvik

•Vaasa

•Kuopio
•Joensuu

•Östersund

*Lake
Region*

•Sundsvall

Jyväskylä   •Savonlinna

Galdhøpiggen
8,100 ft
(2,469 m)

S W E D E N

Ljusnan

•Pori   •Tampere

•Mikkeli   •Imatra
•Lappeenranta

•Rauma   •Lahti

•Bergen

•Hønefoss

•Falun   •Gävle

•Turku   **Helsinki**
•Espoo

•Kotka

•Haugesund   Drammen•   ⊛Oslo

Klarälven

Svealand   •Uppsala

*ÅLAND
ISLANDS*

Gulf of Finland

•Narva

•Stavanger   •Skien

Karlstad   •Västerås

•Tallinn

•Örebro

Hiiumaa

E S T O N I A

*Lake
Peipus*

Fredrikstad

Mälaren   ⊛Stockholm

Saaremaa

•Pärnu   •Tartu

Kristiansand•

Vänern   •Norrköping

Vättern   •Linköping

Skagerrak

•Göteborg

*Gulf of
Riga*

•Valmiera

•Borås   •Jönköping

Visby•

Ventspils•

⊛Riga   •Rēzekne

Götaland

Gotland

L A T V I A

Western Dvina

*NORTH
SEA*

•Ålborg

Kattegat

•Öland

Liepāja•   Jelgava•   Daugavpils•

Helsingborg

Šiauliai•

•Panevėžys

•Århus
JUTLAND

D E N M A R K   ⊛Copenhagen

•Klaipėda

L I T H U A N I A

Esbjerg•   •Odense   *Sjælland*   •Malmö

Neman

•Kaunas

Fyn

Bornholm

KALININGRAD
(RUSSIA)

⊛Vilnius

B E L A R U S

BALTIC SEA

P O L A N D

0 — 100 miles
0 — 150 kilometres

NORTHERN EUROPE

THE BALKANS

UKRAINE

AUSTRIA

HUNGARY

Maribor
SLOVENIA
Ljubljana ⊛

⊛ Zagreb
Rijeka

CROATIA

Pula

Osijek

Zadar

Prijedor
Banja Luka
Doboj
BOSNIA AND
Zenica Tuzla
HERZEGOVINA
Sarajevo ⊛
Split
Mostar

Subotica

Novi
Sad

Zrenjanin

Šabac Pančevo
Belgrade ⊛

Smederevo

SERBIA
Kragujevac
Čačak   Kraljevo
Kruševac
Leskovac Niš

Prishtinë ⊛
MONTENEGRO Pejë
KOSOVO
Podgorica ⊛ Prizren
Ferizaj
Shkodër Tetovo ⊛ Skopje
Durrës ⊛ **NORTH MACEDONIA**
Tirana ⊛
Elbasan • Bitola
ALBANIA
Vlorë

Satu Mare Botoşani
Baia Mare Suceava
Zalău Iaşi MOLDOVA
Oradea **TRANSYLVANIA** Piatra
Neamţ Bacău
Cluj-Napoca Târgu-Mureş
Arad Deva Alba Iulia
Timişoara Sibiu Braşov
Reşiţa Galaţi
Brăila
Râmnicu Tulcea
Vâlcea Buzău
Drobeta- Ploieşti
Turnu Piteşti
Severin ⊛ Bucharest
Craiova Constanţa

ROMANIA

Transylvanian Alps

Iron Gate
Dam

Danube

Ruse
Dobrich
Pleven Shumen Varna
Teteven Dryanovo
Tryavna
Sofia ⊛ Stara Zagora Burgas
Sliven
Plovdiv

BULGARIA

BALKAN MOUNTAINS

BALKAN

RHODOPE MTS.

PENINSULA

Kavála

Thessaloníki
Halkidikí

Olympus
9,570 ft
(2,917 m)

Lárissa Vólos

GREECE

Pátra
Corinth
Olympia
Sparta

Píreas Athens ⊛
Kallithéa

PELOPONNESUS

Lemnos

Lesbos
(Mitilíni)

Chios

Sámos

Ikaría

CYCLADES

Náxos

Thíra
(Santoríni)

Sea of
Marmara

Dardanelles

TURKEY

Rhodes

Rhodes

DODECANESE

SEA OF CRETE

Iráklio
Crete

DINARIC ALPS

DALMATIA

ADRIATIC SEA

ITALY

Strait of Otranto

IONIAN
SEA

IONIAN ISLANDS

Corfú

Gulf of Messinía

AEGEAN SEA

BLACK SEA

Drava
Sava
Drava
Tisza
Sava
Danube
Dniester
Prut

Map Key

- ⊛ Country capital
- • • • City or town
- ⋯⋯ Country boundary

0   100 miles
0   100 kilometres

Former Yugoslavia, 1991

**Yugoslavia, or 'Land of the Southern Slavs',
was created in 1918 as a country of many ethnic
groups, but it started coming apart when Slovenia
and Croatia became independent in 1991. Yugoslavia
ceased to exist in 2003, when the country changed its
name to Serbia and Montenegro. In 2006, Montenegro
declared independence, as did Kosovo in 2008.**

AUSTRIA HUNGARY
Former Yugoslavia
Border (1991)
SLOVENIA ROMANIA
CROATIA
BOSNIA
AND
HERZEGOVINA SERBIA
ITALY BULGARIA
MONTENEGRO KOSOVO
NORTH MACEDONIA
GREECE TURKEY
Adriatic Sea
ALBANIA

NORTHERN CYPRUS
(recognised only by Turkey)
CYPRUS Nicosia
• Limassol
Same Scale as Main Map

326

Map Key

⊛ Country capital
••• City or town
····· Country boundary

0   200 miles
0   300 kilometres

NORWAY

BARENTS SEA

•Murmansk   *Kolguyev I.*

Vorkuta•

Kola Peninsula   ARCTIC CIRCLE

Karin Peninsula

Usinsk•

SWEDEN

Ob

WHITE SEA

Pechora•

FINLAND

Severodvinsk• •Archangel

Sosnogorsk•

EUROPE-ASIA BOUNDARY

Gulf of Bothnia

Ukhta•

Northern Dvina

Zheleznodorozhnyy•

•Petrozavodsk

U R A L

Gulf of Finland

Lake Ladoga   *Lake Onega*

Syktyvkar•

•Kotlas

M O U N T A I N S

ESTONIA

St. Petersburg

Sukhona

Berezniki•

BALTIC SEA

Lake Peipus

•Cherepovets   •Vologda

•Pskov   •Velikiy Novgorod

Rybinsk Reservoir

•Kirov   Perm'•

LATVIA

Velikiye Luki•

•Rybinsk   •Kostroma

Izhevsk•   *Kama*

KALININGRAD (RUSSIA) LITHUANIA

•Tver   •Yaroslavl'

•Ivanovo

•Nizhniy Novgorod

Ufa•

N O R T H E R N   E U R O P E A N   P L A I N

Moscow⊛   •Vladimir

Kazan'•

Naberezhnyye Chelny•

Magnitogorsk•

•Smolensk

BELARUS

Oka   *Volga*

Ul'yanovsk•

Sterlitamak•

•Kaluga   •Ryazan'

Cheboksary•

POLAND

•Tula

•Saransk

Syzran'•   Tol'yatti•

Belaya

•Bryansk   *Oka*

•Penza

Samara•

Novotroitsk•

•Orel   •Lipetsk

•Tambov

Orenburg•

Orsk•

Dnieper

CRIMEA
Russia invaded Crimea in 2014 and, after secession from Ukraine was approved in a disputed and boycotted referendum held in Crimea, the Russian parliament voted to annex Crimea into the Russian Federation. The United Nations General Assembly subsequently adopted a nonbinding resolution declaring the annexation invalid and affirming Ukraine's territorial jurisdiction. As of 2019, Russia administers and controls all aspects of the peninsula, while Ukraine continues to maintain that Crimea is its sovereign territory.

•Kursk   •Voronezh

Saratov•

Balakovo•

•Belgorod

Engels•

KAZAKHSTAN

Kamyshin•

Don

Ural

ROMANIA

Donets

UKRAINE

Volgograd• •Volzhskiy

Volga

C A S P I A N   D E P R E S S I O N

•Shakhty

Don

Line of Russian control

•Rostov

•Taganrog

Astrakhan'•

SEA OF AZOV

CRIMEA

•Krasnodar

Simferopol'•

•Stavropol'

C A S P I A N

BULGARIA

Sevastopol'•

Boundary claimed by Ukraine

Maykop•

Pyatigorsk•

B L A C K   S E A

Sochi•

El'brus 18,510 ft (5,642 m)

CHECHNYA

•Groznyy

Makhachkala•

•Vladikavkaz

C A U C A S U S   M O U N T A I N S

S E A

GEORGIA

TURKEY

ARMENIA   AZERBAIJAN

IRAN

EUROPEAN RUSSIA

10 TOWERING FACTS ABOUT UNUSUAL BUILDINGS

Dog lovers visiting Cottonwood, Idaho, U.S.A., can check into a beagle-shaped residence called the **Dog Bark Park Inn.**

LOCATED ON ONE OF BOLIVIA'S SALT FLATS, THE PALACIO DE SAL HOTEL IS MADE ALMOST ENTIRELY OUT OF SALT.

India's National Fisheries Development Board is headquartered in a three-storey building shaped like a fish swimming in midair.

THE OUTSIDE OF THE **RIPLEY'S BELIEVE IT OR NOT! MUSEUM** IN NIAGARA FALLS, CANADA, INCLUDES A **COLOURFUL SIDEWAYS SCULPTURE** OF THE **EMPIRE STATE BUILDING** TOPPED WITH **KING KONG.**

The inspiration for the **warped shape** of the **Crooked House** in Sopot, Poland, came from Polish fairy-tale illustrations.

BONHOMME'S ICE PALACE WAS CONSTRUCTED FROM NEARLY **2,000 135-KILOGRAM** (300-LB) FROZEN BLOCKS FOR THE 2018 QUEBEC WINTER CARNIVAL.

Visitors flock to **HUAINAN, CHINA,** to see a **BUILDING** shaped like a massive **GRAND PIANO** and **VIOLIN.**

The parking garage of the **Kansas City Public Library** in Missouri, U.S.A., is decorated with **two-storey-tall book spines** showcasing **42 titles.**

A **THREE-STOREY DONUT** atop Randy's Donuts in Inglewood, California, U.S.A., has been **GREETING CUSTOMERS** for more than **SIX DECADES.**

VISITORS TO THE **UPSIDE-DOWN HOUSE** IN HARTBEESPOORT, SOUTH AFRICA, CAN CHECK OUT A HOME THAT'S FLIPPED ON BOTH THE OUTSIDE AND INSIDE.

THE ORIGINAL 7 WONDERS of the WORLD

More than 2,000 years ago, many travellers wrote about sights they had seen on their journeys. Over time, seven of those places made history as the 'wonders of the ancient world'. There are seven because the Greeks, who made the list, believed the number seven to be magical.

THE NEW 7 WONDERS of the WORLD

Why name new wonders of the world? Most of the original ancient wonders no longer exist. To be eligible for the new list, the wonders had to be human-made before the year 2000 and in preservation. They were selected through a poll of more than 100 million voters!

THE PYRAMIDS OF GIZA, EGYPT
BUILT: ABOUT 2600 B.C.
MASSIVE TOMBS OF EGYPTIAN PHARAOHS LIE INSIDE THIS ANCIENT WONDER — THE ONLY ONE STILL STANDING TODAY.

HANGING GARDENS OF BABYLON, IRAQ
BUILT: DATE UNKNOWN
LEGEND HAS IT THAT THIS GARDEN PARADISE WAS PLANTED ON AN ARTIFICIAL MOUNTAIN, BUT MANY EXPERTS SAY IT NEVER REALLY EXISTED.

TEMPLE OF ARTEMIS AT EPHESUS, TURKEY
BUILT: SIXTH CENTURY B.C.
THIS TOWERING TEMPLE WAS BUILT TO HONOUR ARTEMIS, THE GREEK GODDESS OF THE HUNT.

STATUE OF ZEUS, GREECE
BUILT: FIFTH CENTURY B.C.
THIS 12-METRE (40-FT) STATUE DEPICTED THE KING OF THE GREEK GODS.

MAUSOLEUM AT HALICARNASSUS, TURKEY
BUILT: FOURTH CENTURY B.C.
THIS ELABORATE TOMB WAS BUILT FOR KING MAUSOLUS.

COLOSSUS OF RHODES, RHODES (AN ISLAND IN THE AEGEAN SEA)
BUILT: FOURTH CENTURY B.C.
A 34-METRE (110-FT) STATUE THAT HONOURS THE GREEK SUN GOD HELIOS.

LIGHTHOUSE OF ALEXANDRIA, EGYPT
BUILT: THIRD CENTURY B.C.
THE WORLD'S FIRST LIGHTHOUSE, IT USED MIRRORS TO REFLECT SUNLIGHT FOR KILOMETRES OUT TO SEA.

TAJ MAHAL, INDIA
COMPLETED: 1648
THIS LAVISH TOMB WAS BUILT AS A FINAL RESTING PLACE FOR THE BELOVED WIFE OF EMPEROR SHAH JAHAN.

PETRA, SOUTHWEST JORDAN
COMPLETED: ABOUT 200 B.C.
SOME 30,000 PEOPLE ONCE LIVED IN THIS ROCK CITY CARVED INTO CLIFF WALLS.

MACHU PICCHU, PERU
COMPLETED: ABOUT 1450
OFTEN CALLED THE 'LOST CITY IN THE CLOUDS', MACHU PICCHU IS PERCHED 2,350 METRES (7,710 FT) HIGH IN THE ANDES.

THE COLOSSEUM, ITALY
COMPLETED: A.D. 80
WILD ANIMALS — AND HUMANS — FOUGHT EACH OTHER TO THE DEATH BEFORE 50,000 SPECTATORS IN THIS ARENA.

CHRIST THE REDEEMER STATUE, BRAZIL
COMPLETED: 1931
TOWERING ATOP CORCOVADO MOUNTAIN, THIS STATUE IS TALLER THAN A 12-STOREY BUILDING AND WEIGHS ABOUT 1,100 TONNES (1,083 TONS).

CHICHÉN ITZÁ, MEXICO
COMPLETED: 10TH CENTURY
ONCE THE CAPITAL CITY OF THE ANCIENT MAYA EMPIRE, CHICHÉN ITZÁ IS HOME TO THE FAMOUS PYRAMID OF KUKULCÁN.

GREAT WALL OF CHINA, CHINA
COMPLETED: 1644
THE LONGEST HUMAN-MADE STRUCTURE EVER BUILT, IT WINDS OVER AN ESTIMATED 7,200 KILOMETRES (4,500 MILES).

MORE MUST-SEE SITES

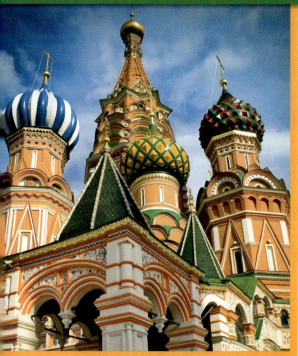

Time and Space

The famous astronomical clock, built in 1410 in Prague, Czechia (Czech Republic), has an astronomical dial on top of a calendar dial. Together, they keep track of time, as well as the movement of the sun, moon and stars.

Cathedral on the Square

The onion-dome-topped towers of St. Basil's are a key landmark on Moscow's Red Square in Russia. Built between 1554 and 1560 to commemorate military campaigns by Ivan the Terrible, the building is rich in Christian symbolism.

The Upright Stuff

The Tower of Pisa in Italy started tilting soon after its construction began more than 800 years ago. It was built on an ancient riverbed, which proved to be a foundation too soft to support a structure weighing 9,525 tonnes (9,375 tons)! By 1990, Italy's famously tilted landmark leaned so much that officials closed it to visitors, fearing it might fall over. But after years of repair work, the marble monument is again open. And although you can't see the difference, it now leans 48 centimetres (19 in) less. To straighten it, some 73 tonnes (72 tons) of soil were dug from below the side opposite the lean. When the ground underneath settled, the tower corrected itself slightly. Officials say it should be safe for tourists to walk up for another 200 years. That gives you plenty of time to plan a visit!

331

A WORKER REPAINTS A SECTION OF THE BRIDGE.

COLOUR CONFUSION

The Golden Gate Bridge was almost given the same colours as a bumblebee! Originally the U.S. Navy wanted to coat the overpass with black and yellow stripes to make it extra visible to sailors. Designers ultimately chose to paint the bridge a bold orange to complement the landscape.

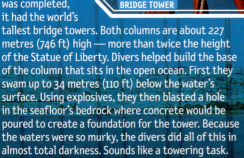

GOLDEN GATE BRIDGE TOWER

TOWER TIME

When the bridge was completed, it had the world's tallest bridge towers. Both columns are about 227 metres (746 ft) high — more than twice the height of the Statue of Liberty. Divers helped build the base of the column that sits in the open ocean. First they swam up to 34 metres (110 ft) below the water's surface. Using explosives, they then blasted a hole in the seafloor's bedrock where concrete would be poured to create a foundation for the tower. Because the waters were so murky, the divers did all of this in almost total darkness. Sounds like a towering task.

IT TOOK EIGHT YEARS FOR WORKERS TO BUILD FORT POINT.

FORT

HIDDEN FORT

Built during California's gold rush in the mid-1800s, Fort Point is tucked into the bridge's south side. It was designed to protect the region and its gold fields from foreign invaders, although it has never seen battle.

SECRETS OF THE
GOLDEN GATE BRIDGE

THIS GROUNDBREAKING STRUCTURE HAS JAW-DROPPING FEATURES.

The Golden Gate Bridge in San Francisco, California, U.S.A., is a real trailblazer! Finished in 1937, it was the world's largest suspension bridge at the time. Get the inside scoop on this innovative bridge.

HIGHS AND LOWS

Travellers crossing the Golden Gate Bridge aren't the only ones on the move. The overpass is often in motion too! It was designed to sway up to 8.2 metres (27 ft) in each direction in high winds. And its length expands and contracts by as much as 0.9 metre (3 ft) as temperatures go from warm to cool and back again. None of this damages the structure or puts people at risk, because the bridge was built to be flexible.

WHALE OF A VIEW

Scientists hold stakeouts on the bridge's overpass, observing and photographing marine life like grey and humpback whales and dolphin-like mammals called harbour porpoises, who munch on anchovies that thrive in San Francisco Bay.

UNITED STATES
— CALIFORNIA
PACIFIC OCEAN
ATLANTIC OCEAN

★ Sacramento
NEVADA
● San Francisco
CALIFORNIA
PACIFIC OCEAN
● Los Angeles

Bizarre Beaches

THE WORLD'S COOLEST COASTLINES OFFER
SO MUCH MORE THAN SANDY SHORES.

BLACK-OUT

WHAT: Punalu'u Black Sand Beach
WHERE: Big Island, Hawaii, U.S.A.
WHY IT'S BIZARRE: The jet-black sand on this skinny stretch of beach is made up of tiny bits of hardened lava, produced over centuries by the nearby (and still active) Kilauea volcano. This cool spot is also a popular nesting place for hawksbill and green sea turtles.

GLASS FROM THE PAST

WHAT: Glass Beach
WHERE: Fort Bragg, California, U.S.A.
WHY IT'S BIZARRE: Decades ago, the water along this beach was a dumping ground for glass bottles and other debris. Now what was once tossed in the ocean has washed up as a rainbow of shimmering sea glass covering the coves.

FOR THE BIRDS

WHAT: Boulders Beach
WHERE: Harbour Island, Bahamas
WHY IT'S BIZARRE: You might expect to see penguins on an icy coast. But these birds like it hot! African penguins splash in the warm waters of this national park next to 540-million-year-old granite boulders.

TIP-OFF

WHAT: Zlatni Rat
WHERE: Bol, Croatia
WHY IT'S BIZARRE: This narrow beach is a real shape-shifter. Its tip — which sticks out as much as 500 metres (1,640 ft) into the crystal blue water — shifts in different directions as a result of wind, waves and currents.

WILD VACATION

EAT ON TABLES AND CHAIRS MADE OF SALT!

SLEEP ON BEDS MADE OF SALT

Salt Hotel

HOTEL TAYKA DE SAL

WHERE Tahua, Bolivia

HOW MUCH About £100 a night

WHY IT'S COOL You've stayed at hotels made of brick or wood. But salt? Hotel Tayka de Sal is made mostly of salt (*sal* means 'salt' in Spanish), including some beds — though you'll sleep with regular mattresses and blankets. The hotel sits on the border of Salar de Uyuni, a dried-up prehistoric lake that's the world's biggest salt flat. Builders use the salt from the more than 10,500-square-kilometre (4,000-sq-mile) flat to make the bricks, and then glue them together with a paste of wet salt that hardens when it dries. When rain starts to dissolve the hotel, it's no problem: The owners just mix up more salt paste to strengthen the bricks.

COOL THINGS ABOUT BOLIVIA

During rainy summer months, Bolivia's Salar de Uyuni salt flat looks like a giant mirror.

The bus station in La Paz was designed by Gustave Eiffel, the same architect who built the Eiffel Tower and the Statue of Liberty.

Every August in Bolivia, dogs are honoured during the Feast of St. Roch.

THINGS TO DO IN BOLIVIA

Snag a *salteña* — a baked pastry filled with spicy meat — from a street vendor in Cochabamba.

Take a boat to Isla del Sol, an island in Lake Titicaca, where motorised vehicles aren't allowed.

Dance with thousands of masked and costumed performers at the Carnaval de Oruro.

QUIZ WHIZ

Is your geography knowledge off the map? Quiz yourself to find out!

Write your answers on a piece of paper. Then check them below.

1 The Elephant Sanctuary Brazil takes in elephants rescued from _____.
a. construction zones
b. circuses
c. zoos
d. amusement parks

2 Singapore's mascot is which mythical creature?
a. a merlion
b. a unicorn
c. a pegasus
d. a dragon

3 Where was the skeleton of the largest *Tyrannosaurus rex* to date uncovered?
a. Sasebo, Japan
b. Sasaram, India
c. Saskatchewan, Canada
d. Sassari, Italy

4 **True or false?** Australia has no native hoofed animals.

5 Which of the following is not considered a geographic feature?
a. glacier
b. canyon
c. river
d. cloud

Not **STUMPED** yet? Check out the *NATIONAL GEOGRAPHIC KIDS QUIZ WHIZ* collection for more crazy **GEOGRAPHY** questions!

ANSWERS: 1. b; 2. a; 3. c; 4. True; 5. d

HOMEWORK HELP

Finding Your Way Around

LATITUDE AND LONGITUDE lines help us determine locations on Earth. Every place on Earth has a special address called absolute location. Imaginary lines called lines of latitude run west to east, parallel to the Equator. These lines measure distance in degrees north or south from the Equator (0° latitude) to the North Pole (90° N) or to the South Pole (90° S). One degree of latitude is approximately 113 kilometres (70 miles).

Lines of longitude run north to south, meeting at the poles. These lines measure distance in degrees east or west from 0° longitude (prime meridian) to 180° longitude. The prime meridian runs through Greenwich, England.

ABSOLUTE LOCATION. Suppose you are using latitude and longitude to play a game of global scavenger hunt. The clue says the prize is hidden at absolute location 30° S, 60° W. You know that the first number is south of the Equator, and the second is west of the prime meridian. On the map to the right, find the line of latitude labelled 30° S. Now find the line of longitude labelled 60° W. Trace these lines with your fingers until they meet. Identify this spot. The prize must be located in central Argentina (see arrow, right).

CHALLENGE!

1. Look at the map of Africa on pp. 264–265. Which country can you find at 10° S, 20° E?

2. Look at the map of Asia on pp. 272–273. Which country can you find at 20° N, 80° E?

3. On the map of Europe on pp. 280–281, which country is found at 50° N, 30° E?

4. Look at the map of North America on pp. 284–285. Which country can you find at 20° N, 100° W?

ANSWERS: 1. Angola; **2.** India; **3.** Ukraine; **4.** Mexico

GAME
ANSWERS

Green Scene
page 140

Litter is shown in yellow; recycling and compost bins are blue.

What in the World?
page 141

Top row: **basketball net, Hula-Hoop, pineapple**
Middle row: **tree trunk, doughnut, key ring**
Bottom row: **swimming ring, dartboard, Saturn**

Find the Hidden Animals
page 142

1. **C**, 2. **A**, 3. **F**, 4. **D**, 5. **E**, 6. **B**

What in the World?
page 145

Top row: **paint set, socks, lollipop**
Middle row: **parrot, cake, crayons**
Bottom row: **sprinkles, umbrella, Slinky**

What in the World?
page 149

Top row: **zebra, flamingo, giraffe**
Middle row: **elephant, mandrill, chameleon**
Bottom row: **leopard, tortoise, African wild dog**

Find the Hidden Animals
page 150

1. **E**, 2. **D**, 3. **F**, 4. **B**, 5. **C**, 6. **A**

What in the World?
page 152

Top row: **plums, yarn, sea fan**
Middle row: **shoelace, starfish, red cabbage**
Bottom row: **crayons, orchid, amethyst**

Signs of the Times
page 153

Signs **#1** and **#5** are fake.

Want to Learn More?

Find more information about topics in this book in these National Geographic Kids resources.

Brain Candy series

Weird But True! series

Just Joking series

5,000 Awesome Facts (About Everything!) series

Beastly Bionics
Jennifer Swanson
June 2020

Ultimate U.S. Road Trip Atlas, 2nd Edition
Crispin Boyer
April 2020

Fetch! A How to Speak Dog Training Guide
Aubre Andrus
August 2020

Girls Can!
*Marissa Sebastian,
Tora Shae Pruden,
Paige Towler*
October 2020

Breaking the News
Robin Terry Brown
October 2020

Cutest Animals on the Planet
National Geographic Kids
March 2021

Top Secret
Crispin Boyer
April 2021

Ultimate Rockopedia
Steve Tomecek
December 2020

Abbreviations:
AL: Alamy Stock Photo
AS: Adobe Stock
DRMS: Dreamstime
GI: Getty Images
IS: iStockphoto
MP: Minden Pictures
NGIC: National Geographic Image Collection
SS: Shutterstock

All Maps
By National Geographic unless otherwise noted

All Illustrations & Charts
By Stuart Armstrong unless otherwise noted

Front Cover
(turtle), David Doubilet/NGIC; (volcano), Lucie/AS; (taxi), Grafissimo/IS/GI; (water bottle), Weera Danwilai/SS

Spine
(turtle), David Doubilet/NGIC

Back Cover
(Earth), ixpert/SS; (chameleon), Vera Kuttelvaserova/AS; (Great Wall), Sean Pavone/SS; (wolf), Gavriel Jecan/GI; (future city), 3000ad/IS/GI; (Holi celebration), ferrantraite/E+/GI; (butterfly), Steven Russell Smith/AL

Front Matter (2-7)
2-3, 500px Prime/GI; 5 (A), Michael Milfeit/500px Prime/GI; 5 (B), ElenaMirage/iStock; 5 (C), pchoui/IS/GI; 5 (D), 3000ad/IS/GI; 6 (A), agefotostock/AL; 6 (B), Photosani/SS; 6 (C), Thomas Sbampato/imageBROKER RF/GI; 6 (D), Dirk Ercken/SS; 6 (E), Coldmoon_photo/IS/GI; 6 (F), Albert Russ/SS; 6 (G), soft_light/AS; 7 (A), tdub_video/IS/GI; 7 (B), Richard T. Nowitz/Corbis; 7 (C), Nick Brundle/Moment Open/GI; 7 (D), Michele Falzone/Stockbyte/GI

Your World 2022 (8-17)
8-9, Michael Milfeit/500px Prime/GI; 10 (UP LE), Caroline Benzel; 10 (UP RT), Stephanie Rousseau/AS; 10 (LO LE), Field Museum of Natural History; 10 (LO RT), Christopher Furlong/GI; 11 (UP), Zero G Kitchen LLC; 11 (LO), Jingmai O'Connor; 12 (UP), Kristian Laine; 12 (LO), Masato Sakai/Yamagata University; 13 (UP), Phil Bex/AL; 13 (CTR), Dmitry Feoktistov/TASS via GI; 13 (LO), Atsushi Tomura/GI; 14 (UP), Ellen Helmke; 14 (CTR), Georgia Institute of Technology; 14 (LO), CBW/AL; 15 (UP), Jiraporn Kuhakan/Reuters; 15 (CTR), Sean Viljoen; 15 (LO), Sean Viljoen; 16 (B), Roblan/SS; 16 (A), SasaStock/SS; 16 (C), Magnus Larsson/AS; 16 (D), Patrick Foto/SS; 16 (E), cougarsan/SS; 16 (F), Uryadnikov Sergey/AS; 16 (G), Alhovik/SS; 16 (H), Africa Studio/SS; 16 (I), Jak Wonderly; 17 (UP), Umit Bektas/Reuters; 17 (CTR), Taxon Expeditions; 17 (LO), Jose Angel Astor Rocha/AS

Kids vs. Plastic (18-35)
18-19, ElenaMirage/iStock/GI; 20-21, trial-artinf/AS; 21 (UP), Jacobs Stock Photography Ltd/GI; 21 (CTR RT), SeeCee/SS; 21 (CTR LE), Norbert Pouchain/EyeEm/GI; 22-23, Steve De Neef/NGIC; 23 (RT), Aflo/SS; 23, photka/SS; 23 (LE), Pete Atkinson/GI; 24 (LE), Clearwater Marine Aquarium; 24 (RT), Clearwater Marine Aquarium; 24-25, Science Faction/GI; 25 (LE), Clearwater Marine Aquarium; 25 (RT), Norbert Wu/MP; 26 (UP RT), Brian J. Skerry/NGIC; 26 (UP LE), Steve De Neef/NGIC; 26 (LO), Brian J. Skerry/NGIC; 27 (A), Levent Konuk/SS; 27 (B), Tory Kallman/SS; 27 (C), Andrea Izzotti/SS; 27 (D), sittipong/SS; 27 (E), Dahlia/SS; 28 (UP LE), KPPWC/AS; 28 (UP RT), Simone/AS; 28 (CTR), eurobanks/AS; 28 (LO LE), Mikhail/AS; 28 (LO RT), Kelpfish/DRMS; 29 (UP), Ivonne Wierink/SS; 29 (CTR LE), Brooke BeckerAS; 29 (CTR RT), PaulPaladin/AL; 29 (LO), Lori Epstein/National Geographic Staff; 30 (UP LE), Steven Sanders/Alamy; 30 (UP RT), Fuse/Corbis/GI; 30 (CTR), unkas_photo/IS/GI; 30 (LO-1), ac_bnphotos/IS/GI; 30 (LO-2), yellowdaffs/SS; 30 (LO-3), jenifoto/IS/GI; 30 (LO-4), Shannon Hibberd/National Geographic Staff; 31 (UP LE), Elena Veselova/SS; 31 (LO), Melica/SS; 31 (UP RT), Maks Narodenko/SS; 32-33, Hilary Andrews/National Geographic Staff; 34 (LO LE), Pete Atkinson/GI; 34 (LO LE), Norbert Pouchain/EyeEm/GI; 34 (LO RT), Science Faction/GI; 34 (UP RT), Melica/SS; 35, Albo003/SS

Amazing Animals (36-87)
36-37, pchoui/IS/GI; 38 (CTR), DioGen/SS; 38 (LO), Nick Garbutt; 38 (UP), lifegallery/IS/GI; 39 (UP LE), EyeEm/GI; 39 (UP RT), reptiles4all/SS; 39 (CTR LE), Hiroya Minakuchi/MP; 39 (CTR RT), FP media/SS; 39 (LO), Ziva_K/IS/GI; 40 (UP), Nataliia Melnychuk/SS; 40 (LO), Verena Matthew/AS; 40 (CTR), Suzi Eszterhas/MP; 41 (UP), ZSSD/MP; 41 (CTR), Rolf Kopfle/AL; 41 (LO), ZSSD/MP; 42 (ALL), Marcel Gross; 43 (UP), Jasper Doest; 43 (LO LE), Jasper Doest; 43 (LO RT), Karine Aigner/National Geographic Staff; 44 (ALL), From Hen Who Sailed Around the World by Guirec Soudée, copyright © 2018 by Guirec Soudée. Reprinted by permission of Little, Brown an imprint of Hachette Book Group, Inc.; 45 (ALL), Dean MacAdam; 46 (UP LE), Steven Kazlowski/Nature Picture Library; 46 (UP RT), Ryan Korpi/IS/GI; 46 (LO), Gary Bell/Oceanwide/MP; 47 (UP LE), Thomas Marent/ARDEA; 47 (UP RT), Mike Hill/AL; 47 (CTR), YAY Media AS/AL; 47 (LO), Cathy Keifer/SS; 48 (UP LE), Klein & Hubert/Nature Picture Library; 48 (UP RT), Kajornyot Krunkitsatien/AS; 48 (LO LE), Juniors Bildarchiv GmbH/AL; 48 (LO RT), Maros Bauer/SS; 49 (UP LE), John Carnemolla/IS; 49 (CTR), Dirk Ercken/SS; 49 (UP RT), Piotr Naskrecki/MP; 49 (LO), Suzi Eszterhas/MP; 50, Cisca Castelijns/MP; 51, Mircea Costina/SS; 52-53, Bornean Sun Bear Conservation Centre; 53 (UP), Siew te Wong/Bornean Sun Bear Conservation Centre; 53 (LO), Bornean Sun Bear Conservation Centre; 54 (LO), Anna Gowthorpe/PA Images via GI; 54 (UP), Abby Wood/Smithsonian's National Zoo; 55 (LO LE), saad315/SS; 55 (UP LE), Andrea Izzotti/SS; 55 (UP RT), Sylvain Cordier/GI; 55 (LO RT), Dr. Axel Gebauer/Nature Picture Library; 56, Staffan Widstrand/Nature Picture Library; 57 (jaguar fur), worldswildlifewonders/SS; 57 (tiger fur), Kesu/SS; 57 (leopard fur), WitR/SS; 57 (lion fur), Eric Isselée/SS; 57 (LE CTR), DLILLC/Corbis/GI; 57 (leopard), Eric Isselée/SS; 57 (tiger), Eric Isselée/SS; 57 (lion), Eric Isselée/SS; 57 (snow leopard), Eric Isselee/SS; 57 (snow leopard fur), Eric Isselee/SS; 58 (RT), Suzi Eszterhas/MP; 58 (CTR), FionaAyerst/GI; 58 (LE), Gerard Lacz/Science Source; 59 (UP), Felis Images/Nature Picture Library; 59 (LO), Jack Bradley; 60 (UP), Image Source/Corbis; 60 (LO), Juniors/SuperStock; 61 (UP), Tom & Pat Leeson/Ardea; 61 (LO), Lisa & Mike Husar/Team Husar; 62-63, Tony Heald/NPL/MP; 63 (UP), Matthew Tabaccos/Barcroft Media/GI; 63 (LO), Matthew Tabaccos/Barcroft Media/GI; 64 (UP LE), Westend61/GI; 65 (UP RT), Roy L. Caldwell; 65 (LO), Helmut Corneli/Alamy; 66 (UP), Design Pics Inc/Alamy; 66 (LO), mauritius images GmbH/Alamy; 67 (UP LE), Kathryn Jeffs/Nature Picture Library; 67 (LO), Tory Kallman/SS; 67 (CTR RT), Design Pics Inc/Alamy; 67 (UP RT), Tony Wu/Nature Picture Library; 68 (UP), Ian McAllister/NGIC; 68 (LO), Bertie Gregory/MP; 69 (UP), Paul Nicklen/NGIC; 69 (LO LE), Paul Nicklen/NGIC; 69 (LO RT), Paul Nicklen/NGIC; 69 (CTR), Ian McAllister/Pacific Wild; 70, Eric Baccega/NPL/MP; 71 (LO), Jordi Galbany/Dian Fossey Gorilla Fund International; 71 (UP LE), Stone Sub/GI; 71 (CTR RT), courtesy Dallas Zoo; 71 (UP RT), Martin Hale/FLPA/MP; 72 (LO), Heidi & Hans-Juergen Koch/MP; 72 (CTR LE), Stephen Dalton/MP; 72 (LE), Michael D. Kern; 72 (CTR LE), AtSkwongPhoto/SS; 72 (CTR), Hitendra Sinkar Photography/Alamy; 73, gallimaufry/SS; 74 (UP), Norbert Rosing/NGIC; 74 (LO), David Pike/Nature Picture Library; 74-75, David Hiser/Stone/GI; 74 (CTR), Alaska Stock LLC/Alamy; 75 (LE), Paul Nicklen/NGIC; 75 (RT), Art Wolfe/The Image Bank/GI; 76 (UP), Jane Burton/GI; 76 (LO), Will Hughes/SS; 77 (LO), Brian Kimball/Kimball Stock; 77 (CTR), Ryan Lane/GI; 77 (UP), maljalen/IS; 78 (LO), Justin Siemaszko; 78 (UP), Shai (Asor) Lighter; 79 (CTR), Malia Canann, The Piggy Wiggies; 79 (UP), Joanne Lefson/Farm Sanctuary SA; 79 (LO), Peter Mares; 80 (UP), Chris Butler/Science Photo Library/Photo Researchers, Inc.; 80 (CTR), Publiphoto/Photo Researchers, Inc.; 80 (LO), Pixeldust Studios/NG Creative; 81 (A), Publiphoto/Photo Researchers, Inc.; 81 (B), Laurie O'Keefe/Photo Researchers, Inc.; 81 (C), Chris Butler/Photo Researchers, Inc.; 81 (D), Publiphoto/Photo Researchers, Inc.; 81 (E), image courtesy of Project Exploration; 83 (UP LE), Sergey Krasovskiy; 83 (UP RT), Dr. Ashley Poust; 83 (LO), National Park Service; 84 (BOTH), Franco Tempesta; 85 (UP), Catmando/SS; 85 (CTR), Franco Tempesta; 85 (LO), Leonello Calvetti/SS; 86 (LO LE), Jane Burton/GI; 86 (UP RT), Tony Heald/NPL/MP; 86 (LO RT), Helmut Corneli/Alamy; 86 (UP LE), Stone Sub/GI; 87, GOLFX/SS

Science and Technology (88-113)
88-89, 3000ad/IS/GI; 90 (UP), C_Eng-Wong Photography/SS; 90 (CTR), Plume Creative/Digital Vision/GI; 90 (LO), Library of Congress Prints and Photographs Division; 91 (UP LE), Rob Stothard/GI; 91 (UP RT), ober-art/SS; 91 (CTR LE), Roman Samokhin/SS; 91 (CTR RT), Chris Ratcliffe/SS; 91 (LO), Naeblys/SS; 92 (UP), Jetpack Aviation; 92 (LO), Solent News/Splash News; 93 (UP LE), Caters News Agency; 93 (LO inset), REX USA/Aaron Chang/Solent News/Rex; 93, REX USA/Aaron Chang/Solent

News/Rex; 93 (UP RT), Bird Photo Booth; 93 (CTR), Bird Photo Booth; 94-95 (ALL), Joe Rocco; 96-97, Mondolithic Studios; 98-99, Mondolithic Studios; 100, Ted Kinsman/Science Source; 101 (A), Sebastian Kaulitzki/SS; 101 (B), Eye of Science/Photo Researchers, Inc.; 101 (C), Volker Steger/Christian Bardele/Photo Researchers, Inc.; 101 (D), ancelpics/GI; 101 (E), puwanai/SS; 101 (F), sgame/SS; 101 (G), kwest/SS; 102 (UP), FotograFFF/SS; 102 (LO), Craig Tuttle/Corbis/GI; 103 (earthworm), Kzww/SS; 103 (mushrooms), Ovydyborets/DRMS; 103-139 (background), Fer Gregory/SS; 103 (seedling), Mathom/DRMS; 104 (UP), SciePro/SS; 104 (LO), R. Gino Santa Maria/DRMS; 105 (LO), cobalt88/SS; 105 (UP), Cynthia Turner; 106 (A), Creator: Odua Images/SS; 106 (B), Creator: Hong Vo/SS; 106 (C), Africa Studio/SS; 106 (D), Sebastian Kaulitzki/SS; 106 (E), Creator: grebcha/SS; 106 (F), Brian Maudsley/SS; 107 (UP RT), AFP/GI; 107 (UP LE), juan moyano/AL; 107 (LO LE), VikramRaghuvanshi/GI; 107 (LO RT), Pasieka/Science Source; 108 (UP LE), Dimarion/SS; 108 (CTR LE), Microfield Scientific Ltd./Science Source; 108 (CTR RT), mrfiza/SS; 108 (LO), iLexx/IS; 108 (UP RT), Eraxion/IS; 109 (UP), Jani Bryson/IS; 109 (CTR), MyImages - Micha/SS; 109 (LO), RapidEye/IS; 110 (LE), Eric Isselee/SS; 110 (RT), sdominick/GI; 111 (UP), Jean-Pierre Clatot/AFP/GI; 111 (CTR), kryzhov/SS; 111 (LO), Lane V. Erickson/SS; 112 (LO RT), iLexx/SS; 112 (UP LE), Mondolithic Studios; 112 (UP RT), Ovydyborets/DRMS.com; 112 (LO LE), kryzhov/SS; 113, Klaus Vedfelt/GI

Culture Connection (114-137)

114-115, agefotostock/AL; 116 (UP LE), CreativeNature.nl/SS; 116 (LO LE), Tubol Evgeniya/SS; 116 (UP), Dave Donaldson/AL; 116 (LO), Pigprox/SS; 116 (LO RT), Stephen Coburn/SS; 117 (LO RT), wacpan/SS; 117 (RT CTR), Zee/Alamy; 117 (CTR), Dinodia/GI; 118 (CTR), 156181766/SS; 119, Chonnanit/SS; 120-121 (ALL), Rebecca Hale/National Geographic Staff; 122-123, Naeblys/SS; 122 (UP LE), Hemis/AL; 122 (UP RT), E.D. Torial/AL; 122 (LO LE), John Kellerman/AL; 122 (LO RT), Jorgen Udvang/AL; 123 (UP), Roman Babakin/SS; 123 (CTR LE), Clarence Holmes Photography/AL; 123 (CTR RT), George Oze/AL; 123 (LO), Roy Conchie/AL; 124 (CTR LE), iStock/Mlenny; 124 (UP RT), maogg/GI; 124 (UP RT), Paul Poplis/GI; 124 (LO LE), Glyn Thomas/Alamy; 124 (UP LE), Radomir Tarasov/DRMS; 124 (LO RT), Brian Hagiwara/GI; 125 (LO RT), Kelley Miller/National Geographic Staff; 125 (LO LE), 'Money Dress' with 'Colonial Dress' behind. Paper currency and frame, Lifesize ©Susan Stockwell 2010. ©photo Colin Hampden-White 2010.; 125 (UP CTR LE), Igor Stramyk/SS; 125 (UP RT), Joe Pepler/Rex USA/SS; 125 (UP LE), Georgios Kollidas/Alamy; 125 (CTR LE), Mohamed Osama/DRMS; 125 (CTR RT), Daniel Krylov/DRMS; 126, Rebecca Hale/National Geographic Staff; 127, Mark Thiessen/National Geographic Staff; 127, Danny Smythe/SS; 128 (A), Nguyen Dai Duong; 128 (B), Ho Trung Lam; 128 (C), Mark Thiessen/NGP; 128 (D), Randall Scott/NGIC; 129 (A), Mark Thiessen/NGIC; 129 (B),

Jeremy Fahringer; 129 (C), Robert Massee; 129 (D), Catherine Cofré; 129 (E), K. Bista; 129 (F), Mark Thiessen/NGP; 129 (G), Jeevan Sunuwar Kirat; 129 (H), Jeevan Sunuwar Kirat; 130 (UP LE), liquidlibrary/GI Plu/GI; 130 (UP RT), Jose Ignacio Soto/SS; 130 (LO), Photosani/SS; 131 (UP LE), Corey Ford/DRMS; 131 (RT), IS; 132-133, Christina Balit; 133, Christina Balit; 134 (UP), Randy Olson; 134 (LO LE), Martin Gray/NG Creative; 134 (LO RT), Sam Panthaky/AFP/GI; 135 (LO LE), Reza/NationalGeographicStock.com; 135 (LO RT), Richard Nowitz/NG Creative; 135 (UP), Thierry Falise/LightRocket/GI; 137 (UP LE), spatule-tail/SS; 137 (UP RT), PictureLake/E+/GI; 137 (CTR), cifotart/SS; 137 (LO), zydesign/SS; 137, Danevski/SS

Fun and Games (138-157)

138-139, Thomas Sbampato/imageBROKER RF/GI; 140, Jeff Hendricks and Viktoriya Tsoy (green city), James Yamasaki (litter, bins), Image Digitally Composed; 141 (UP LE), Corbis; 141 (UP CTR), Max Power/Corbis; 141 (UP RT), Supapics/Alamy; 141 (CTR LE), Zoom (192) Time/Imagemore/GI; 141 (CTR), Demkat/SS; 141 (CTR RT), Corbis/Jupiterimages; 141 (LO LE), ViewofAmelie/IS; 141 (LO CTR), Simple Stock Shots; 141 (LO RT), hideto999/SS; 142 (A), Gerard Soury/GI; 142 (B), Constantinos Petrinos/Nature Picture Library; 142 (D), Art Wolfe; 142 (E), Andy Rouse/MP; 142 (F), Christopher MacDonald/SS; 143 (A), Jim Brandenburg/MP; 143 (frog in profile), Photolukacs/SS; 143 (frog facing forward), Dirk Ercken/SS; 143 (agouti facing left), Jaymi Heimbuch/MP; 143 (kinkajou sitting), Roland Seitre/MP; 143 (toucan eating), Visuals Unlimited, Inc./Gregory Basco/GI; 143 (kinkajou portrait), Ali Atmaca/Anadolu Agency/GI; 143 (kinkajou hanging), Roland Seitre/MP; 143 (frog from above), Christian Ziegler/MP; 143 (agouti facing right), Thomas Hertwig/Alamy; 143 (toucan), Eduardo Rivero/SS; 144, Jason Tharp; 145 (UP LE), Pete Turner/GI; 145 (LO RT), Garry Gay/Alamy; 145 (UP RT), Jeffrey Hamilton/Digital Vision/GI; 145 (UP CTR), Elena Schweitzer/SS; 145 (UP LE), EldoradoSuperVector/SS; 145 (LO CTR), Andriy Bondarev/; 145 (CTR RT), botulinum21/SS; 145 (LO LE), Shannon Alexander/SS; 145 (CTR), Oleksandra Naumenko/SS; 146 (ALL), Gary Fields; 147 (UP), Bullstar/SS; 147 (CTR RT), Greer & Associates, Inc./SuperStock; 147 (CTR LE), Penny Boyd/Alamy; 147 (LO), Stone Sub/GI; 148, Jim Paillot; 149 (LO CTR), Peter Steyn/Ardea; 149 (UP LE), Alexey Petrunin/DRMS; 149 (UP CTR), Bandersnatch/SS; 149 (UP RT), PhotoDisc; 149 (CTR LE), jeep2499/SS; 149 (CTR), ElisabethAardema/IS; 149 (CTR RT), For Out/SS; 149 (LO LE), Volodymyr Burdiak/SS; 149 (LO RT), Ondrej Prosicky/SS; 150 (C), B&S Draker/Nature Picture Library; 150 (B), Adegsm/IS/GI; 150 (C), Steven Kazlowski/Nature Picture Library; 150 (D), Taja Planinc/IS/GI; 150 (E), Don Paulson Photography/Purestock/Superstock; 150 (F), Roy Toft/NGIC; 151, Dan Sipple; 152 (UP LE), Bill Boch/Foodpix/Jupiterimages; 152 (UP CTR), Ingram Publishing/SuperStock; 152 (UP RT), Darryl Torckler/GI; 152 (CTR LE), Francisco Cruz/

Superstock; 152 (CTR RT), Firstlight/GI; 152 (LO LE), William Thomas Cain/Reportage/GI; 152 (LO CTR), Wendell Webber/Botanica/Jupiterimages; 152 (CTR), Ferenc Cegledi/SS; 153 (1), Paul Souders/Stone/GI; 153 (2), Yagil Henkin/Alamy; 153 (3), robertharding/Alamy; 153 (4), Jonathan Blair/NGIC; 153 (5), Jonathan Tourtellot/NGIC; 153 (6), Danita Delimont/GI; 153 (7), Peter Dazeley/The Image Bank/GI; 154 (UP), otsphoto/SS; 154 (CTR LE), Cosmin Manci/SS; 154 (LO), Helena Queen/SS; 154 (CTR RT), cynoclub/SS; 155, Dan Sipple; 156, Strika Entertainment, Inc.

Space and Earth (158-179)

158-159, Coldmoon_photo/IS/GI; 160 (UP), NGIC; 160 (LO), Joe Rocco; 161 (UP), Ralph Lee Hopkins/NGIC; 161 (UP LE and RT), Visuals Unlimited/SS; 161 (CTR LE), Visuals Unlimited/Corbis; 161 (CTR RT), Dirk Wiersma/Photo Researchers, Inc.; 161 (LO LE), Charles D. Winters/Photo Researchers, Inc.; 161 (LO RT), Theodore Clutter/Photo Researchers, Inc.; 162 (UP LE), raiwa/IS; 162 (LO LE), Albert Russ/SS; 162 (UP RT), MarcelC/IS; 162 (CTR RT), Anatoly Maslennikov/SS; 162 (LO RT), IS; 163 (UP LE), didyk/IS; 163 (UP RT), Mark A. Schneider/Science Source; 163 (LO LE), Ben Johnson/Science Source; 163 (LO CTR LE), Kazakovmaksim/DRMS; 163 (LO RT), oldeez/DRMS; 163 (LO CTR RT), Ingemar Magnusson/DRMS; 163 (UP CTR), Joel Arem/Science Source; 163 (UP LE), Meetchum/DRMS; 163 (UP CTR LE), Albertruss/DRMS; 163 (UP RT), 123dartist/DRMS; 163 (UP CTR RT), Igorkali/DRMS; 164 (LO CTR), ODM/SS; 165, Mark Shneider/Visuals Unlimited/Corbis; 165 (UP FAR LE), Dzarek/SS; 165 (UP CTR), Kevin Hewitt Photography Inc.; 165 (UP CTR), photolibrary.com; 165 (UP CTR RT), Danny Smythe/SS; 165 (UP CTR RT), Trinacria Photo/SS; 165 (UP RT), Smit/SS; 165 (LO LE), John Madden/IS; 165 (LO RT), Dai Haruki/IS/GI; 166, Frank Ippolito; 167 (UP LE), All Canada Photos/Alamy; 167 (CTR LE), NASA; 167 (CTR RT), Diane Cook & Len Jenshel/NGIC; 167 (LO LE), Image Science and Analysis Laboratory, NASA-Johnson Space Center. "The Gateway to Astronaut Photography of Earth."; 167 (LO RT), Douglas Peebles Photography/Alamy; 167, NG Maps; 168 (UP LE), Florian Neukirchen/AL; 168 (UP RT), Victoria Chekalina/AS; 168 (LO LE), Franco Tempesta; 168 (LO RT), Keystone Press/AL; 169 (UP), Image courtesy of New Zealand American Submarine Ring of Fire 2007 Exploration, NOAA Vents Program, NOAA-OE; 169 (CTR LE), iofoto/SS; 169 (CTR RT), Derek G. Humble/SS; 169 (LO), Sean Pavone/SS; 170-171 (CTR), Mark Garlick/Science Photo Library; 170 (LO), NASA/CXC/IOA/A Fabian Etal/Science Photo Library; 171 (UP), NASA, ESA and M.J. Jee (Johns Hopkins University); 171 (LO), M. Markevitch/CXC/CFA/NASA/Science Photo Library; 172-173, David Aguilar; 174, David Aguilar; 174 (LO), NASA/JHUAPL/SwRI; 175, David Aguilar; 176 (UP), EHT Collaboration/NASA; 177 (A), Allexxandar/IS/GI; 177 (B), Walter Myers/Stocktrek Images/Corbis/GI; 177 (C), Tony & Daphne Hallas/Photo Researchers, Inc.; 177 (D), Don Smith/Photolibrary/GI; 178 (UP), John Madden/IS; 178 (LO), Image courtesy of New Zealand

American Submarine Ring of Fire 2007 Exploration, NOAA Vents Program, NOAA-OE; 178 (CTR), NASA/CXC/IOA/A Fabian Etal/ Science Photo Library; 179 (UP), pixhook/ E+/GI

Awesome Exploration (180–197)

180-181, soft_light/AS; 182 (UP), Mark Thiessen/NGP; 182 (CTR LE), Steffen Foerster/ SS; 182 (CTR RT), Nick Dale/AS; 182 (surf-board), Steve Collender/SS; 182 (LO), Jeff Mauritzen; 183 (UP), Alize Bouriat; 183 (CTR LE), Jeff Mauritzen; 183 (CTR RT), Salome Buglass/Charles Darwin Foundation; 183 (LO), Tomas Kotouc/SS; 184 (UP), Tyler Roemer; 184 (LO LE), Tyler Roemer; 185 (LO LE), Randall Scott/NGIC; 185 (UP LE), Jacqueline Faherty/NGIC; 185 (LO), National Geographic Channels/Michael Stankevich; 186-187 (ALL), Joel Sartore, National Geographic Photo Ark/NGIC; 188-189 (ALL), Wes C. Skiles/NGIC; 189, Andrew Hounslea/GI; 190 (UP), Agustin Fuentes; 190 (LO), Frans Lanting/Frans Lanting Stock; 191, Arctic-Images/Corbis; 191 (LO LE), Arctic Images/AL; 191 (LO RT), Arctic Images/AL; 192, Thomas Cabotiau/SS; 193 (UP), Tony Campbell/SS; 193 (LO), SS; 194, Mattias Klum/NGIC; 195 (UP), Brian J. Skerry/ NGIC; 195 (LO), Michael Nichols/NGIC; 196 (UP RT), Steffen Foerster/SS; 196 (LO RT), Arctic Images/AL; 196 (UP LE), Wes C. Skiles/NGIC; 196 (LO LE), National Geographic Channels/ Michael Stankevich; 197, Grady Reese/IS.com

Wonders of Nature (198–219)

198-199, tdub_video/IS/GI; 200 (LE), AVTG/ IS.com; 200 (RT), Brad Wynnyk/SS; 201 (UP LE), Rich Carey/SS; 201 (UP RT), Richard Walters/IS.com; 201 (LO LE), Karen Graham/ IS.com; 201 (LO RT), Michio Hoshino/MP/ NG Creative; 202 (UP), Dobermaraner/SS; 202 (LO LE), guentermanaus/SS; 202 (LO RT), Pete Oxford; 203 (UP), duangnapa_b/ SS; 203 (CTR LE), THAWISAK/AS; 203 (CTR RT), snaptitude/AS; 203 (LO), Janne Hamalainen/ SS; 204 (LE), cbpix/SS; 204 (RT), Mike Hill/ Photographer's Choice/GI; 204-205, Chris Anderson/SS; 205 (LE), Wil Meinderts/Buiten-beeld/MP; 205 (RT), Paul Nicklen/NGIC; 206, Steve Mann/Shutterstock; 207 (UP), Chasing Light-Photography by James Stone/GI; 207 (LO), James Balog/NGIC; 208 (UP), Stuart Armstrong; 208 (LO), Franco Tempesta; 209 (Statue of Liberty), Chris Parypa Photography/SS; 209 (bus), Rob Wilson/SS; 209 (paper boat), Nadiia Ishchenko/SS; 209 (orca), Christian Musat/SS; 210 (LO RT), Eric Nguyen/Corbis; 210 (LO LE), Alan and Sandy Carey/GI; 210 (CTR RT), Brand X; 210 (UP LE), Richard T. Nowitz/Corbis; 210 (UP RT), gev-ende/IS/GI; 211 (LO), Richard Peterson/SS; 211 (1), Leonid Tit/SS; 211 (2), Frans Lanting/ NG Creative; 211 (3), Daniel Loretto/SS; 211 (4), Lars Christensen/SS; 212, Digital Vision/ GI; 213 (UP LE), Lori Mehmen/Associated Press; 213 (LO LE), Jim Reed; 213 (EF0), Susan Law Cain/SS; 213 (EF1), Brian Nolan/IS.com; 213 (EF2), Susan Law Cain/SS; 213 (EF3), Judy Kennamer/SS; 213 (EF4), jam4travel/SS; 213 (EF5), jam4travel/SS; 214-215, 3dmotus/

SS; 216, Galen Rowell/Corbis/GI; 217 (UP LE), Aikman/Newspix/GI; 217 (UP RT), Australian Reptile Park; 217 (LO), Xinhua/Stringer via GI; 217 (LO INSET), Banaras Khan/AFP via GI; 218 (CTR RT), duangnapa_b/SS; 218 (UP), cbpix/ SS; 218 (LO), Alan and Sandy Carey/GI; 218 (CTR LE), Aikman/Newspix/GI

History Happens (220–251)

220-221, Nick Brundle/Moment Open/ GI; 222 (LO), Fengling/SS; 222 (UP LE), DeAgostini/GI; 222 (UP RT), LibraryTuul/ Robert Harding Picture; 223 (LO RT), Yoshio Tomii/SuperStock; 223 (LO LE), Kenneth Garrett/NGIC; 223 (UP), Adam Woolfitt/ Robert Harding Picture Library; 224-225 (UP), Mondolithic Studios; 224 (UP RT), Seamas Culligan/Zuma/Corbis; 224 (LO), Roger Ressmeyer/Corbis; 226 (UP LE), Andrey Burmakin/SS; 226 (UP RT), Sean Pavone/SS; 226 (LO LE), Edwin Remsberg/ AL; 226 (LO RT), Wong Chi Chiu/AS; 227 (UP), Johnstocker/AS; 227 (CTR LE), Artokoloro/ AL; 227 (CTR RT), Frederic J. Brown/AFP via GI; 227 (LO), Caoerlei/DRMS; 228 (treasure map paper), EcOasis/SS; 228 (gold frame), Iakov Filimonov/SS; 228-229 (old paper), val lawless/SS; 228, Matjaz Slanic/E+/GI; 228 (LO), Mari Lobos; 229 (gold oval frame), Winterling/DRMS; 229 (UP), Mari Lobos; 229 (LO), Mari Lobos; 230 (UP LE), Metropolitan Museum of Art, Munsey Fund, 1932; 230 (UP RT), DEA/A. De Gregorio/De Agostini/GI; 230 (LO), Look and Learn/Bridgeman Images; 231 (UP LE), Purchase, Arthur Ochs Sulzberger Gift, and Rogers, Acquisitions and Fletcher Funds, 2016/Metropolitan Museum of Art; 231 (UP RT), Metropolitan Museum of Art; 231 (LO), Heritage Images/GI; 232-233, CTON; 234, U.S. Air Force photo/Staff Sgt. Alexandra M. Boutte; 234, U.S. Air Force photo/Staff Sgt. Alexandra M. Boutte; 234 (UP INSET), Leemage/Universal Images Group/GI; 234 (square gold frame), Iakov Filimonov/SS; 234 (LO INSET), The Granger Collection, New York/The Granger Collection; 234 (LO), NinaMalyna/SS; 235, courtesy Navigea LTD.; 235, Corbis/GI; 235 (LO RT), Chris Jackson/ GI; 235 (CTR INSET), William Essex/The Bridgeman Art Library/GI; 235 (LO LE INSET), Hans the Younger Holbein/The Bridgeman Art Library/GI; 235 (LO LE), Ninell/SS; 235 (LO RT INSET), Nikreates/Alamy; 238, Jozev/IS; 241, February/GI; 242, Anton Petrus/GI; 247, Pavol Kmeto/DRMS; 250 (UP), Sean Pavone/ SS; 250 (CTR RT), LibraryTuul/Robert Harding Picture; 250 (CTR LE), DEA/A. De Gregorio/De Agostini/GI; 251, Christopher Furlong/GI

Geography Rocks (252–337)

252-253, Michele Falzone/Stockbyte/GI; 259 (LO), NASA; 259 (UP), Mark Thiessen/NGP; 261 (UP CTR), Maria Stenzel/NG Creative; 261 (LO CTR), Bill Hatcher/NG Creative; 261 (LO RT), Carsten Peter/NG Creative; 261 (UP RT), Gordon Wiltsie/NG Creative; 261 (LO LE), James P. Blair/NG Creative; 261 (UP LE), Thomas J. Abercrombie/NG Creative; 261 (BACK), Fabiano Rebeque/Moment/GI; 262, iStock/GI; 263 (UP), AdemarRangel/GI; 263 (CTR RT), Iko/SS; 263 (CTR LE), Edward Stanley; 263 (LO), eAlisa/SS; 266, Klein &

Hubert/Nature Picture Library; 267 (CTR), Mark Conlon, Antarctic Ice Marathon; 267 (UP), Achim Baque/SS; 267 (LO), Stephen Nicol; 267 (CTR RT), Flipser/SS; 270, P Deliss/ The Image Bank/GI; 271 (UP), Jon Arnold Images/Danita Delimont.com; 271 (CTR RT), Nancy Brown/Photographer's Choice/ GI; 271 (CTR LE), John Downer/MP; 271 (LO), slowmotiongli/AS; 274, Arun Roisri/Moment RF/GI; 275 (UP), Andrew Watson/John Warburton-Lee Photography Ltd/GI; 275 (CTR LE), Adam Fletcher/MP; 275 (CTR RT), David Wall Photo/GI; 275 (LO), Martin Valigursky/ AS; 278, Guillem Lopez/Cavan Images; 279 (UP), Roy Pedersen/SS; 279 (CTR LE), Thomas Lohnes/GI; 279 (CTR RT), Richard Becker/AL; 279 (LO), Aleksandr Volkov/AL; 282, Gavriel Jecan/GI; 283 (UP), Rodrigo Arangua/GI; 283 (CTR LE), Beth Zaiken; 283 (CTR RT), Neirfy/SS; 283 (LO), Mint Images RF/GI; 286, hadynyah/ IS/GI; 287 (CTR RT), DC_Colombia/GI; 287 (UP), Soberka Richard/hemis.fr/GI; 287 (LO), Keren Su/GI; 287, Eraldo Peres/AP/SS; 293, Kelly Cheng/GI; 294, Uros Ravbar/DRMS; 298, Renate Wefers/EyeEm/GI; 301, ferrantraite/ E+/GI; 302, DaveLongMedia/IS/GI; 306, Nikolai Sorokin/DRMS; 309, Michael Runkel/ AL; 314, Steve Lovegrove/SS; 328 (UP LE), M L Pearson/AL; 328 (UP RT), Exotica/AL; 328 (LO LE), Kenishirotie/AL; 328 (LO RT), Oleksandr Prykhodko/AL; 329 (UP), Rubens Abboud/AL; 329 (CTR), Angela Hampton Picture Library/ AL; 329 (LO), Themba Hadebe/AP/SS; 330 (A), David Sutherland/The Image Bank/GI; 330 (B), Ferdinand Knab/The Bridgeman Art Library/Gatty Images; 330 (C), Ferdinand Knab/The Bridgeman Art Library/GI; 330 (D), Ferdinand Knab/The Bridgeman Art Library/ GI; 330 (E), Wilhelm van Ehrenberg/The Bridgeman Art Library/GI; 330 (F), Ferdinand Knab/The Bridgeman Art Library/GI; 330 (G), DEA Picture Library/GI; 330 (H), Holger Mette/SS; 330 (I), Holger Mette/SS; 330 (J), Jarno Gonzalez Zarraonandia/SS; 330 (K), David Iliff/SS; 330 (L), ostill/SS; 330 (M), Hannamariah/SS; 330 (N), Jarno Gonzalez Zarraonandia/SS; 331 (UP RT), Taylor S. Kennedy/NGIC; 331 (LO), Iourii Tcheka/SS; 331 (UP LE), Gilmanshin/SS; 332 (LO), S.Borisov/ SS; 332-333, Justin Sullivan/GI; 332 (CTR), Justin Sullivan/GI; 332 (UP), Andy Freeberg; 333, Nick Ut/AP Photo; 334 (UP LE), Danita Delimont/AL; 334 (LO RT), Gardel Bertrand/ GI; 334 (UP RT), ArtyAlison/IS/GI; 334 (LO LE), Ian Cumming/ZUMApress/Newscom; 335 (ALL), Red de Hoteles Tayka; 336 (LO), Maria Stenzel/NG Creative; 336 (CTR), Beth Zaiken; 336 (UP), Eraldo Peres/AP/SS

National Geographic Kids Books
gratefully acknowledges the following people for their help with the *National Geographic Kids Infopedia.*

Bryan Howard of the
National Geographic Explorer Programs

Amazing Animals

Suzanne Braden, Director, Pandas International

Dr. Rodolfo Coria, Paleontologist,
Plaza Huincul, Argentina

Dr. Sylvia Earle, National Geographic
Explorer-in-Residence

Dr. Thomas R. Holtz, Jr., Senior Lecturer,
Vertebrate Paleontology,
Department of Geology, University of Maryland

Dr. Luke Hunter, Executive Director, Panthera

Nizar Ibrahim, National Geographic Explorer

Dereck and Beverly Joubert,
National Geographic Explorers-in-Residence

"Dino" Don Lessem, President, Exhibits Rex

Kathy B. Maher, Research Editor (former),
National Geographic magazine

Kathleen Martin, Canadian Sea Turtle Network

Barbara Nielsen, Polar Bears International

Andy Prince, Austin Zoo

Julia Thorson, Translator, Zurich, Switzerland

Dennis vanEngelsdorp, Senior Extension Associate,
Pennsylvania Department of Agriculture

Culture Connection

Dr. Wade Davis, National Geographic
Explorer-in-Residence

Deirdre Mullervy, Managing Editor,
Gallaudet University Press

Wonders of Nature

Anatta, NOAA Public Affairs Officer

Dr. Robert Ballard,
National Geographic Explorer-in-Residence

Douglas H. Chadwick, Wildlife Biologist and Contributor
to *National Geographic* magazine

Susan K. Pell, Ph.D., Science and Public Programs Manager,
United States Botanic Garden

Space and Earth
Science and Technology

Tim Appenzeller, Chief Magazine Editor, *Nature*

Dr. Rick Fienberg, Press Officer and Director of Communications,
American Astronomical Society

Dr. José de Ondarza, Associate Professor,
Department of Biological Sciences, State University
of New York, College at Plattsburgh

Lesley B. Rogers, Managing Editor (former),
National Geographic magazine

Dr. Enric Sala, National Geographic Explorer-in-Residence

Abigail A. Tipton, Director of Research (former),
National Geographic magazine

Erin Vintinner, Biodiversity Specialist,
Center for Biodiversity and Conservation at the
American Museum of Natural History

Barbara L. Wyckoff, Research Editor (former),
National Geographic magazine

History Happens

Dr. Sylvie Beaudreau, Associate Professor,
Department of History, State University of New York

Elspeth Deir, Assistant Professor, Faculty of Education,
Queens University, Kingston, Ontario, Canada

Dr. Gregory Geddes, Professor, Global Studies,
State University of New York–Orange,
Middletown-Newburgh, New York

Dr. Fredrik Hiebert, National Geographic Visiting Fellow

Micheline Joanisse, Media Relations Officer,
Natural Resources Canada

Dr. Robert D. Johnston,
Associate Professor and Director of the
Teaching of History Program, University of Illinois at Chicago

Dickson Mansfield, Geography Instructor (retired),
Faculty of Education, Queens University,
Kingston, Ontario, Canada

Tina Norris, U.S. Census Bureau

Parliamentary Information and Research Service,
Library of Parliament, Ottawa, Canada

Karyn Pugliese, Acting Director, Communications,
Assembly of First Nations

Geography Rocks

Dr. Kristin Bietsch, Research Associate,
Population Reference Bureau

Carl Haub, Senior Demographer,
Conrad Taeuber Chair of Public Information,
Population Reference Bureau

Dr. Toshiko Kaneda, Senior Research Associate,
Population Reference Bureau

Dr. Walt Meier, National Snow and Ice Data Center

Dr. Richard W. Reynolds, NOAA's National Climatic Data Center

United States Census Bureau, Public Help Desk

Since 1888, the National Geographic Society has funded more than 12,000 research,
exploration, and preservation projects around the world. The Society receives
funds from National Geographic Partners, LLC, funded in part by your purchase.
A portion of the proceeds from this book supports this vital work.
To learn more, visit natgeo.com/info.

For more information, visit nationalgeographic.com, call 1-877-873-6846,
or write to the following address:

National Geographic Partners, LLC
1145 17th Street N.W.
Washington, DC 20036-4688 U.S.A.

For librarians and teachers:
nationalgeographic.com/books/librarians-and-educators

More for kids from National Geographic: natgeokids.com

National Geographic Kids magazine inspires children to explore their world
with fun yet educational articles on animals, science, nature, and more.
Using fresh storytelling and amazing photography, *Nat Geo Kids* shows kids
ages 6 to 14 the fascinating truth about the world — and why they should care.
kids.nationalgeographic.com/subscribe

For rights or permissions inquiries, please contact National Geographic Books
Subsidiary Rights: bookrights@natgeo.com

Designed by Kathryn Robbins and Ruthie Thompson

**National Geographic supports K–12 educators with ELA Common Core Resources.
Visit natgeoed.org/commoncore for more information.**

The publisher would like to thank everyone who worked to make this book come
together: Angela Modany, associate editor; Mary Jones, project editor;
Sarah Wassner Flynn, writer; Michelle Harris, researcher; Lori Epstein, photo
director; Mike McNey, map production; Chris Philpotts, illustrator; Anne LeongSon
and Gus Tello, design production assistants; Joan Gossett, editorial production
manager; and Molly Reid, production editor.

Trade paperback ISBN: 978-1-4263-7206-3

Printed in the United States of America
21/WOR/1